MICHAEL TILSON THOMAS

MICHAEL TILSON THOMAS
Viva Voce

Conversations with Edward Seckerson

faber and faber
LONDON · BOSTON

First published in 1994
by Faber and Faber Limited
3 Queen Square London WC1N 3AU

Printed in England by Clays Ltd, St Ives plc

A CIP record for this book is available from the British Library

ISBN 0 571 16738 1

2 4 6 8 10 9 7 5 3 1

Contents

List of Illustrations

Acknowledgements

The following, either through editorial assistance or encouragement, have made this book possible: Paul Bentley, Linda Indian, Joshua Robison, Judith Salpeter, Helen Sprott, Ed Victor, Jan Younghusband, and the staff at Faber and Faber.

For my Parents
Roberta and Ted

Preface

MAKING MUSIC IS one of man's basic needs. For some, it is as necessary as food or drink or breath. So it is for me.

I often feel as if I have a personal relationship with the composers whose music I play, many of whom are no longer living. It is unnerving sometimes to feel such a profound friendship with people who are departed. As I play over their scores, it is as if I can hear them speaking through the phrases, asking, 'Can you hear me? Do you understand?' But music does have that strong power of evocation that makes one feel that one is in the living presence of someone from another time. There are two poems which express why I am a musician.

> Ideal and dearly beloved voices
> of those who are dead, or of those
> who are lost to us like the dead.
>
> Sometimes they speak to us in our dreams;
> sometimes in thought the mind hears them.
>
> And for a moment with their echo other echoes
> return from the first poetry of our lives –
> like music that extinguishes the far-off night.
>
> Cavafy, Voices (translation: Rae Dalven)

> I live my life in growing rings
> which stretch themselves out through the things
> of the universe.
> Perhaps I will not complete the last ring,
> but I will try.

I am circling around God, around the ancient tower,
and I have been circling for a thousand years;
and I still don't know: am I a falcon, a storm
or a great song.

Rilke

Michael Tilson Thomas, London, 1994

Michael Tilson Thomas

Introduction

One of my very, very first memories is of my parents' house in Los
Angeles. In the late afternoon the light would come through windows
at one end of the house. There were venetian blinds and the blinds
would be open so the light would come into the room in bands of
light, because there was a lot of dust in the air in San Fernando Valley
in the summertime especially, and in these bands of light there were
motes of dust, dancing in the light; and my first musical memory, I
think, is watching those particles of dust moving, and reaching way
up over my head to the keyboard of this big old upright rosewood
Steinway grand that my parents had, and trying to play notes that
would accompany this dance of the dust.

MICHAEL TILSON THOMAS'S first music statement? The technique may
have been flawed, but the spirit was willing.

Michael Tilson Thomas was born on 21 December 1944 to Theodor
and Roberta Thomas. The place: Cedars of Lebanon Hospital, Hollywood.
Actually, the family name was Thomashefsky, traceable back two hundred
years or more to the Ukraine, to Kiev and Odessa. We can probably go
further still. Artur Rubinstein once told him that anybody with the name
Thomashefsky had to have originated from the village of Thomashov on the
border between Russia and Poland, depending of course upon the date. The
Thomashefskys were singers from a long and distinguished line. His grandfather Boris was a quite famous boy soprano soloist with one of the foremost
Jewish liturgical choirs in Russia. And that was to be the foundation of his
career when he arrived to begin his new life in the United States. He later
married Bessie and together they founded and became stars of the American
Yiddish Theatre in New York.

So the stage was set for Tilson Thomas's formative years. The key
elements were all in place: mother Russia and her music, singers and songs,
the theatre. His childhood was acted out in the midst of a thriving movie
community. The house was more often than not filled with actors and musicians, reminiscing, even performing. Many were Russian – a valuable link

to the past with Stanislavski, Chaliapin and the like. He was raised on tales of old Russia. So many of them. His grandmother would tell of market day in Kiev when it was impossible to talk for the sound of church bells. And she would sing to him – lively, catchy tunes he later recognized as the folk-tunes of Stravinsky's *Petrushka* and *The Firebird* ballets. This was a household where people readily sang: Broadway songs, Yiddish theatre songs, Italian opera from the family gramophone. His father wrote and sang songs: Gershwin had taught him the piano. It was an intoxicating environment in which to grow. And years later, even as he became swept up in the brilliant rhythmic gyrations of Stravinsky and others, he would always think back to the singers and their songs. *Cantabile. Legato.* The little turns of expression in the voice, the bluesy notes, the falling away of the breath, the *vibrato* or lack of it. He learned early: when in doubt about how something should go, sing it.

He would play the piano 'by ear', just as his father before him had done. But his parents were concerned that, unlike his father, he should be able to read music. And this is where Dorothy Bishop came in. She provided his first really serious instruction at the University of Southern California preparatory school. Her style of teaching was deeply rooted in the art of improvisation, and through her Tilson Thomas made his first contact with the faculty of the university itself. He enrolled there in 1962 with 'advanced standing', impressed by the mix and balance of what was on offer. He came to view the faculty of USC a little as we once viewed Berlin – in terms of the German and Russian sectors. Here were two very distinct schools: German intellectualism versus Russian instinct. He recalls how in one moment he could find himself in a class of Schenkerian analysis, dealing with complicated concepts of thematic augmentation or diminution in Schumann, while in the next he might be playing Schumann with Jascha Heifetz or Gregor Piatigorsky. On those occasions, any attempt to theorize would invariably be met with a gentle rebuke: 'I know all those words,' Heifetz would say, 'but I also know that at any given moment in the piece, you must know what must sound and how it must sound.' But Tilson Thomas was lucky with his teachers; no one expected him to swear undying allegiance to one group or the other. He enjoyed the best of both worlds. Among his luminaries was the harpsichordist Alice Ehlers, a pupil of the great Wanda Landowska and friend of Alban Berg; his piano teacher, John Crown, pupil of Moriz Rosenthal (Liszt's pupil), master of 'the generous, leonine romantic style'; and, most significant of all, Ingolf Dahl, his conducting and composition teacher. Dahl was an enormous influence on Tilson Thomas. He taught him about form and the projection of form, he taught him to look at the design of a piece as its single most expressive element.

Los Angeles was an exciting place to be at the time, still a melting-pot for the many European émigrés who had come, seen, and stayed. And for the musical, or just simply the musically curious, there was only one place to be on Monday evening, and that was at Monday Evening Concerts. His parents – avid concert-goers – took him regularly. In fact, he insisted. This was where new music enjoyed a committed showcase, where LA's distinguished musical immigrants came out to play. Igor Stravinsky was one, the one for Tilson Thomas. In fact, he couldn't remember a time before *Petrushka*, *The Firebird*, or *The Rite of Spring*. His grandmother's singing and a few well-worn 78s saw to that. Of course, it was a newer, sparer, and stranger Stravinsky that he more often than not heard during these formative years in some instances the very first readings of works-in-progress. But Tilson Thomas himself should, and shall, relate his personal recollections of the great man. Suffice it to say that in 1963, when Ingolf Dahl took him on board as orchestral pianist and subsequently conductor of those 'Monday Evening Concerts' (keyboards in Webern's Six Pieces for orchestra was his baptism), Stravinsky, the man, the music, and the myth finally became a reality for him. Between 1963 and 1968 he participated in premières of works by composers as diverse as Boulez, Stockhausen, Copland, William Kraft, Ingolf Dahl, and, of course, Stravinsky. He accompanied Heifetz and Piatigorsky (thereby hang some tales), he began to learn about performing, communication, the showbiz of music.

Tilson Thomas graduated *summa cum laude* from USC in 1967, having spent the previous year as a student of Friedelind Wagner and musical assistant at the Wagner shrine, Bayreuth. He took on the post of Chief Conductor at the Ojai Festival, he made the première recording of the piano, four hands, version of Stravinsky's *The Rite of Spring* (with Ralph Grierson). He was ready for that big breakthrough. And it came, in 1968, with a conducting fellowship at Tanglewood, the Boston Symphony's fertile breeding ground for the young and talented in the hills near Lennox, Massachusetts. Leonard Bernstein had made his mark there in the summers of 1940–3 under the watchful eye of Serge Koussevitzky. Even Tilson Thomas concedes that comparisons were inevitable: the surplus of energy, the voracious appetite, the bravura in just about every skill – piano, composition, conducting. At any rate, this prodigious audacity won him the coveted 'Koussevitzky Prize'. A week or two later he was enjoying his first audience with Leonard Bernstein. Again, that and other 'Lenny' stories must be his, though I will pick up on one significant incident. During this revealing close encounter, Bernstein asked him to nominate his favourite musical moment. Tilson Thomas duly went over to the piano and picked out the oscillating minor thirds which precede the first oboe solo in the last movement of Mahler's *Das Lied von der Erde*. It was an important moment for both of them. Those few notes were right at the centre of everything that Bernstein held most dear: so simple, so ambiguous; so much suggested because of how much is left out. A kinship had been established and cemented.

Winning the Koussevitzky Prize opened doors for Tilson Thomas, and one door in particular – the Boston Symphony Orchestra. He was appointed Assistant Conductor the very next year at the age of twenty-four. What followed has a familiar ring to it. On the afternoon of 22 October 1969, only ten days after his appointment, William Steinberg, the orchestra's Music Director, was taken ill mid-concert at New York's Avery Fisher Hall. Enter Tilson Thomas, stepping decisively into the breach just as Bernstein had so famously done when an ailing Bruno Walter expedited his sensational New York début in 1943. The outcome was similarly dramatic. Tilson Thomas conducted thirty-seven concerts with the Boston Symphony during that 1969–70 season. In 1970 he was appointed Associate Conductor and toured Europe with them – the youngest American-born conductor ever to achieve international recognition.

Four outstanding Deutsche Grammophon recordings underline his achievement during those early Boston years. It was almost as if he were serving notice, staking claims on the cornerstones of his repertoire: the American pioneers, Ives and Ruggles; Debussy (so much a part of Boston's French inheritance and even then central to his nervous system); and his Russian past and present – Tchaikovsky and Stravinsky. I effectively came in with these recordings. Tilson Thomas was a dynamic newcomer with a hot reputation, but what came off these discs for me was something mellower and seemingly long-considered. I remember the sounds almost as well as I remember the original LP sleeves: an exceptionally ripe and detailed Debussy *Images*; Tchaikovsky's First Symphony, truly the stuff of 'winter daydreams' from the moment that limpid, rather wistful woodwind tune ambles in over shimmery G minor triads in the strings. One might even be tempted to ask if his grandmother had ever sung the misty-eyed, hugely nostalgic horn melody of the slow movement – so authentically homespun does it sound. Then there is his highly individual *Rite of Spring*, notable above all for its folkloric character and cast. When he was preparing the piano version with Ralph Grierson, their meetings with Stravinsky were constantly illuminating for the way in which he would sing and articulate particular phrases: so shapely, so flexible. Tilson Thomas's reading grew from there. And the Americans: Charles Ives, whose very particular brand of impressionism illuminates *Three Places in New England*, and Carl Ruggles's *Sun-treader* striding confidently across great open spaces. In my mind, Tilson Thomas's Ruggles will always be associated with Buffalo, where he was appointed Music Director of the Philharmonic in 1971. He stayed a full eight years and effectively put that orchestra on the American map. On record they gave us *Gershwin Overtures* and, uniquely, *The Complete Ruggles*. The latter won them a Grammy nomination and *Stereo Review*'s 'Album of the Year'. Aficionados of musical America had found a new champion.

Time now, though, to focus on Tilson Thomas, the conductor, the interpreter, the communicator. First impressions. When he mounts the podium, we see a tall, elegant figure – he might easily have stepped out of a 1930s Hollywood musical. Second impressions. He is charismatic, a sense of urgency and quickening involvement informs his every gesture. The long arms are particularly expressive, reaching out to cue and to encourage key musical lines, tracing phrase shapes and *rubatos*, sweeping across and away from the body to convey length and breadth. Then again, he can almost disappear in moments of intense *pianissimo*, crouching mouse-like one second, pouncing the next to galvanize and redouble the sound in moments of high drama.

But these are merely the physical manifestations of a commanding and flexible technique, the gestures that ultimately encourage, coax and cajole the music off the page at the moment of performance. First comes the exploration, the hours spent alone at the piano. What are these notes really saying, what is the psychological and emotional subtext? And how to communicate these ideas, these feelings? During the twelve months of our collaboration for this book, I have observed, eavesdropped, in a sense participated in a period of intensive and highly diverse work with two very different musical organisms: the New World Symphony Orchestra, America's national training orchestra – where he is in every sense the orchestra's Columbus, being both its founder and spiritual godfather; and the London Symphony, of whom he became Principal Conductor in September 1988. Working with an orchestra like the LSO – or indeed any of the world's major symphony orchestras – is of course the acid test for any conductor. As Tilson Thomas himself says, you are collaborating with musicians of considerable experience and expertise, musicians with fully formed and often wonderful perspectives on particular pieces of repertoire. Very often there are long-established traditions of style to take on board, too. You have to be absolutely certain about what it is you want to say and how you want to say it. There isn't a lot of time to experiment with concepts. Time is a player's livelihood. Tilson Thomas has a way with words, a way of enlivening even basic technical information: '*Tutta forza*, everybody – take no prisoners'; 'Violins, just take this out of the air – just graze the string … I want you to play this minuet as if "on pointes"; horns, that was beautiful but put the sound someplace over in the next valley – more distant.' During one rehearsal for Stravinsky's *Symphony of Psalms*, he royally entertained the LSO Chorus with well-practised impersonations of the great man, hunched over his score like some wizened bird of prey. He was seventeen when he first heard the piece – from the piano, under the composer's direction. 'What was so great about Stravinsky's own reading was this blocked, hieratical feeling it had; somehow it all came out of this clear, detached beat … let's see if we can get that … give me your best devotionally carnivorous sound … now this is raunchier – this is more Carl Orffish: your best happy fishwife sound … now, the nicest cradle singing you can give me, really make these minor seconds into major events …!' And so on.

Tilson Thomas's teacher always told him that he would learn to handle different orchestras as a director handles different actors. He would learn to enjoy and make capital of their different characteristics. He does. Over in Miami, the New World fledglings bring out the teacher in him. But it's a two-way street: he gets back a lot of what he puts in. Young musicians ask a lot of questions, they prompt him to re-evaluate, re-consider: look for new ideas, new solutions to age-old problems. They feed his natural curiosity. And, of course, time is on their side. Time to experiment. No one at NWS is likely to be thinking: 'Forget the history lesson – do you want it louder or softer?' Another of the year's most absorbing weeks was spent watching Tilson Thomas take apart, and then reassemble, Charles Ives's seminal Fourth Symphony. Eighty years on, and this amazing collage of the sights, sounds and songs that are America still defies and transcends reason. These players came to it without preconceptions; Tilson Thomas could use that innocence, even share it. I remember him turning to his first violins during a rehearsal for Mozart's Symphony No.34. He was about to begin the slow movement. They were tense. 'It's OK to be nervous, you should be nervous,' he said. 'Just imagine the music is already happening in your head: listen to it, hear it before making a sound.'

In 1971, the very same year that he was appointed Music Director of the Buffalo Philharmonic, Tilson Thomas also became Director of the New York Philharmonic Young People's Concerts. For the next six years, a string of CBS TV relays spoke for themselves: 'I Love Tchaikovsky', 'Piano vs. Orchestra', 'What is Noise? What is Music?', 'What Makes a Gershwin Tune a Gershwin Tune?'. Tilson Thomas's communication skills had found another natural outlet. TV liked him. Cut to 1986, and a BBC special 'Playing By Heart' – a televisual essay, a moment by moment, prank by prank tour of Richard Strauss's 'Till Eulenspiegel'. That programme opened a lot of eyes – and ears. It was, if you like, more of a 'discovery' than anyone knew. With Tilson Thomas now poised to take the helm of the London Symphony Orchestra, a highly successful series of 'Discovery' concerts was born. The objective: to 'unlock', de-mystify, re-discover key works in the repertoire. London audiences were quick to respond. Tilson Thomas had things to say, theories to share, and entertaining ways of sharing them. Besides, he was good theatre.

Beethoven's Third Symphony, the 'Eroica', was one of the works under his spotlight. And, as ever, he began as he meant to go on: 'Ludwig van Beethoven – 164 years after his death and the man and the music still obsess us ... The Olympics open with a synthesized version of his *Ode to Joy*, rendered unintelligible, no doubt, to promote better understanding. We hear his music as we're put on "hold" (cue Minuet in G); recently I heard the most intimate piece he ever wrote played by a lorry warning me that it was backing up (cue *Für Elise*). But when we seriously think of Beethoven, we think of the fist-shaking, fate-defying creator – the deaf, lonely eccentric – crying his sorrows, rage, triumph across the ages. This is the Beethoven we first discover in the symphony called the "Eroica".' Cue an explosive illustration from the first movement development. The curtain is up. 'I think the "Eroica" is best understood as a kind of musical journal of Beethoven's life between 1800 and 1805 years of great social and political change for Europe, and years of great personal change for him.' And with that, the 'journal' comes to life: Beethoven's own words are heard in dramatic conjunction with the music. Movement by movement, sometimes bar by bar. Tilson Thomas is a passionate, erudite guide. We are invited to play detective, tracing the origins of the symphony right back through these turbulent times to a bizarre (but, we are assured, reliably corroborated) confrontation between Beethoven and his musical nemesis, one Daniel Steibelt – world-famous piano virtuoso, improvisationalist, showman. This is Tilson Thomas's punch-line, his 'dénouement': a reconstruction of the aforesaid incident in which Beethoven, angered by Steibelt's brilliant but cynical improvisation on a theme from his Trio, Op.11 for piano, clarinet, and cello, was said to have snatched the cello part of Steibelt's own Quintet from the stand, turned it upside-down (intentionally?), picked out the first four notes, and proceeded to improvise. The same four notes, played 'upside-down' in the treble clef, give us the pivotal bass-line motif from the Finale of the 'Eroica' – four notes from which the entire symphony effectively sprang. But you have to imagine Tilson Thomas's zealous performance at the keyboard for this 'revelation' to have its full effect, just as you have to hear his reading of the symphony in its entirety (as was the pattern in Part Two of these 'Discovery' concerts) in order to put flesh on his lively analysis. Consider his words as we arrive at the Finale's glorious *andante* variation, the climax of the symphony. 'Why does this music affect us so deeply? Of course, because of its expressive harmonies. But also because it returns to the texture and mood of the funeral march. It serves as a kind of happy ending to the march, showing us a transfigured vision of the hero in glory. Suddenly there is this noble hymn and Beethoven is showing us just how overwhelming he can make even this very silly theme. A wonderful epilogue then seems to move away from this heroic world and take us back to Beethoven at his desk striving to do his best. Note the parallel here to the A flat major episode of the funeral march. All at once, an abrupt and very short Coda brings the whole drama to a close. Just as he did in real life, Beethoven rushes from the room exclaiming at us all: "You are fools! Fools!"' Perhaps, but now we were listening intently.

Tilson Thomas still works from the very first score he ever possessed of the 'Eroica'. Like all his scores, it was duly leather-bound and personalized in gold-leaf engraving by an old established book-binder in New York. Every marking he ever made on those pages is still there – a history of preparation and performance in a thousand scrawled messages to himself: key notes and phrases, crucial accents and *sforzandi* are all circled. On the title page he has written: 'Form, Character, Expression. Arrive at a style; adjust tempo to style.' And then, at the beginning of the first movement: 'Beginning of a journey.' An important side-bar to this 'Eroica' project was a series of master-classes with students from the Barbican's neighbouring Guildhall School of Music and Drama. In one particularly illuminating session, three young conducting students gathered around the Green Room piano for an hour's informal coaching. Tilson Thomas's first words of advice were – know the composer, know his life, know his other music. Know the score. You can only start hearing, really hearing, the music when you've got beyond the mechanics. Then you figure out how to bring it off the page.

From the top, he began playing his way through the first movement. 'The first thing you'll find is that players instinctively want to shape the theme: keep the distribution of time absolutely even – establish your pulse and hold it. Be careful the fourth bar doesn't sag: you can die in the fourth bar. The theme is in real danger until it turns the corner and grows confident. All these twists and turns, these little journeys into different keys are about setting up the dominant … Now be careful not to squeeze expression from the second subject.' On his score he had written: 'Careful: *romanza,* no *sforzandi*!'. 'Ask yourself, what is the meaning of this bar or that, this chord or that: is this, perhaps, a brief moment of nostalgia? Is this a stab of pain? Something lost? Ask yourself where the key moments, the key turning points are.' He begins quizzing the students. They come back with some keen observations. We are into the development section: 'This is one of Beethoven's wild and wonderful improvisations – imagine him pounding it out … I'll bet he played this note with his thumb! This moment here is Bambi meets Godzilla: these flourishes from the strings are entirely percussive – Berlioz would have added six snare drums. And now the trumpets: Maurice Murphy (the LSO principal) generally gives me *Rhinegold* here.' And onwards to the funeral march: 'Think of the grace-notes in the bass line as a voice catching with emotion. This is public grief now … Again you must decide exactly where you are going to be "in tempo" and where you are going to take a fraction more time … And remind me to show you how to beat the last bar – I made such a hash of that when I first did it. Above all, remember – pulse, momentum. You can relax the tension without slowing. Be particularly careful where the music gets softer. But at the same time, give your soloists plenty of expressive freedom within that greater framework. I like to hear how this or that player will shape a solo – it's all part of an orchestra's character.'

When one of the students asks how he might tactfully take issue with a horn player who is consistently playing too loudly, Tilson Thomas suggests a little sleight of hand. 'You could, for instance, ask the strings to give less so that the horn can play as quietly as he wants! That could do the trick. And remember, you don't always have to be telling an orchestra, try asking them: what can we do to make this better?'

In various interviews over the last few years, Tilson Thomas has repeatedly laid down his creative priorities. Audacity, creative audacity, that's the key. Keeping things ardent and special for himself and for others; making music on the highest emotional level – that keeps him alive as a performer. Increasingly, he is looking to develop a more personal style of playing among his orchestras, a more personal approach to the core repertoire, striving, if you like, to make great classics like the 'Eroica' less 'ceremonial' than they can sometimes seem to the listening public. But how should we define a classic? These words, delivered as part of his opening address to the 1991 Pacific Music Festival, eloquently encapsulate his musical philosophy.

What is a classic? It means different things to different people. To some it is a play or a statue or a poem, a song, a car. Classics are Hamlet, Rodin's *The Thinker*, *The Tale of Genji*, Beethoven's Fifth, a '55 Corvette, or the song 'As Time Goes By'.

And that's the point – classics do define their time, and they also transcend time. They are great and intriguing the first time and keep meaning more as we come back to them over our own lives, or from one generation to another. They stick with us; they are universal.

Our classical music is a rich tapestry woven from the thread of many musical traditions – folk music, religious music, dance music, victorious processions, funeral marches, lullabies, love songs, all the rich and varied occasions and feelings of life given shape and order by the wisdom of the mind. This is the balance we must understand in the music we play.

So what is the significance of this disciplined music in our age of teen idols, mega-hits, mega-marketing and blasting backbeat – where rock records sell five million copies and classical records maybe fifty thousand. Does any of our work still have meaning? Well, let me tell you a story. While walking to the market near my home in New York City, I saw a bunch of kids playing baseball in the street. There were boys and girls about ten years old wearing sweat-pants, ripped T-shirts, purple sneakers, and squashed baseball hats worn at crazy angles. Their pitcher threw the ball and the batter hit it way down the block – a home run for sure. He stood there for a second to see just how far the ball was going, and giving a little shiver of delight, ran around the bases like a crazy disco dancer, dodging the oncoming cars and singing *Eine Kleine Nachtmusik*.

I thought of Mozart writing *Eine Kleine Nachtmusik* for that special aristocratic audience of eighteenth-century Vienna – and of that piece travelling through all levels of society, all countries, oceans, continents – not to mention generations and centuries – to live in the consciousness of a New York City street kid. This boy's utter delight in hitting his home run is probably much like what Mozart felt at the moment when he wrote those joyous notes over two hundred years ago … It's as if he had written those notes especially for the boy and for the childhood he never had. Somehow, Mozart was speaking to this boy, as all the masters of the past are speaking to us saying, 'We lived, we loved, we tried – this is what we learned. This is tradition.'

As you will see from the pages of this book, ideas tend to germinate as Tilson Thomas speaks. Time and again during our conversations, a casual thought, a fleeting recollection, an incidental detail would fire his enthusi-asm. I could greet a tired man – but moments later he was buoyant, revital-ized, flying off in some new direction. Then again, in the next moment, he might become distant. I quickly learned not to violate the long pauses, the reflective silences, just as I learned not to divert him when his mind was moving in a particular direction. There was the time we were due to discuss Mahler but wound up re-investigating Brahms's Second Symphony. That was the preoccupation of the day. After years of performing the piece, he felt he had finally come close to unlocking it. Brahms was suddenly more relevant to our understanding of Mahler. Both discussions were greatly enhanced.

Tilson Thomas's insatiable curiosity, his wide-ranging tastes in all things have pulled him in many different directions – and continue to do so. He's regarded as a Russian specialist, an American specialist, prime mover for the music of Ives and Ruggles, champion of Gershwin, keeper of the Bernstein legacy; he's a natural Mahlerian, a devoted Francophile, a willing activist in the cause of new music. If I might be permitted to turn critic for a moment and cast my mind back over just one year's events, then the broader picture might begin to emerge. Mahler. Tilson Thomas's temperamental kinship speaks for itself. Mahler's closest friends all recalled his quixotic changes of mood, his volatile emotional extremes. Our debate on Mahler would see Tilson Thomas break down over a tiny detail in the Eighth Symphony. And since we're talking here about instinct beyond any received wisdom, I think anybody who has seen him at the keyboard, in the driving seat of Gershwin's Second Rhapsody – tantalizing, fanciful, opulent – will understand how the spirit of improvisation lives in everything he does. It enables him to be both precise and infinitely free with his Debussy, for instance. *Jeux* was new to the LSO when they first tackled it with him, but he was able to harness their quick-reflex style of playing to piquant effect – now you hear it, now you don't. A still greater testament to his growing influence over the orchestra was his resurrection of Debussy's *Le martyre de St Sébastien* – perhaps the critical success of the 1991 autumn season. For those of us familiar only with the somewhat skeletal 'symphonic suite', it was as if this rare and beautiful music (much of it never heard) had been reborn. In effect, it had. With Leslie Caron as narrator, Debussy's shot-silk score was effectively reunited with Gabriele d'Annunzio's 'divinely decadent' text; Parsifalian meditations – at once passionate and chaste – regained their dramatic context. But what had pleased the conductor more than anything was the orchestra's awareness and realization of the style – that word again. Refinement without preciousness. Perhaps he could yet persuade them that there was more to Tchaikovsky than a few cheap thrills. He was working on it.

In the case of Leonard Bernstein, much of the stylistic ground-work had already been laid down by the man himself. The LSO have this music as well and truly under their fingers as any American orchestra, and in this of all years they were going to prove it. The 'Lenny' tributes – including the world première of the Suite from his opera *A Quiet Place*, fashioned in part by Tilson Thomas himself – punctuated an entire season. But the mother of them was still to come, and that would resonate long after the event: a sensational semi-staged revival of LB's very first Broadway show *On the Town*. The show's collaborators, lyricists Betty Comden and Adolph Green, were on hand to advise and participate, a dream cast was assembled, cut songs reinstated, the original orchestrations restored and spruced up, and the whole thing was immortalized on record and film. The Barbican concert hall even acquired a New York skyline. But you had to have seen first-hand the care that Tilson Thomas and his cast lavished upon the fine-print of each and every number to know why it worked so well. I recall his intensive preparation with Tyne Daly (power-casting for tell-it-like-it-is Hildy), each session finding notes even she didn't know she had. Cleo Laine dropped in to resurrect one of the 'lost' numbers, 'Ain't Got No Tears Left' – Tilson Thomas joined her at the piano. The 'band' took everyone's breath away: they were Broadway-bound and the heat was on – one blistering dance episode after another, the very life-force of the score. At the end of it all, the song on everyone's lips wasn't 'New York, New York' but 'Some Other Time' – one of the great Bernstein numbers, more pertinent, and more poignant now than ever: 'Where has the time all gone to, haven't done half the things we want to ...'

There never is enough time. As I write, Tilson Thomas begins another season and looks forward to the future when he takes up his new position as music director of the San Francisco Symphony. 'You want to know what it is like being a performing musician?' he asks. 'In a sense you are like somebody working on the ancient Chinese texts. A scholar in the Eastern tradition finally looks at the ancient texts in a version which has no punctuation, no editing, nothing – and according to where you put the punctuation, the meaning of the text entirely changes. Your achievement as a scholar is getting to the point where you abandon all the readings and all of the interpretations of your teachers and mentors and whoever else, and just say: "Here is the blank text and now I am going to punctuate it." That is so much like what it is to be a performing musician, an interpretative artist.'

Time to talk.

Edward Seckerson, August 1992, London.

Part One

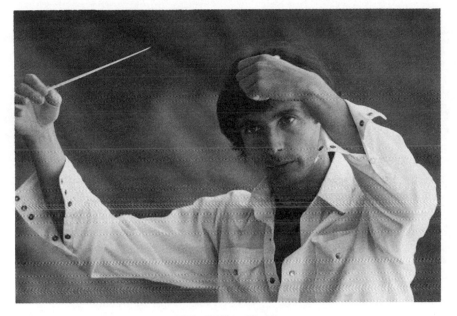

Michael Tilson Thomas

On Conducting

The Role of the Conductor

ES: *Why not begin as we mean to go on, with an impossible question. What is the role of a conductor?*

MTT: The conductor is there because someone must unify all the different talents, perspectives, past histories, reaction times and perceptions of a number of different people who have come together to perform a given piece of music. Those people may have very different ideas of what the piece is about.

This is terribly important: performers have such different pasts with respect to a piece, and such different ideas about what the piece is. They must be in agreement about what the reading will be on one particular occasion. So in a piece of orchestral music it's the conductor who's trying to indicate the leading edge of the performance.

If it's a soloist's piece, such as a big aria or a big violin concerto, the orchestra will be influenced by the way the soloist leads. Maria Callas used to say that the true definition of a prima donna is the person from whom the energy and the direction, the thrust of the performance, comes. But in the case of the orchestra, everyone is a prima donna or primo uomo in some way, and they have to coalesce. Nowadays the conductor is particularly important because the people who sit at the back of a very large orchestra do not hear things that are going on in the centre or on the opposite side in the way that ideally they should – at least not in most halls. So the conductor is also there to be a guide, to listen, and give indications of balance, phrasing, breathing and pacing; to caution and to encourage.

Subtext and Imagery in Music

ES: *Would you accept that music on the page is dead until the first note is sounded?*

MTT: Certainly.

ES: *So the art of the re-creator is far more crucial than many people think.*

MTT: Yes. The score no matter how intricate is only an approximation of the broader outlines of the music. Musical notation is a kind of glyph attempting to describe the subtlety of a phrase that was once sung, played or dreamt by the composer. The performer has to have the vision to see through the notation to the music the composer really meant. That's why performers who say, 'I only do what it says in the score' are to me pretenders.

It is crucial to come up with performing priorities. Is the main point of the phrase the injection of the melody, the inexorable pace of the crescendo, the interruption of one instrument by another? Only the conductor can say. Maybe instead of using the word priorities it's better to think of the word subtext, because any performing musician knows that as you are playing a piece you should have a subtext in your mind. You should have a sense of what the music is actually saying, what it means, and how you are trying to make that clear in the performance. This allows you to sort out what the priorities should be. In a large symphonic work performers might have very different ideas about what the subtext is. Maybe because the subtext is in some other part of the orchestra, or maybe there are various subtexts which are in concord or discord or at cross purposes with one another. Each section of the orchestra has only one part in front of it. The conductor's the only guy who's got the whole score, the whole picture; so it's his responsibility, in the absence of the composer, to sort it out.

The truth is that most musicians who play in orchestras don't have a subtext for what they play. Or no longer have it. Perhaps that's part of the difficult and somewhat brutalizing aspect of life as an orchestral musician; you play pieces so many times that they can become just tasks to be got through, and you lose sight of what they originally meant to you. One of the most important things that a conductor can do is to risk a certain amount of parody and ridicule by discussing what a piece is about. There are always those in the orchestra who say, 'Oh, give me a break; louder or softer, faster or slower?' Bernstein had one of the greatest comebacks of all – to a player in the Boston Symphony, in fact. He was making his return to the BSO after many years, conducting Beethoven's Ninth Symphony, and in the slow movement he was talking at some length about *Innigkeit* and peace, and one of the players said, 'Lenny, what do you want, louder or softer?' And Lenny paused for a moment and said, 'I'd like it louder ... and softer ... and a lot of other things.'

Once, with the Chicago Symphony, I was conducting *Zarathustra*, again on very little rehearsal, and they were bantering with me, having a very good time. They were saying, 'Ah, the last person that dared do this piece was Fritz Reiner; you know, we haven't done this piece since Fritz, nice to see it again.' So we came to a particular passage and I stopped and said, 'Now violins, here I would like you to add ...' And I couldn't quite put into words what I wanted, and I was saying 'er, um, ah', and stammering on, and they began to imitate me. They were all going 'er, um, ah ...' I said, 'All right, all right, four bars happy, and then suddenly, on the G flat, sad.' And they looked at me and they said, 'Right, okay, great', and they did it, and it was better than what we had done before. And they all recognized that too. I just gave them very simple things, four bars of happy and two bars of sad, that was all, and suddenly there was a completely different performance. It had animation, it had a reason.

ES: *You like to conjure up images and anecdotes.*
MTT: Well, I'm the child of actors. I mean, I grew up around actors and theatre people, so, of course, that's the way I think of anything, because what an actor tries to do is get a take on something, and you don't generally get that in the theatre by endless study and preparation. If you're out there on the boards, a lot of the time you say, 'The idea is in this or that gesture, it's conveyed by this body language, it's that image' – which is a very clear way of quickly demonstrating a vision of a piece, and a lot of Romantic era musicians use it. Both Horowitz and Sviatoslav Richter, in the few conversations that I had with them, talked about music in this kind of way. They would say, 'This section of the piece is like rain, this is like the

Teaching conducting with Yakov Kreitzberg, 1981

world slowly crystallizing into ice.' Very old-fashioned images, the kind that were ridiculed by orchestras when I first came into the profession. 'And here the sun comes up,' a conductor would say. 'Oh yeah?' But now we need to remember that, yes, the sun does come up here, or that suddenly everything is all right, or that all at once we're in a mood of complete lassitude, or whatever it may be. This is important, and it's easier for us to think of specific pictures and images – whether they are something literary or something descriptive – than to think in abstract concepts.

ES: *Working with those student conductors yesterday, you described a passage in Beethoven's 'Eroica' Symphony as 'Bambi meets Godzilla'. Now that immediately sums up the nature of the conflict.*
MTT: Sure. I particularly enjoy that sort of bizarre imagery – pushing things to the extreme. But one reason I do that is it's a more efficient way of working, and it's more fun too. If everyone laughs, great. Let's laugh together, but make the point.

Once I was on tour with the London Symphony Orchestra, playing Mahler in Salzburg. Great. We felt we were at the top of the musical universe. One day off, and the next day we find ourselves due to play in a nightclub dance hall outside Ravenna ... with purple lights under the seats, and an absolutely dreadful acoustic, purple upholstered couches and open bars where the public is drifting in under the flickering light of mirrored globes in the ceiling. Such a terrible place! We have to play Tchaikovsky's Fifth Symphony, which we've not played at all on the tour, and we have forty-five minutes to sort it out. Also there is a soloist coming that we've never worked with before. It's just one of those things that can happen sometimes on the road. We were meant to have a proper rehearsal, but the van has broken down and the instruments haven't arrived, and suddenly there you are in one of those situations, looking at these purple lights and thinking, 'How on earth did we get here?' Nonetheless, you have a few things to sort out, like what's going to happen in Tchaikovsky's Fifth. So we rehearse a little bit here and there, and we start the third movement, and quite predictably and rather appropriately under the circumstances, some members of the orchestra begin quietly singing the famous words to that movement, 'Once I was a virgin, now I am a whore; once I used to hate it, now I like it more and more and more and more ...'

We play the concert in the nightclub, and a day or so later we are in Rome, and now we really have to play the Tchaikovsky Fifth – this is a serious concert. And again we have very short rehearsal time to see what we can do. So we work out a few points in the first movement, and we come to the third movement, and I say to the orchestra, 'Now, at the beginning of this movement, you know what would be wonderful? If you could play this opening phrase as if you were *really* saying, '*Once* I was a virgin'. You'll get it right if you can play like that. Could we try it please?' And the strings come out with such a gorgeous, ravishing sound. We're all entranced. After that the whole movement worked. We got it.

And afterwards I said to them, 'You see, we agree, you've always known the correct words for the first line, "Once I was a virgin". But the next line isn't, "Now I am a whore", it's actually, "It was long ago". Those are the real words that the notes of the next phrase evoke. Once we agree on them we can really make music.'

Deciding to Be a Conductor

ES: *When you started out on your musical life, was conducting always there? Or did you ever perhaps think of being an instrumentalist instead?*

MTT: I thought about being involved in the world of music. I can't say there was a specific moment when I thought, 'I want to be a conductor.' Maybe in high school I began to think I could be a conductor, which was an outcome of the fact that I already was a pianist, and playing chamber music and taking some ensemble responsibility. But much more important was that earlier I had already decided to become a musician, perhaps long before I even realized it myself; certainly long before I told my parents that that was my intention.

What it really goes back to is my realizing as a very, very small child that life was going on and people were talking to one another, commenting upon what was happening around them – but in fact the most important things that were happening around them, or perhaps within them, were not being discussed at all, or else were being discussed in such a veiled or confused sort of way that the messages weren't really getting through. And in music I discovered, or felt intuitively, that the message was very much getting through, that there was a kind of expression, a kind of companionship, a kind of closeness that I felt from a very early age towards Bach, Brahms, Stravinsky, Schoenberg, Prokofiev, that I actually didn't feel towards other people or other children, particularly of my own age. And I felt that the things that were being said to me in music were the most profound and most significant communications I was receiving.

ES: *And you wanted to communicate those things to other people, presumably?*

MTT: I wanted to be in that world, I wanted to be part of that world, whatever it was, I couldn't imagine what it was, but the idea that there was a musical accompaniment, a musical subtext, a musical sub-song, to all events of life, was something I latched on to very early.

One of my very, very first memories is of my parents' house in Los Angeles. In the late afternoon the light would come through windows at one end of the house. There were venetian blinds and the blinds would be open so the light would come into the room in bands of light, because there was a lot of dust in the air in San Fernando Valley in the summertime especially, and in these bands of light there were motes of dust, dancing in the light; and my first musical memory, I think, is watching those particles of dust moving, and reaching way up over my head to the keyboard of this big old upright rosewood Steinway grand that my parents had, and trying to play notes that would accompany this dance of the dust. I can remember that very vividly. And then I remember that every time I was out walking round in the big garden we had, or at school on the playground or anywhere, at any time, if I was not actually talking with somebody else, there was constant music going on in my head, whether it was music that I'd been hearing on my parents' gramophone or just a continuous original stream of music in my mind.

It was really my parents who recognized that I was so involved with music and playing everything by ear, just anything that I wanted to. My parents gave me music lessons so that I would learn to read notation, because they were worried that I would become a tremendous 'by ear' musician, like my father, but not actually able to read. So they first gave me some piano lessons, just to learn to read music, so I'd have that skill, with no other thought beyond that. There were teachers who were saying, 'Well, Michael is talented and he should go to a better teacher, and he should practice many hours a day,' and my parents absolutely did not want me to do that. They were dead set against the idea of my becoming a prodigy; so I just practised what I wanted to, and I think I probably improvised and made up things just as much as I played the actual lessons I was supposed to be doing.

ES: *And when did you first pick up a baton and stand in front of an orchestra?*
MTT: The very first time was in junior high school, well, maybe even before that. In a way it was back in nursery school. I remember that we had a teacher who would come a couple of times a week, and she would play music on the piano; we had various instruments, tambourines, wood blocks, things like that, and we were supposed to tap the rhythm of what she was playing, and she would shift from one rhythm to another, and I remember that I could always change rhythm immediately, and then I would notice

certain other children who weren't changing rhythm, and I would stop and look over at them and tell them that they should be changing to this other rhythm. I must have been, what, three or four at that point.

But really the first time I conducted was in junior high school, when I was playing the oboe in the school orchestra one day, and the teacher didn't show up, and there was a substitute teacher who was sent in who was actually a physical education instructor, a kind of assistant football coach. This poor fellow came in and he was supposed to be conducting a Sammartini symphony of all things, and of course he didn't know what was happening, so he said, 'Well, is there anybody here who can do this?' And I said, 'Yes, I can' (I was around twelve or thirteen), and I got up and conducted that rehearsal.

So the very first piece I ever conducted was some symphony by Sammartini. I think it was in G minor.

ES: *How old were you when you first conducted a major orchestra – the Boston Symphony, say?*
MTT: I was twenty-four when I first conducted the BSO.

ES: *Did you feel confident? Or apprehensive?*
MTT: Oh, completely confident in the repertory that I knew. Maybe that's the thing, especially when you're a young conductor. There are certain pieces you really do know well – and others you're still trying to figure out, of course. I was very lucky at that time because the orchestra had a lot of experienced people in it, and there was I, saying, 'I really love these pieces, they are so important, let's do them even better ...' They were very co-operative, very generous, great colleagues.

To Begin at the Beginning

ES: *What would you say is the single most difficult thing about conducting a concert?*
MTT: The bow at the beginning.

ES: *You're kidding.*
MTT: No really. Look – you work your way up to a performance of a score. You explore the subtext more and more. You try to interiorize the subtext more and more. You try to bring the piece and the world of the piece into yourself spiritually. But it also physically affects you. Your body feels quite different when you perform different composers. Its mass, shape, size and

centre of gravity seem to change with the stylistic and psychological density of the piece you're performing. Each composer and each work demands a physical equilibrium different from the one you use in real life. You perform in an altered state of consciousness that you must find anew as you walk on to the stage.

It can be terribly hard, this transition from the real self to the idealized musical self. Various things can make you absolutely crazy or furious during this time. Suddenly one of your waistcoat buttons chips, or the tie won't tie itself quite properly, or you suddenly think you must have another look at one detail of the score, or you remember something you didn't quite get round to rehearsing, or you really do need another cup of coffee, or someone was supposed to come backstage and say hello and pick up tickets and you don't know if they've got there or not. Maybe your shoulder is hurting and you think you should take some aspirin before doing the performance, or maybe the hall is too cold. It can be very distracting. You can really get so upset about something so silly and trivial.

Then, of course, there's all the hustle and bustle of the backstage – the orchestra's got to get on, the concessionaires have to stop, the personal manager comes to tell you that we are down two violins who are ill, the house manager wants to know when there should be a pause for latecomers, the stage manager is rounding up the orchestra to get on to the stage, there are announcements, people are taking leave of me, and I have to face this moment where I have to tell myself, 'Okay, we're on.' I shake hands with the leader backstage, we wish each other good luck, or say something rude and obscene in Russian or German, or some traditional showbiz backstage line. He goes off. I hear the applause for him and then I must walk out.

And the first thing I have to do, if I am in England, is negotiate a series of idiotic steps in full view of the public to get up to the platform. I certainly prefer to walk straight out on to the platform. But no, I have to walk out and then I have to get myself up these little steps and walk on to the platform. By now the orchestra has stood up. I come round and then shake hands with the leader and the violinist standing next to him and bow to the audience. Then I have to turn around, seat the orchestra, wait a moment for everything to quiet down, and get myself ready to begin the piece. It's all part of the concert ritual.

This taking a bow moment is in fact very difficult for me. I know who I am off-stage. I can feel my own nervousness and my own excitement. But I have to walk out as myself on to the stage and relate as myself to the orchestra and to the audience and then somehow turn all this around and begin actually making the music. This means I have to become the composer as much as I can. And becoming the composer and becoming the music has nothing to do with these conventional rituals. You must go back to the place in which the music was actually conceived.

My key to this transition has been the great Hebrew prayer, the Schehecheyanu. This prayer in English says, 'Blessed art Thou, our Lord God, King of the Universe, who has granted us life, who has sustained us, and who has brought us to this place.' I say this prayer to myself just before I go onto the stage. Then I can cross over the border. I can float up the stairs. I can come round the orchestra. I can adjust my pacing so it will work out right as I step on to the platform itself. I can greet everyone. I can do everything that I have to do – and yet I'm already in the place where the music is going to begin.

On the Podium: Technique

ES: *So you're there, on the podium, and there are of course technical preoccupations. But for a conductor pure technique is probably less important than it is in instrumental playing. What's important surely is actually communicating the thoughts and feelings and emotions, and getting the balances right. Would you say that's true? Or do you attach great importance to basic stick technique?*

MTT: There is a classical orthodox stick technique, which is very important, that was primarily mastered by people who came from the traditional school of operatic conducting, in European opera houses. The technique was extremely necessary because like as not there was no rehearsal at all, and you had to be able to get through an opera, with all the recits and arias and alternative versions (not to mention catastrophes), without any comment to the orchestra at all. So there was a sort of lingua franca of baton moves, and that was the sort of education in conducting I first had from my teacher Ingolf Dahl, who had worked in German opera houses a lot and in Zurich. I still go back to that at times. That is still the centre of what I try and do.

One of the first things I was told by Ingolf was that conducting technique is a terribly simple thing because there are only three possible ways you can beat: up and down is one. If you beat up and down, that will cause the music to go faster. If you beat from side to side, the music will go slower, it will become more sustained. Away from you, in front of you, will make the music louder; close to you, backwards, will make the music softer. It really does have that effect when you work with an orchestra. So, there are the only three possible ways you can conduct. Everything else is just a combination of those moves. It's terribly easy. It's working out all the spaces in between those moves which is the difficult bit. You need to become acquainted with that space, what can happen in that space.

Technique in conducting is a curious thing because it's sometimes altered by the people with whom you are working. You sense the general reaction time of the group. The reaction time of each orchestra is very different, and the way they respond to a particular conductor is very different. But in itself the orchestra has a kind of collective reaction time which one has to learn to work with. If members of a different orchestra have to come together, to play together, in some festival situation, it can be very difficult for them to do so.

When we had the memorial concert for Leonard Bernstein in New York, we had an orchestra which was composed of members of the London Symphony Orchestra, the Vienna Philharmonic, the Israel Philharmonic, the Academy of Santa Cecilia, the New York Philharmonic and the Boston Symphony. I took the first rehearsal, and the first piece to be done was a meditation from Lenny's Mass. This is a piece which opens with a unison attack for percussion, harp and strings. We had a concert-master from the Vienna Philharmonic, a second violinist from the Academy of Santa Cecilia, a principal viola from Israel, a cellist from Vienna, a bass player from Moscow, two New York percussionists, and a keyboard player from, I think, the Orchestre National of France. I gave an upbeat and then the opening downbeat – and there were at least five discernible attacks – it sounded like a quintuplet. It was that different. The whole first part of the rehearsal was spent resolving amongst ourselves when we were going to play. You know the old joke of how Furtwängler conducted the Berlin Philharmonic: they used to say his beat was so vague that they would all play when he got the stick down to his third waistcoat button. So there is a whole question of reaction time, of the ensemble perceiving what that time is, and learning to mould that.

The other day I rehearsed the backs of the sections. These are the people in the orchestra who need to have the most highly concentrated awareness of what's going on because they are on the edges, they really have to be clued into the conductor and the centre of the orchestra. That's what makes a really great orchestra, how much they are involved. It's in tribute to them that I always shake hands with the violinist standing next to the leader when I'm taking a bow. But the feeling of making music or working with an orchestra is not so much one of starting something or stopping something, although there are moments when you have to have the ability to do that very quickly and efficiently, but the more important aspect of making suggestions, suggesting that some quality might come to the surface, or that the pacing might just move on a trifle. I may sometimes stop and say,

'Play these notes as slowly in the tempo as you can. Play these as quickly and bouncily in the tempo as you can; in the tempo, or maybe different sides of the tempo. Play this on the right side of the beat, play this on the left side of the beat, on the front edge or the back edge of the note' – which, although it is only a matter of a millisecond in time, makes an enormous difference.

Pop musicians have an incredible sense of this. Years ago, for a few days, I went on tour with James Brown, the famous soul singer. This was at the time that his big international hit was 'Sex Machine', and he had this band that he had tuned to an amazing level of precision. He had a rhythm section which consisted of a drummer playing a drum set, a hand drummer playing conga drums, and an electric bass player. He wanted the kit drummer to play on the front edge of the beat, he wanted the hand drummer to play on the back edge of the beat, and he wanted the bass player to play right in the middle. And he could actually discern just those relationships even while singing and boogalooing his brains out. In the middle of a song he would reel around and yell, 'Conga too far front, bass too far back.' He'd fine the players for not playing exactly as he demanded. By crafting the stroke of the beat he was defining just how long now really is. He was really determining the width and length and time of the present. That is a very interesting and sophisticated concept that's not even approached by most musicians, especially not classical musicians.

Classical music is different. It doesn't deal with time in that sort of way. It deals with time in a way much more related to inflection. That's what the interpretation of classical music is – it's inflection. It's punctuation and inflection. And for that a different kind of technique is necessary. It's feeling in space where the music actually is. Using space as an allegory of time to indicate the sort of pacing, the kind of feel, the kind of mood that the music should have.

I learnt more about that through working with clay than from anything else in my life. Very early on, about the time I was first playing piano and first playing music, I was also in a pottery class in San Fernando Valley and we were all seven- or eight-year-old kids, you know, learning to make silly things that would please our parents. But so many of these things were based on rolling a coil of clay. And when you work with clay you very soon discover that if you try and force the clay to make a coil, it will not do it, it just becomes square and then breaks up into fragments and dries up. But if you just use a very light pressure that suggests to the clay what you would like it to do, it will quite rapidly turn itself into a coil. With the potter's wheel, even more so. You have to find exactly the right level of pressure,

Clay class at about seven years old, c.1952

you just suggest to it that it should come up into a nice cone. It's such an art, the art of suggestion. Not doing too much, just that little bit at the right time, not overdoing it. It's difficult because you have to control your own enthusiasms and insecurities and your own need perhaps to be physically involved in some way. Conductors generally live a long time, perhaps because they do aerobic kinds of things, physical activities, a lot. And what is so interesting is that the conductors who have died on the podium, or just after being on the podium, have all died after conducting slow movements, because actually in very, very slow movements there's a kind of intensity which is somehow much greater than just beating rapidly.

Actually a wonderful way to learn about conducting is my favourite programme on British television, *One Man and His Dog*.

ES: *Ah yes, the sheepdog and border collie competitions.*
MTT: It's my favourite programme because it reminds me of such important lessons about conducting. First of all, you always notice it's the old sheepdogs that win. The sheepdogs have to bring the sheep down from the mountain, around a hedge, over a brook, across a meadow and into a pen at the bottom. The young dogs are so eager to get the sheep to go around this particular hedge or over that particular brook that they go wildly after the sheep, who go crazy and run much too far, scattering in all directions. Then

the young dogs have to go madly chasing after them and try and get them back on the correct track. But the older dogs see the sheep dawdling or becoming a bit wayward, and they just lean forward a little and quietly and a bit menacingly growl, 'Woof.' The sheep think, 'Oh, yes, yes, quite right,' and they go exactly where they are supposed to.

That's very much like some of the most important principles of conducting, which, as a young conductor, one has to remind oneself of all the time. That's why I know that in my early career some of the best performances I did, especially with some of the great Romantic orchestras, were when I was either tired or ill. Because somehow that aged me, it put another twenty years of experience on me. In a way it slowed everything down a bit.

Conducting often feels as if you are piloting a dirigible or very large oil-tanker. This enormous thing's in motion and it's making majestic progress, and you can't just say, 'Oh, let's stop.' It has to be allowed to stop in good time, so you have to look around and say, 'Soon, we are going to stop,' and communicate this to the engine room. That's very much the case in conducting minimalist compositions. It's quite fascinating in those pieces because it's all about playing time. You know, a jazzer would play time, very, very strict time, with an incredible evenness. And what you discover is that everyone's perception of time is different, and the whole art of playing a piece is finding what someone else's perception of time is and then linking

One Man and His Dog

Conducting *The Desert Music*, Brooklyn Academy of Music, 1984

in with them. And in a very long piece, like *The Desert Music* by Steve Reich, or something like that, you can start to feel one particular player in the ensemble is perhaps moving a little bit ahead. You cannot make any physical gesture, certainly not any rapid, violent gesture, to try and bring that person back into the fold, back into synch with the others, because if you do it will upset all of the other things that are happening. You have to just look at that person and arch one eyebrow, perhaps, or raise your chin slightly, tilt your shoulders one way or another, to caution them, or alert them that they should perhaps listen just a little bit more. I'm sure that in the classical repertory there are many times in which one has to do that. I expect I'll discover more of those in the future.

There are moments when the conductor is really necessary, and moments when he is not. If the players truly know the piece and have lived through it, and know exactly what they're doing, then they really can play it, a lot of it, by themselves. This became very clear to me when I was around nineteen years old. There was an orchestra which was called the Beverley Hills Symphony Orchestra – an orchestra of pick-up musicians which was put together now and then to play for Stravinsky. The old man was doing a suite from *The Firebird* and a few pieces from *Petrushka*. He got up in front of the orchestra, they stood to attention as they always did, and then sat down. He

began conducting a kind of jerky three. And against these silent movie ges-
ticulations the double basses, perfectly together, played the opening of *The
Firebird*. He carried on for a couple of bars, then he stopped and looked at us
in bewilderment and said, 'Oh no, *Petrushka, Petrushka*.' He had been conducting the opening of *Petrushka*, and the double basses, absolutely perfectly, absolutely gorgeously, had played the opening of *The Firebird*. There'd
been a mistake about the order of rehearsal. We all had a good laugh. But I
thought, 'Well, that's really interesting; you see, if the orchestra really
knows a piece they can play it, even if the conductor is conducting an
entirely different work.'

The truth is that it's not really necessary for me to give endless clear
beats to indicate tempi to the musicians I'm privileged to work with. It's
other things I have to communicate. Questions of phrasing or the general
mood or colour balance or little expressive accents and details, and things
within the whole picture. I don't have to keep giving time signals, particularly if it's a piece that's in repertory. A lot of what I do is quite unorthodox;
it's horrifying for me sometimes, or surprising anyway, to see a film of
myself and to think, 'Oh my goodness, I'm not really doing that, am I?'
Nonetheless it seems to work.

The sort of techniques that I initially learned were so strongly connected
with contemporary music, though, that I have to be aware that I'm not
dealing with the same sort of reaction time in Beethoven or Schubert or
other parts of the repertory. It's more necessary in late Stravinsky or Boulez.

ES: *You mean precise, angular gestures?*
MTT: Yes, instantaneous attacks and cut-offs.

ES: *When the musicians are utterly dependent on those signals?*
MTT: Right.

ES: *Of course visual information is important for the audience, as well as for the
musicians. For example, if an audience feels the emanations of the conductor in a particularly intense* pianissimo, *then they are going to get more drawn into the moment.
I think people overlook that. It's like in a Mahler symphony, when Mahler instructs
his wind players to lift the bells of their instruments in the air — it is not just to
change the sound and make the moment more prominent, it is actually to pull focus
visually, surely?*
MTT: Yes, that's one part of it.

ES: *Conversely, when they watch a conductor in the concert hall, people might say,*

'Oh my goodness, he's very showy',or ,'He's very extrovert, is it really necessary?' It was often said about Bernstein.
MTT: Sure.

ES: *But the fact is that at this level of communication, those moments that excite players into giving that little bit more are surely what it's all about?*
MTT: Well, it is about that. You see, in the conducting profession they say that you can have a piece in your head, but do you have it in your arm yet? Having a piece in your arm is a different thing, because it means that you've actually moved through space and time with that piece of music, you can actually feel the plasticity of the notes within time, in your arm, your body, your face – everything becomes expressive of how you mean the contour and the intensity of the music to be played, to be heard.

Bernstein would always say, 'Forget about conducting and just play the music, just play the music as if it were in space, as if it were on an instrument, the orchestra is an instrument.' But of course he also had to begin, as everyone else does, with a first performance of a piece, and find that space, find the sort of line that would give him the confidence to project exactly what it was he wanted. Ultimately you arrive at a place where the music is totally interiorized – it's written into your molecular structure. When you arrive at this point you're totally unconscious of what you're physically doing. It's all part of existing in the past/present/future of the work.

First Rehearsals

ES: *When you get into the first rehearsals, how much of the detail is pre-set, and how much comes out in the course of rehearsal and the actual performance?*
MTT: You mean when I'm first doing a piece?

ES: *Well, maybe both. When you're first doing a piece and when you've done a piece many times before.*
MTT: When you're first doing a piece, no matter how much you have studied it, how much you have analyzed it, it's still the first time, and you are inevitably just exploring it. You are trying to sculpt and shape, and make little cairns and signposts, and an Ariadne's thread to keep things connected and on course. The more you know the piece, the more you have a methodology of setting it out. You know just how you're going to rehearse it, and how you're going to perform it.

But that can change. That's one of the most difficult things, I think, about conducting. Sometimes you have certain feelings about a piece, and you learn it, and it's very focused, the way it's supposed to be. Then you don't do that piece for some time. And you come back to it again and you may find you are actually uncomfortable with what you did earlier. But you don't have the time or the will to deconstruct your interpretations as thoroughly as you would like to, to change some of the conceptions which still remain from the way you first learned it.

Let me give you a specific example: Stravinsky's *The Rite of Spring*. I worked with terrific intensity on this piece, first on piano for four hands, playing it for Stravinsky, and then with the Boston Symphony Orchestra, going into every little detail of the piece, every little inflection, over the course of a whole season. There were people in the orchestra who had played it with Koussevitzky and with Monteux and others, it was such a total experience. Now, although I have done *The Rite of Spring* since, and I've done some hair-raising performances, especially with the LSO, I have not yet been able to take the next step with the piece as I really would like to. The amount of study necessary to do it would be enormous. Moreover, I fear I would wind up with a conception of the piece which would be so detailed that it would necessitate rehearsing it in the Celibidache style, where I would become too fussy, too specific about the exact nuance of each phrase. It might turn out wonderfully, but I think I would drive myself crazy trying to do it, and perhaps everyone else working with me.

I know the direction I would want to go with it. I would want to perform it much more like village music, like Rimsky-Korsakov, and less like twentieth-century, hard edge, contemporary music. Because all the inflections are there, all the folkloric twists, all of the little funny breakings in the voice and the funny squeaky sounds of village instruments. They're all there, that's what the dissonances and the odd orchestration is meant to suggest – and then blow it up. If you took a little village orchestra in Russia and gave them all contact microphones and plugged them into the Grateful Dead's speaker system, you'd have the effect of what Stravinsky was trying to do.

ES: *But isn't that an interesting point, that whatever else the piece has or hasn't got, it must have a sort of first-time shock about it? I've heard you say about a particular phrase that some conductors would make sure that all these solos were absolutely metronomical and precise, whereas you like to feel that the soloist has room to create something of their own.*

MTT: Right. But a piece like *The Rite of Spring* is very frustrating for me because I can't play every part myself. I'd much rather play it on the piano now, maybe, than play it with the orchestra, because I just know, I can feel under my fingers, exactly how I want every little bit to be.

Interpretation and the *Zeitgeist*

MTT: You see, the great thing about these pieces we all perform, the 'classics', is that they don't reveal themselves at first reading. They have many aspects which change all the time, different things can be seen in them at different times in your life, at different levels of your experience. So there is a change in the interpretation, in the performance, as you go through life. The important thing about the great pieces is that they can never completely be defined, there is no definitive performance.

There are performances which present a particularly striking view of a piece at a particular time for a particular audience. In more provocative times in my life I used to say interpretation is a polite word for distortion. What does an interpreter do? He looks at a work which is a big universal masterpiece, vast in its expression, and he sees something in it which is particularly relevant to people of the interpreter's own time. And he performs the piece, emphasizing those aspects of it in such a way that the audience feels, 'My goodness, this piece is so fresh, it's as if it's just been written, it has so much to say to us.' And that is considered at that particular moment a very vivid and important interpretation.

It's easy to understand this as we compare interpretative views of Bach. Liszt, Busoni and Schoenberg appreciated in Bach the crazy chromaticism, the expressive 'Mathias Grünewald at the organ' aspect of his music. They saw his music as a precursor of their late romantic vision. Schweizer and Landowska saw Bach as an expressive hierarchy of small to large musical designs. This fitted in with the Schenkerian analytic conception of their day. Stokowski saw in Bach a bravura theatricality. He transcribed the overwhelming sonorities of the organ pieces to virtuoso turns for orchestra and conductor. Glenn Gould emphasized glittering articulation, spareness of sound and intellectual design – almost a preview of the electronic versions of Bach that were to follow. And most recently the original instrument crowd has placed historical correctness and research above intuitive performing instinct. But all these artists did what they did because they loved Bach and they wanted to make him more relevant to the audiences of their times.

But as we have already seen, a generation later, or in the sort of world we're living in now, five years later, people say, 'Oh well, that view was part of that time,' and, 'Oh yes, we've heard that, we know all that, and we want something new now.' The way people perceive what is genuinely felt, or truly significant, changes according to what their perceptual bias may be, and of course the most difficult thing to perceive is that your perception itself has a particular bias, a particular twist.

One thing that I find so amusing to observe is the question of forgeries. I'm very interested in art forgeries. Fakes of Vermeer were done in the 1930s and were accepted worldwide as his paintings. You see those paintings now, and immediately the whole world of 1930s expressionism leaps out at you. The look on their faces, the sort of body language in the pictures, makes it obvious that they are not paintings of the seventeenth century. They're not from that world at all, but from some world in which the disturbing currents of the twentieth century are already very evident in the people being portrayed. But at the time that they were presented, the painter who did the forgery and people in general were looking at the whole world in the same way. So they couldn't see that the painting was a forgery. Something like that is relevant to musical performance and musical interpretation.

ES: *Are you saying that if you brought Furtwängler back and put him on at the Festival Hall next week, that the whole experience would be something alien; that it might even be laughed off the stage?*
MTT: Yes, it might be laughed off the stage, but probably it wouldn't be, because in the case of Furtwängler you had someone who was so convinced about what his vision was, what his view was, that it carried the whole audience, the whole orchestra, the whole world with it.

Belief

ES: *We're into a very interesting area here – belief.*
MTT: Well, I'll tell you a wonderful experience I had of belief. Years ago I was conducting the Chicago Symphony Orchestra one summer at Ravinia. We had very little rehearsal time, and one of the pieces in the week was Brahms's Second Symphony. At that time Frank Miller was the principal cellist of the orchestra. This man was a great artist, a legendary cellist and section leader, and he had worked for donkey's years under Toscanini, Walter and everybody that had been in Chicago. In the rehearsal we finished the second movement, in which there is an enormous cello passage, and, while the orchestra took a break, I turned to Mr Miller and said, 'Frank, tell me the truth, what do you think of what I am doing with this cello passage, is it all right?' And he said in a wonderful lion-like, smiley way that he had, 'Michael, we've done these pieces so many different times

and places, we don't know any more what's right or wrong or anything like that. All we know is that every once in a while somebody comes along and he's got an idea, and he's really convinced about it, and it goes over, and that's good.' That is one of the truest, real-life statements about the way music performance actually works.

ES: *Yes, yes. It's like what you were saying the other day about the Adagietto in Mahler's Fifth. You said that when you first performed the movement you took it slightly up tempo, because all the evidence suggested that Mahler preferred to take it faster. And then you asked Leonard Bernstein what he thought.*
MTT: And he said, 'When you make up your mind what it really means to you, and how you mean it to go, then it'll be just fine.'

Pressures on Performers

Tremendous pressure exists in the life of a conductor (and it exists in the life of all musicians now). It comes from the way modern society expects us to work: the number of pieces we are expected to perform, the number of concerts, the very short preparation period, the lack of time for absorption in a piece. Symphonies such as Mahler's Second, Strauss's *Ein Heldenleben*, Beethoven's Ninth, the big pieces, were meant to be performed by an orchestra that had probably rehearsed the piece for at least a week or perhaps even longer.

Most of Beethoven's symphonies were first played at Academy concerts in Vienna. Beethoven would do one of these a year. The première of each new piece had a sense of occasion about it. It was this sense of occasion that led to the mega-symphonies of Bruckner, Tchaikovsky and Mahler. These pieces were conceived as vast undertakings, the combined efforts of performers over weeks, culminating in one, or maybe two apocalyptic performances that would be talked and argued about for months.

Mahler, for example, would never have imagined that a group of musicians would, as we do now, have a rehearsal on a Wednesday, then Thursday maybe have a couple of rehearsals, the next day a final rehearsal, and then perform the piece that night. Or possibly another three or four nights, if it's an American orchestra. Mahler would never have imagined that his pieces would be used in that sort of way.

It's terribly difficult as a performer, as a conductor, to go out on stage and do a piece which is about some little matter like birth, life, enchantment, disillusionment, rage, death, resignation, resurrection – and do it with a couple of days' notice, and then four or five times in a row. It's hard to re-experience all of those things, to come up with all the inner strength you need, with consistency, and the fierce intensity of repetition often demanded. In another way, it is very difficult for the musicians here in London to put together a huge programme over a few days, perform it, and then immediately go on to something else, and it might need a completely different sort of sensibility.

For example, we did a programme of Bernstein and Stravinsky, then moved on to a programme of Taverner and Beethoven, then next week on to Strauss and Brahms, then suddenly we had to make the shift into Debussy's *Jeux* and *Le martyre de St Sébastien*. Well, these are such different pieces, they are poles apart, and the public is asking the musicians to make great psychological leaps, and that's very exhausting. It can lead to a kind of emotional exhaustion which can very easily become part of the performance, if you're not careful.

What it also means is that the conductor faces the problem of trying to enlist the co-operation of the musicians in creating moods and atmospheres which are not necessarily related at all to the mood and the atmosphere of the real lives we are all leading, or the conditions under which the work is being prepared. For example, you come in from a difficult morning, commute to the Barbican, park your car, having maybe dealt with paying your taxes on the way, or some other vexing matters from the long list of things which assail us all in modern times, and you come as a musician into the rehearsal. There are a number of things to be done, and time is limited. To try and find a mood of utter tranquillity, relaxation, gratefulness, spirituality, is difficult. It's much easier to say, 'Could you play it louder, or shorter, or faster?' It's difficult to say, 'Now, in the remaining thirty-five seconds, could you give me utter serenity, tranquillity, and a sense of eternal peace?' Those kinds of qualities require a long time, and a kind of patience, on the part of both the conductor and the performers. Patience to say, 'Well, it's not quite as beautiful as it could be, not quite as wonderful, but it's nobody's fault, it just needs a little more time, a little bit more thinking, or relaxing with the piece.' That time should be there somehow, but it's not there in most working situations in music in the world today, and it's one of the most difficult things for the conductor to find and to create together with the people who are performing. With most of the orchestras that I conduct, certainly the LSO and the American orchestras, there is an immense capacity for virtuosity, and tremendous peaks. Some of these orchestras can play very loudly, very softly, very articulately – but the most difficult thing for us to find together is the sort of easy, no one's in a hurry, everything's all right, gentle tranquillity, this sense of total security, a feeling of 'nothing could possibly disturb this'. I have to focus my own energies most acutely to try and create that sort of feeling, that kind of sense of easy tranquillity, with the LSO, or with any orchestra. That's partially me, partially the LSO, but it's also the twentieth century. We don't live lives where we have a sense of easy tranquillity.

Planning, Rehearsing and Performing

ES: *How do you cope with the whole nonsense of having to plan years in advance? How do you manage to surmount the difficulties of finding yourself, say, in two years' time with a series of dates and a series of works that may not be in your spirit or soul at that particular point in time? Do you somehow have artificially to wrench yourself back into the thinking of those pieces?*

MTT: You do, and it's easier for some people than others. It's very hard for me because my relationships with music and life are so inter-related; and events in life, events in the world, change my feelings about things, and therefore I want a certain kind of music at a particular moment. Of course, I may be committed to doing a particular piece. I must do it. But I refuse to book myself, as many artists do, three, four, five years in advance. They have this big masterplan: this year they'll do Bruckner's Second and then the next year it will be Bruckner's Third.

I realize now that there are pieces that I am not going to perform, ever. It's actually a very liberating and exciting feeling just suddenly to say, 'I'm not going to do those pieces. I have now chosen to concentrate on certain pieces which mean more to me, or perhaps write some new music myself.' I'm not going to perform *Lohengrin,* much as I may admire things in it. I'm not going to perform the Bruckner Second Symphony, it's not going to happen. I'm not going to perform *Pénélope* by Fauré. I may never perform anything by Fauré.

ES: *Are there any other pieces you can't see yourself returning to in years to come?*

MTT: I can't see myself performing a great deal of Vivaldi in the near future, except in an exploitative way. Yes, if I had a concert to do with two marvellous trumpets or a terrific mandolin player, or something like that, I would certainly programme one of his concertos, but I wouldn't do a whole evening of it. And if I had a choice between doing something like the Vivaldi *Gloria,* or a comparable piece by Monteverdi or Pergolesi, I know exactly what my preference would be – for someone other than Vivaldi. Perhaps that just has to do with the recognition of what I think my strengths are. I'm interested in giving shape and defining contrast in music, and doing interesting and perhaps provoking things with the inflection of the music, mercurial things with the inflection of the music. But when the point of the music is to be just nice and all right and on course, just modulated with a certain general kind of sound and texture all the time, then I don't find myself so interested. There are others who can handle these eleven minute sound bites better than I.

ES: *But it must occasionally happen that you find yourself due to conduct a piece that you're not in the mood for with three hours to get inside it. If you're not in the mood, is it possible to counterfeit your feelings, or do you have to resort to purely technical matters to persuade players, like balance, loud, soft and phrasing?*
MTT: The conductor must be a source of energy for what's going on in the rehearsal and in the performance, and even if you are tired and scarcely able to connect your thoughts you still somehow have to have a thread that keeps the rehearsal moving, keeps the performance moving. I don't have a problem in performances, because the experience of performing is still so exciting to me that whatever the circumstances there is an edge that's always there. And even in rehearsals I recognize that there is a kind of reaction that happens in me, so that I actually have a burst of energy in the last quarter of an hour. Just as everyone's energy is low, like a long-distance runner coming into the last lap, I suddenly feel, 'Aha, now I'm going to really accomplish something, you know, wrap this up.' Some musicians find that very daunting – 'Oh God, he's off again!'

There are lots of old homilies about performing. One of the first things I heard about being a musician was, 'Being a professional musician means that you play well even when you don't feel like it.' I have been trying to change that in myself, and in the other people with whom I work, by saying, 'Being a professional musician means that you will always find the way to feel like playing well.'

ES: *That's what I was getting at; and then communicating that feeling to the players.*
MTT: Of course, there are different styles of conducting. Take Bernstein. Lenny wanted to be the centre of everything. And, particularly in the earlier days when I first saw him, he would rehearse in Boston or New York in a way which was incredibly obsessive about details, to such a point that they would never have played through the whole piece before the performance, or at least not since the very early rehearsals. He relied on his magnetism and excitement as a performer to pull all of the details together in the performance. A scary and dangerous thing to do, and not something that

Serge Koussevitzky, signed by Olga Koussevitzky

orchestral musicians really like, because they want to feel that they have played the piece and know where they are. What made the last part of Lenny's career as a conductor so great was that he'd arrived at the point where he could be absolutely obsessive about detail, but still have time to do the entire performance, because he had entered that nirvana of conductorial existence, the world of unlimited rehearsal, an ecstasy of eternal overtime. That was always there for him to use, and he always used it wonderfully, and nobody objected because they recognized that it was a very extraordinary experience to work with him at that time of his life.

Koussevitzky was very funny about that – about a conductor's perceptions of orchestral musicians. When Koussevitzky developed the Boston Symphony Orchestra he did a very clever thing. He got very wonderful players from France, Germany, Russia, mostly from those places, and brought them all to Boston. They were all living in Boston, all speaking different languages, all adjusting to a new country, all very confused about everything. They had only one thing in common – Serge Koussevitzky. He was their employer and the one person who spoke all of their languages. He was the centre of everything. His first plan was to have constructed, next to Symphony Hall in Boston, a very large apartment house, a huge block of flats, in which he proposed that all the members of the orchestra would live. He said, with his Russian accent, 'It vill be vonderful in my building, they vill have vonderful time, and then I vill press button that vill ring bell, and zat vill mean ve vill rehearsing be.' And he was quite astonished to discover that the musicians didn't want to live like that.

Conductors like Koussevitzky and Stokowski were such inspired people, yet so much of what they both did was just to say, 'It can be better, it can be better.' And in the case of Koussevitzky, it was wonderful, because when he spoke English he was always translating from some other language, mostly Russian or French, so his big phrase to the Boston Symphony used to be 'Gentlemen, we will do it again, we will do it again, and we will do it again and again until it will not be beautiful.' Which is, in French, *'Jusqu'il ne sera beau.'* So he was translating it literally. And Stokey would just say, 'It can be more beautiful. Yes, of course, of course.'

Great Performances

ES: *Can you explain why one day there may be an extraordinary magic in a performance, and the next day, nothing? Yet basically it's the same reading.*

MTT: No one knows what makes a great performance. For me, some of the greatest have been evenings when I've relinquished conscious control over many things that were happening in the orchestra. The nature of my training was to be supremely aware of all kinds of detail and occurrences in the orchestra, to anticipate and react to them; but in recent years I've recognized that some of the best work that I've actually done has been on a particular occasion where somehow I was able to surrender all of those questions to the extraordinary virtuosi with whom I'm so lucky to work, and start to mould the music at some higher level. Almost listening to the performance and saying, 'Well, here it should grow more intense, here it should grow more tranquil, here it should start to become more halting, slightly but inexorably pulling back, here it should race ahead.'

It's very difficult to express this in words – the changes in levels of emotional intensity. I don't know exactly how they are communicated. But I do know that there are some evenings where it does happen, and the effect of the music on those nights is so overwhelming to everyone in the orchestra and in the audience that people come back and say, 'That was so extraordinary,' and I don't know what to say to them, I cannot speak to them. I'm still so far out there in the realm of the music, where this spirit has inspired the music. I so appreciate that they come back to say hello or say something nice, but I can't react to what they're saying, because I've just gone so far away.

I became a musician because I didn't feel I would ever be able to communicate with other people through words, through life, as well as perhaps I should, or as comfortably as I wished I could. But through music I felt, 'Well, this is a way I can really be with other people in the kind of loving and sharing way that I would like to be.' But as this new aspect of what it really means to do one of these kind of transcendent performances becomes clearer to me, it's frightening. Because in fact the music is leading to a lonelier and lonelier place. I never expected that that would happen. And it's a very strange thing to be thinking that the best present, the most wonderful thing I can actually do for all these people that I care for in the audience, in the orchestra, everyone, is to go out to this far realm where in fact I am so alone, so absolutely alone, that I sometimes fear whether I can ever really come back. It's very scary.

ES: *Yes, I've noticed in the short time that I've been around you that you're someone who does become totally absorbed – perhaps even obsessed – with the task in hand.*
MTT: It's not only the task. For example, say I'm working on the 'Eroica'. It just keeps on going through my mind, and I feel as if Beethoven is there saying, 'Don't forget me, I'm trying to say *this* to you, and I'm trying to say *this*. Do you hear what I'm saying? Do you hear what these notes are saying? Don't forget me, don't lose this.' That is devastating, that feeling that someone who's in another room, a wall away or a time away, or in a tomb, is still saying, 'Can you hear me, can you hear me?'

I've been doing the music of Debussy recently. I feel absolutely certain in this music. My way of measuring how well I know it is aiming to say I know exactly what every single bar, every single note, of this music is getting at. I know what he is trying to say in these bars. That is what it is all about. At the beginning, finding out what it is that's supposed to be said is the joy of it, is the fun of it – and then discovering that there's always more to be found out. That is what is interesting. That's what makes the pieces interesting over a longer period of time. But at a certain point it's in a way accomplished. I mean, yes, what I have to do, a person my age and at this point in my career and all that, the challenge for me now is to say, 'Okay, knowing that I know exactly what I feel about every single note, how can I now make that clear enough to the performers and through them to the audience?' That's a whole other level of technique and psychology and many other things.

But if suddenly tomorrow I found out that I could never perform *Jeux* again, or never perform the 'Eroica' again, or whatever, it really wouldn't bother me that much because I know what those pieces are saying. Even if I never hear them again, I have inside me what they are supposed to be saying, and what message the audience are supposed to have inside.

Sometimes you are walking around in the lonely nights, the lonely streets, wherever, and something happens which enables you to draw upon the message which comes from one of those pieces. If the message is in your heart, your soul, it comes out, you can gather strength from it, you can gather wisdom and consolation. That is the purpose of the music. Yes, it's nice if there is a brilliant performance, but ultimately the brilliance of the performance will vanish, will be supplanted by some other performance – but did you really get what the music was all about? Did the performer, did the interpreter assist you in getting the message?

For me, this is summed up in a stanza from Walt Whitman's 'Song of Myself'. He talks about walking through the street, which is littered with leaves, falling leaves, and every single leaf is a message from God. All of these messages are written to me, and I have to understand what the writing means:

> I find letters from God dropt in the street,
> and every one is signed by God's name
> and I leave them where they are for I know that
> wheresoever I go others will punctually come for ever and ever

What the composers are saying is more important than the music itself. It's when you're all by yourself in some situation in your life, and you realize that music is still with you. It springs into your mind, comes into your heart, in instant recollection. I think that's why these people were writing, that's why people do write. We have lost so much of that in the twentieth century, because people are so obsessed with being original that they lose sight of the fact that the reason to write music is because you have something to say to someone else. And although I really don't know if I'll go on performing and making music for ever, I'm absolutely certain that I have the message of certain composers, and once you have that ...

A Conductor's Repertoire

ES: *Giulini also says it has to be a part of his soul before he will do it. But I think then you're in a dangerous area, because you are not fully exploring a composer's work. There will be some pieces you will return to more often than others, but surely to embrace the whole œuvre of a composer is important, at least initially? To put the works you do perform in some kind of context?*

MTT: Yes, I agree that it's important to study a composer's entire output, just as it's important to study music history from the Middle Ages until now. A performance of any work benefits greatly from a sense of context. The musical, historical and spiritual context of a composition and its composer helps you to determine the interpretative priorities for that piece. But study is one thing. It's a lifelong commitment for any musician. Performing is quite another. Taking a piece out on to the stage must be a very personal committment. The musical establishment these days is obsessed with cycles and 'completeness'. It tells you that you can't just do one Bruckner symphony; you've got to do them all. And if you're going to do Bruckner, you should also of course do Schmidt and Pfitzner – the list gets more exhaustive as the repertoire and scope of recordings extends; there is always something else they think you *should* be doing.

I saw a concert with Gunther Wand, a Bruckner symphony. It was very impressive, because, like Furtwängler, he's so convinced, he's so at home in his view of the world. He has a real sense of pacing and all these things about him. And that's the world in which he wants to be. There are all these pressures on him because of the need of the orchestra he's conducted at various points to do other repertoire, but why should he do anything else other than what he wants to, unless he really has something to say? Michelangeli, a great pianist, in the same way, has found a particular repertoire, and he really does it very specially. And they are some of the people I most admire. I'm not doing that, but I feel sometimes I should be.

It is exciting to know that that potential is there, because for myself I believe that if you really spend time on it you can understand a particular composer. But at a certain point in your life you have to start asking, 'Do you really want to spend the time doing that?' I think this is something that people who write about music, music journalists such as yourself, sometimes don't recognize. It's not a question sometimes of whether someone understands a piece or not. You say, 'Well, so-and-so's not a Beethoven pianist, or so-and-so's not a this or that ...' But they could be. Anyone with a certain degree of talent and imagination can do whatever they want to do if they spend the time to become comfortable doing it. That's also true of orchestras. 'This band's not a Mozart orchestra, but it's a Mahler orchestra.' This just means they happen to have played Mahler quite a lot for some reason, but they could very easily make themselves into a Mozart orchestra or whatever they want – if they have the time to do it.

So much has changed in the role of the conductor. It's been caused by the international music scene and the sort of pace at which everything moves. Some conductors, like Wand, naturally feel drawn to a particular kind of repertoire, and feel comfortable with a certain century or a certain composer. But there is the question of an international career, and there is a kind of pressure on conductors to do everything. You're a conductor, you're an international figure, a kind of brand name, a trade mark, and if it's a big trade mark then of course you are going to do everything. You know, like Marks and Spencer – you're going to do woollen jumpers, chicken tandoori and household items.

I mean, there is a great deal of pressure upon me, not in a negative way, but in a charming and inviting way, to conduct opera. Everyone says, 'You have such theatrical instincts, why don't you conduct more opera?' I don't conduct more opera because, on the whole, my experience of opera houses has been frustrating. Yes, there are certain operas which I'd like to conduct; when I was in the opera world again in Salzburg this last summer, I thought, 'This is something I really would like to do.' But I also have to ask myself, 'How many hours are you going to actually be conscious, how many years are you going to be alive? What do you want with the time you've got?' And what I feel now is that my first priority after my responsibilities to the ensembles I work with has got to be writing my own music. I'm seriously behind in music I should have written up to this point.

Practicals

Rehearsing Mahler's Third and Brahms's Second Symphonies

MTT: Playing music together in an orchestra is a fusion of will, many people's wills. Incredibly subtle levels of give and take are involved. I'm experiencing that very much right now, working on Mahler's Third Symphony. It is such a difficult work. It's a work which demands the highest level of technical brilliance, and total sensitivity and stamina from everyone involved. And the LSO is really accomplishing this with amazing grace and ease. It's extraordinary how easily it's coming together, perhaps because I did this piece and recorded it with them three years ago, and there is a great deal of the foundation of the last performance still there. But also because the piece is so challenging that everyone's concentration is very focused. They're thinking, 'We really have to be at our very best to do this.' The piece is a kind of vast musical pageant, or perhaps it's a movie score to a psychological landscape. And although it does contain many small and very subtle fluctuations of nuance and shading, its world is nevertheless very 'theatrical'. You can look on Mahler's Third Symphony as a series of nature portraits, but also perhaps as scenes taken from an opera. So much of it is like a big recitative that would normally be sung by a baritone or tenor, but which happens to be given to the horn section, or solo trombone, or whatever it may be.

Quite to the contrary is the experience I'm having working with the orchestra on arriving at a comfortably resolved performance of Brahms's Second Symphony. Now why should that be? Here's a piece which is nowhere near as long, and for the most part not nearly so difficult technically as Mahler's Third, yet it's so much more difficult for an orchestra to play.

ES: *Why is that?*
MTT: There are many reasons. But all of them trace back to the personality and lives of Brahms and Mahler themselves – their histories, their methods of working as expressed in the works they left to us.

With the London Symphony Orchestra, 1993

Brahms is a far more secretive and difficult personality for us to understand, even though his music sounds 'easier'. He was primarily a composer of songs, choral music, piano music and chamber music. Orchestral music is a very small portion of his output and not a genre in which he was anywhere near as daring or as at home as in these more 'hands on' formats he favoured. Brahms expected that his music would be played by friends who knew him already through his songs and piano pieces. Therefore they (the musicians) would play his symphonies recognizing the nuances they already knew from his folkloric transcriptions, intermezzi, trios, etc. But, of course, today most musicians do not know this other side of Brahms. They only know the big symphonic artifacts. So the process of rehearsal is inevitably a voyage of discovery back to the levels of vulnerability of nuance and shading of the smaller works.

Mahler, also a song composer, knew from the beginning he was going to 'blow up' his songs into symphonies. So he made his symphonic versions hyper-exact notations of every curse, every shudder, every sigh his song world suggested. It's much more exacting. Yet, by being more specific in its demands it's easier for the second clarinettist to grasp.

Both Mahler's and Brahms's music is strongly based on many vernacular musical forms – dance music, folk music, religious music. So we're up against the problem of how, within the parameters of modern orchestral life, we can create a long, deep, personal history with works such as these. For those of us who are playing the piece for the first time, or with each other for the first time, there are many challenges, especially since the LSO has just finished a recording session of Steve Reich plus a recording of *La Traviata*, symphonies of Tchaikovsky and Shostakovich, and more besides. Now the orchestra must collect its thoughts and look at a Brahms piece which has the most particular demands.

Subtlety of Phrasing

So, you're trying to get an orchestra to inflect a phrase with tonal shadings that suggest the sort of subtlety that a *lieder* singer would bring to similar musical lines. What is so difficult is that in a *lieder* singer's performance, even in a sustained, *cantabile*, *piano* passage, there will be little changes of coloration, varying intensities of breath, changes in the phonemes – all of which can happen within a sustained mood. The singer can sing a long phrase which you may perceive as, yes, a *tranquillo* phrase, yet within that there are all kinds of quicksilver, swiftly moving, stream-of-consciousness coloration, indications of psychic state, of security, insecurity, ardency, fear. And somehow I've come to a point where I can imagine these same kinds of coloration happening in a viola section, a second violin section.

But how to get that to happen in practice? It's still a dream I'm pursuing. I cannot be content just to listen to a generalized, lovely, glowing *mezzo* forte sort of noise, although that can be very charming, and there are orchestras in the world, 'Romantic orchestras', which do play in such a manner and seem to have no problem. But the interpretive challenge is to go a step beyond that.

ES: *How?*

MTT: I've begun by editing the parts much more carefully, and indeed the parts of these Brahms symphonies of mine are now on their way to resembling the parts of a Mahler symphony, or a Berg orchestral piece. There are many more indications of fingerings, of dynamics, of specific articulation; here play *legato*, here play *tenuto*, here play *marcato* but *sostenuto.* These things may ultimately become compulsive, but I recognize it's too much to ask musicians to absorb them quickly. Even if the instruction is written on their parts, they say, 'Well, we already know how the phrase is meant to go, so what are those words that are written there? Oh yes, it says *legato*, it says *marcato*, it says *poco a poco più agitato*, it says *giocoso* ...' But nonetheless it can't be absorbed in five seconds, because there is too long a history behind it; and moreover it means that the players must suspend their own disbelief to make a try for something which is more highly coloured, more personal, more theatrical, whatever the terms may be.

Differences between Orchestras

ES: *How would the approach to your parts differ between, say, the Vienna Philharmonic and the London Symphony Orchestra? To what extent do they bring something of their own? a style, a history?*

MTT: This is a very interesting area, because when you talk about the London Symphony Orchestra, you are talking about a superb twentieth-century orchestra. Anything written right on the cusp of the century and into the twenty-first century, anything requiring very brilliant, forward, rhythmic, virtuoso playing, is something they can do instantly with astonishing panache. There is never a moment when you have to look round and say, 'Right, when you hear the whistle we throw ourselves out of the trench and go on to the next one and take no prisoners.' That's never a worry. They are fearless.

But then it comes to a moment of turning inwards and saying, 'Now, can we try and explore together this sense of loneliness or vulnerability that exists as we leave E minor?' Just for an instant the raised third degree of the scale, the G sharp appears, and for one haunting moment there's a shadow of A flat minor, a six chord, which is just fleetingly hinted at. How could that sense of loneliness be suggested? By just a small hesitation in the quaver accompaniment, and perhaps a *tenuto* played by the violas really *flautando*, with a very, very airy and somewhat hesitant sound? And then, just at a pivot-point here, it moves quickly off in another direction. Again, little quicksilver changes of thought suggested in the tone, but not disturbing the immense calmness and generosity of expression. And it's a real test for me to try to articulate these things, and communicate them more simply and more directly. I've now come to realize it's all not going to be achieved in one performance.

Afterwards, thinking back on a performance I can say, 'Ah yes, I can see that last time we really did settle these particular issues, and next time we can build on that.' This is done in places like Dresden and Vienna over generations of performances, over generations of musicians who play the piece, teach it to their students, bring those students into the orchestra and sit beside them. On the other hand these places cannot approach new music – in which the tradition must be created at this moment – in the same way that we can.

How to Attain the Ideal Interpretation

Thinking again about Brahms and Mahler, it's so interesting to look at the orchestral material by other composers that Mahler conducted. When you look at Beethoven, say, there really is very little marked in it, so Mahler didn't feel obliged to write in a lot of instructions for players; but from accounts of him we know he rehearsed them obsessively, endlessly stopping and starting, and insisting on all these tiny changes of articulation. He could only work with an ensemble for so long and then they just couldn't take any more. I think that when you look at the sort of performing instructions there are in Mahler's compositions, you have a perfect idea of what he must have been asking people for in the performances of other composers' music. These shadings of vibration, slight dynamic changes and little changes of balance are just the sort of thing he was asking them to play in Wagner, Beethoven and Martucci, and in all the very wide range of composers' music on which he worked.

When I go back to the piano, when I have a period of playing these scores myself, I'm so happy to come back to this sense of responsibility for playing every single note, and for the joy of exploring how individual and special phrasing can be, how the shape of the music can become really clear. And indeed, all musicians are. If you put musicians in the position of playing chamber music, or playing solo music, we're all willing to devote endless amounts of time to the particular inflection, the most engaging inflection, for an individual phrase.

Nevertheless, the thing that now interests me about the standard repertoire is the combination of very personal inflection of every phrase with a way of indicating that in the shape of a rehearsal. I'm interested in getting many levels deeper into the possibility of personal inflection.

Experiments with Orchestral Sound in the Concert Hall

Then there's the question of what actually is heard in the hall, and the questions of new instruments, old instruments, how big the orchestra is, all that. And the final question is, what do people actually hear in the hall? So, yes, I am doubling the winds in the Brahms symphonies, because in certain places I think that's a wonderful sort of sound. It's only now that I am finding the courage to say, 'Look, in this place I would like to have four flutes, four oboes, four clarinets, two bassoons and only one-third of the string section,' because here I would like to have this whole looming presence of organ sound in the orchestra, and the strings are just a shadow of that. You have all these wind instruments playing together, but playing very quietly, and then suddenly this organ sound vanishes, and we are left with one little, reedy wind soloist, who is now playing against a great, deep carpet of slowly vibrating strings.

I'm just beginning to take up these kinds of thoughts. I recognize that, of course, they are influenced by the perspective of recording. So often I'm up there on the box, listening to the sound, and I think, 'But it should have a certain bloom around it, it should have a certain aura.' And I have to ask myself, 'Well, is it really that the players are not doing this, or is it that I've got an idea of the aural perspective for this? I want to hear this at a distance, as if heard through the ambient mikes. Is that what I'm searching for?' I used to discuss this with Glenn Gould, who was experimenting at that time with recording the piano from different distances. At the time I thought it was quite eccentric, but it strikes me now as a quite natural direction in which to go. It started with my performances of the Beethoven symphonies, where I first did the pieces with a very small orchestra; then I did them with a large orchestra, but cut down the numbers of players at one point or another during the symphony as a way of clarifying texture, sometimes only having one on a part, and sometimes having many more. I did this in pieces like 'Eroica' as a way of relieving the continuous grandiosity of it all.

Of course things like this have been done before in the history of orchestral music. Piatigorsky told me that when he was the principal cellist in the Berlin Philharmonic they would do certain phrases where one of the principal players would play *mezzo forte*, very *espressivo*, a sort of focused *mezzo forte*, and then everyone else in the section would play so lightly that they were nearly inaudible. And that produced a soloistic leading edge with, I suppose, a kind of great cloud of reverberation around it. A halo of sound that they used to great effect. They would experiment with that sort of thing. They had time to do things like that. I think maybe it's time for ideas like this to be taken up again.

Certainly the idea of where the sound comes from in the section is very interesting. I recognize that I'm being influenced by Ives here too. Ives loved having lines played by the last player in the section, playing a solo or something in the distance. So in Mahler's Third, first movement, where Mahler says 'half the strings play here' (it's supposed to be a very quiet passage, where the major march begins), I had that played by the back stands, around the whole orchestra. It produced a very spooky, very distant sound. It's another kind of perspective, and I find this a very interesting area for investigation.

Orchestral Homogenization

ES: *Do you think we are reaching a time when the individual character of an orchestra is diminishing, where there is a more unified and 'international' style?*
MTT: Yes, orchestras are becoming more homogenized, more internationalized.

ES: *Is that because the world's got smaller, in terms of communication and travel, or what?*
MTT: It's just because we're living lives inextricably bound up with one another. We hear so much music from other places, we're so influenced, not perhaps directly by one another, but by the semblance of each other. Maybe this all goes back to when we were warned by God not to have any graven images. Maybe recordings are the ultimate graven image. We think we hear a performance on a recording, we think this is the way something should sound – but of course it is so technologically flattened, its dynamic range is so compressed, its tonal variance is less than ideal, no matter how much it tries to represent the truth.

It's back to the days of the reproducing piano and the confrontation that occurred between Schnabel and the representatives of the Welte Mignon company. He came to record some reproducing piano rolls, and they told him, 'Ach, Herr Schnabel, we are so happy to tell you that we have now perfected the Welte Mignon Klavier so that it can reproduce twelve discernible nuances.' He said, 'Ach, too bad, I have thirteen.'

The Ultimate Challenge in Music

But going to a concert of new music the other night, very wonderfully played new music, I was struck by the incredible organization of new music, the enormous demands, the incredible specificity of everything. The exact nuance, the exact balance, the exact articulation in almost every single instant, and to what a remarkably virtuoso degree the players were able to meet those demands. However, the danger of such total notational exactitude is that it leads towards a conception of performance as a search for sonic congruity. Every live performance attempts to line up exactly with a kind of acoustic template. Perhaps this is an area best explored by electronics.

I find it so curious when I look to the next century, and ask myself what is the most daring and difficult area to explore. Where do you put yourself out on a limb, truly, deeply exposing yourself? It seems to me it is the area of *legato*, *espressivo* playing. This is absolutely opposite to what I would have said at one time. But if you asked me right now, which is more difficult to sing, Berg's *Lied der Lulu* or 'Pace, Pace' from Verdi's *Forza*? the answer would unquestionably be 'Pace, Pace'.

ES: *I think that's because we've now had the experience of the other music, which seemed so fierce at first. As we go deeper and deeper into this century, and the complexities increase, we are probably beginning to realize that the most difficult thing in the world is sustained, simple control.*

MTT: Yes. I mean, that's not to say that there is not a kind of clarity and simplicity which is also completely appropriate to new music, to contemporary music. A wonderful example of this is the percussion ensemble Nexus. You can hear them play works of Cage which in other hands sound like a collage of sounds, and in theirs sound like very specific lines, with quite clear nuances making their telling emotional points. There's a great art to just holding claves in your hand, and playing a quintuplet figure so that the shape of the quintuplet is clearly perceived. We do keep coming back to the same words in these conversations, don't we? Shape, gestalt, nuances, inflection, subtext.

Who Are We Making Music for?

It amuses me when I read some critic or other in the papers really taking an artist to task – and doing it with a kind of very angry, vengeful tone which I never really understand. Yes, it's possible there are some people who are lazy from time to time, but I always remember Piatigorsky's wonderful statement that no one is deliberately trying to do his worst. It's very difficult to sit down and play a piece of music and deliberately do your worst. There may be things that are distracting you, or for some reason something's not working – but it's not a deliberate act. All these different conceptions of music are important in that they represent in most cases a desire on the part of a performer to get a point across. Perhaps the point doesn't get across, but he is trying, and if the piece is a universal masterpiece it can stand that. It can contain everything within it.

ES: *Yes. But still there are self-indulgent performers who so plainly use pieces for their own ends.*
MTT: It's a question of which audience you're playing for. There are people who have probably got more out of hearing Bach played by the switched-on Bach computer, a synthesizer recording, than from any very erudite performance practice group. And there are probably some who would get the message of Bach played on the Atlantic City organ, or played in a schmaltzy Paul Whiteman or Liberace style.

On the other hand, I'm reminded of a young Russian pianist I once met in Israel. She was a remarkably talented woman. We performed Rachmaninov's Third Piano Concerto together. Rachmaninov is very specific about his performance directions, so I was very surprised when, each time the composer indicated faster and rhythmic, she played more slowly and expressively. And where the composer indicated rubato, she played like a humourless five-year plan. When I asked her why she did just the opposite to the composer's suggestion, she said, 'This is an opportunity to display personality.'

ES: *Yes. That's where I think a critic may be entitled to get angry. When I met Thomas Hampson recently, he talked a lot about this obsession we have of presenting things in a different way and how, in the period performance movement, we are becoming obsessed with the idea of style – pasting a style on to music as to opposed to arriving at it through understanding.*

Searching

MTT: It comes back to what I was saying before about Brahms. I guess that when I think of Brahms's Second or Brahms's Fourth, I'm actually not thinking of it as a piece being played by an orchestra, but of all the lines in the piece, and that they all have a particular inflection and expression, as if they were being played as a solo sonata. I hear a particular passage and think, 'Well, if this were in a violin sonata, how would this line be played? Or if this were in a string quartet, how would this line be played?' Or if this were being sung by a soprano, how would this be sung? In this case it happens to be played by sixteen people in a violin section, therefore how should they all play it?'

Sometimes, if I ask an orchestra to try for a certain thing, they may look at me and say, 'What you're asking us is crazy, this doesn't relate to the way an orchestra plays this piece.' And I say, 'Of course it doesn't. You are absolutely right, it doesn't.' But what I am asking for, what I am searching for, is the opposite of the slowed-down reaction times of sixteen people trying to follow one another and be together. I want them to be completely conceptually linked, and to react with a much faster, much more varied style of playing. That is what I am searching for. I'm not there yet, but at least what it is that I want to do as an interpretative performer over this next period of my life is becoming clear to me. Actually I find this much more interesting now than conducting those pieces that I know exactly how to perform.

Legato, legato. Tenuto. Cantabile. It all comes from the fact that I grew up in a household where people sang songs. My father sang and wrote songs. I learned all these Broadway songs. I learned all these Yiddish theatre songs. I listened to records of Italian opera. I've spent so many of my years being obsessed by the rhythmic drive of twentieth-century music. But the fundamental thing that I am left with at the end of the day is song. The *legato*, the little turns of expression, the bluesy notes, the falling away of the breath, the change from *vibrato* to non-*vibrato*, the artfulness of a singer.

ES: *With the human voice being the most natural form of expression in the end.*
MTT: Yes. Enchantingly, sometimes infuriatingly, the voice is the beginning and end of musical expression. If the voice itself is beautifully handled it can make the issue of what is being sung seem secondary. In George du Maurier's classic novel *Trilby*, the heroine sings a programme of Mozart, Schumann and 'Sweet Alice Ben Bolt' in her diva-enchantress personality, saying afterwards, 'What difference does it make what I sing for I am La

Svengali and you will know nothing, think of nothing but Svengali, Svengali, Svengali!' Of course, there are many kinds of beauty. Kiri te Kanawa has a beautiful voice, but then again, so does Joe Cocker.

Brahms's Personality

ES: *You say that Brahms is first and foremost a song composer. Do you think there was a particular reason for that? Was it something about his personality?*

MTT: Brahms's personality is an elusive thing. Brahms as a composer is someone who frequently disguises his real feelings. He was a composer who lived such a strange semi-reclusive existence. He was a handsome young virtuoso who made himself into an eccentric professor, submerging himself in flesh, facial hair, untidiness and cigars. He got up from his deathbed and destroyed all of his private papers, sketchbooks and journals, leaving his only portrait as portrayed in his published manuscripts. This man has so much to say, but is also so concerned with the way in which he is going to say it. A certain sense of reticence and personal dignity, is a great part of that. Occasionally, he surrenders that reserve and dignity, giving us a brief glimpse of how intensely he is feeling. For one moment he will allow himself to break away from his rules of musical rhetoric before withdrawing again into the autumnal veiled space that he's created for himself. It was to preserve the sanctuary of that space that he burned his papers before he died.

Of course there are a couple of pieces which are exceptions to this. The First Piano Concerto, which is a very young man's assertive, aggressive piece. The opening of the First Symphony, which also is still a very aggressive statement. But very often the pieces begin in a veiled mood, a kind of self-conscious, pastoral quality – 'Oh yes, we're just out for a walk here now, and as we're out here various thoughts come into our mind. Some of those thoughts are about that sad summer, how many years ago is it now? How long it is now, sometimes it just seems like yesterday.'

Brahms's Second Symphony

In the Second Symphony one sees this in each movement, in one way or another. The piece has a fascinating opening, an evocation of a sort of D major pastoral world, with these horn-call figures going back and forth.

This brings to mind a very interesting question, because the first movement of the Symphony has the tempo marking *allegro moderato*. It has no metronome mark, it just says *allegro moderato*. And the theme consists of a minim followed by a crotchet. Now of course there's another symphony which starts with a theme which has a minim followed by a crotchet, and that's the 'Eroica' by Beethoven, but the tempo marking in the 'Eroica' is *allegro con brio*. Our sense of priorities is so confused that very often one hears the 'Eroica' performed in a tempo which is actually as slow or slower than the tempo at which Brahms's Second Symphony is meant to begin.

So where is the threshold of *moderato* and *brio* with respect to these two *allegros*? An interesting point to consider. The real issue is decided by what occurs on the third beat of the bar. The *allegro con brio* of the 'Eroica' implies that the crotchet on the third beat somehow leads, in a breathless, energetic sort of way, on to the rest of the phrase, whereas the Brahms *allegro moderato* is a theme which wants to linger imperceptibly on the last crotchet of the bar. The difference between Brahms's and Beethoven's third beat crotchets is in real time probably a hundredth of a second, but in subjective time, the pace – the mood – is entirely different. None of these points is marked by Brahms with any indication of expression. He expects the performer to understand intuitively.

ES: *So why did he mark it* allegro *at all?*
MTT: Because he obviously felt it as an ongoing, moving stream of music. But this sort of almost expressive dawdling that exists in the first subject is quite apart from what occurs later. Then the music goes into quavers, long streams or rivulets of quavers, that must run through, sometimes shaped into groups of four bars or more. Great long, unbroken streams of notes. Sometimes they're in smaller groups, each one implying that there is a small *tenuto* at the beginning of each group.

This term, this wonderful term *tenuto*, to hold the first note a little bit. *Tenuto* is again one of those almost lost arts of music-making. To be able to steal a little time within the tempo, to prolong a note without accenting it, without pushing it, but within the calmness to create this slightly generous distribution that points up ever so gently, but in spirit generously, the design of the music. It's a delicate question, though, inflection. If the audience notices it, it's done too much, but if it's flat, and has no profile at all, it's nothing.

And you won't find anything in the score to help you. If you're one of those conductors who says, 'I just do what's in the score,' well, you won't do anything. You have to see what is really implied in the score, and do it.

Touch

Therefore the music must move, the sound must move, the emotional projection must move, through the notes. Don't we always say about a performance, 'It touched me deeply'? Well, the effect of a touching performance, the creation of a touching performance, comes back to the actual physical touching of their instruments by the players. It means that they must touch their instruments with the same sort of subtle and affectionate vocabulary that they would touch the people they love and care about. There is such a huge vocabulary there.

I first became aware of this when one of my first teachers, Dorothy Bishop, had a preparatory school at USC, and I was playing a Bartók sonatina. There's a simple little tune at the beginning which has to be played in a very artless but slightly melancholy way, a sort of melancholy singsong. I was playing it, and she said, 'No, no, it has to be touching, it has to be expressive. Look, I'll show you.' And she took my arm and she played the notes of the phrase on my arm. Her touch was a revelation, the subtlety, speed, depth, contact, pressure, all of these things. Again, I was doing a piece by Bach, and she showed me the kind of contact she had in playing the opening phrase in a Bach Prelude. That was a great moment in my life. A real moment of, 'Right, I understand what this is.'

So when I start working on a piece by Bach, Brahms or Mahler, I have to ask, 'How much do I care about this note? What do I understand about this note? What and how much do I want to communicate? How can I make this phrase, this performance "touching"?' For me, that is what making music really is about.

Part Two

Childhood home, c.1944

Beginnings

A Hollywood Childhood

MTT: I was born in Los Angeles. More specifically, in Hollywood, in the Cedars of Lebanon Hospital, and I grew up in North Hollywood, which is a suburb just within the San Fernando Valley. Los Angeles is an enormous city, fifty square miles, divided by mountain ranges. At its very roots it was an agrarian Spanish-speaking community that dated back to the very earliest days of the settlement of the city, to the old Spanish land grants. Groups of migrant workers still worked the land around us.

The San Fernando Valley is the extensive area that had been developed first for agriculture and then for residential settlement by the introduction of water there, as is outlined in the film *Chinatown*. A lot of people from the studios lived there. It was quite rural. We had dirt roads, and few of the streets were paved. We lived on high ground which sloped rapidly down towards the Los Angeles river, a meandering ditch which flooded every winter and burned every summer. It would get so dry that all the brush growing along the river bank would burn. That's how we measured the year, by the burning or the flooding of the river.

We were surrounded by large orchards of citrus fruits, walnuts, persimmons, and turkey and horse farms. We lived in about an acre of property on a little street, along which ran a stand of huge eucalyptus trees, planted in a straight line. It was the remains of a wind-break that had been planted by one of the big agricultural developments at some earlier time. It ran for over a mile. What else was in that neighbourhood? A few strange stone houses, which had the reputation of having been used by some kind of religious cult or utopian community back at the turn of the century. The nearest market was several miles away. The air was clear and beautiful, the sky was dazzling blue, the purple mountains that surrounded us were in plain view. That's what it was like in the San Fernando Valley until I was about five years old.

That world changed completely when they paved over the river. The river was finally dug out to an immense trench, and sheathed in concrete. From that time on it was known as the Wash, and the flooding and burning stopped. For the first couple of years afterwards we were overrun by possums, skunks, pheasants, and all kinds of critters trying to take refuge from their lost homes in the river bank. Finally the animal population stabilized – I guess that's a polite way of saying they died out. Then they built the freeways, the first apartment houses and the horror of LA urban sprawl began. All this was a part of prosperity mercilessly despoiling the beauty and charm of the land.

The first school I attended was a socialist co-operative nursery school. So many of the parents who were connected with the film studios were involved in one radical group or another. They created a co-operative nursery school where most of them could come in and teach some of the time. We were entertained by people from the movie business – directors, writers and out-of-work actors – coming in to keep the kids amused. Later I went into the regular public school system and grew up with large classes of Jews, Italians and Mormons.

Parents' House

Our house was a modest ranch-style dwelling crammed to bursting point with books, records, scripts, exotic cooking pots and musical instruments. It was surrounded by a garden in which fruit trees and abundant asparagus beds ringed by volcanic rocks were locked in eternal conflict with huge stands of cactus. This little Eden was the creation of my parents' spirits. They were very intelligent, very caring people. They didn't care much about careers or possessions, but were passionate about beauty, art, friendships, community spirit and education. They first came out to Los Angeles in 1938 to work in the movies. They had had some wonderfully exciting times in the film world, but for much of my childhood my father was a struggling screen writer and my mother a school teacher. We had very little money but our house was a warm and generous place, open to everyone. I guess one could call it a somewhat Bohemian place. People were always dropping by – actors, song writers, painters, designers, musicians, political scientists – all pals of my mom and dad from their New York days. Everyone was radical, intellectual and very much fun. My parents and their friends all seemed to burn with great curiosity about the world and the arts. George Tobias, a famous character actor, loved music and would rush in to play us the newest Louis Armstrong or Prokofiev recording. My mother would bring home a huge volume of paintings from the Prado to look at after dinner. My father would entertain us all for hours playing Gershwin and his own music at the piano. Other friends came by with new books or new recipes for vegetables from their gardens. Something was always happening. As I was an only child I participated in all of these adult adventures.

I also shared a great relationship with my grandmother, Bessie Thomashefsky. Bessie had been one of the greatest stars of the Yiddish theatre – a major headliner. We sat for hours talking about the story of her life in Russia, the founding of the Yiddish theatre in America by my grandfather Boris and all their great years of repertory and touring. I knew the names of the great Yiddish actors and plays of the turn of the century but not the name of a single baseball player or even a baseball team in all America.

This was my world as a child – a few hours of rather prosaic school and then back home for plays, mythologies, poetry, history, love and above all music.

Bessie Thomashefsky, c.1905

Piano with Dorothy Bishop

We had an old Steinway upright piano that I couldn't stay away from. I played first with my father and then began improvising and picking things up by ear. By the time I was seven I had a little repertoire of pieces I could play for doting relatives. But, I couldn't read music. One of our musical friends must have panicked. I was sent to a local teacher just to learn my ABC's. But my real musical education began a few years later. Around the age of ten, I was taken to the University of Southern California preparatory school to play for the head of the school, a remarkable woman named Dorothy Bishop. What she must have thought of me at that first meeting I can't imagine. I 'auditioned', playing bits and pieces of Bach and Gershwin strung together with 'improvements' of my own. It must have been shocking. Fortunately for me, her style of teaching was based on improvisation and on Bach. She saw that I had talent, but no discipline, so she gently, but firmly, took me back through the basics. There were studies and exercises, but there was also keyboard harmony, transposition, modulation, things like this. Sometimes we played games with the pieces we studied, like reversing the parts of Bach inventions, playing the soprano part in the bass and vice versa. She gave me technique and freedom at the keyboard in a way that didn't destroy my imagination. Without her I would never have become a musician.

Alice Ehlers

Through Dorothy Bishop I began to have contact with the faculty at the university itself. That was when I first met Alice Ehlers, the harpsichordist who had been a pupil of Wanda Landowska, and later a colleague of Landowska and Schweizer, and also had been very much on the scene during the whole great years of the Second Viennese school. She was quite friendly, so she said, with Alban Berg. She always said, 'Ach, Alban, so talented, so modest, so beautiful to look at.' She was a very eccentric and very dedicated woman, whose grasp of reality was somewhat diminished, but whose ability to remember exactly the phrasing that should be used in the fifth contrapunctus of the *Art of Fugue* was available at a moment's notice.

She was a very influential teacher for me, in that she taught in a way that made me conscious of every musical action. Many people found this frustrating, because she appeared sometimes to be telling you what to do, then, if you did what she said, the next week she would seemingly contradict herself. It took a long while for me to realize that she was really saying, 'If you

With Alice Ehlers, c.1960

have played the first phrase in this way, then you must follow through in
the second phrase in a way that makes sense with what you've already done,
and in a way which will ultimately build up a musical design that will be
reflective, a whole structure of the piece.'

When I first studied with her at the age of twelve, she assigned me the
Bach C minor Partita, and I learned the first four or five movements of it,
expecting to play them all next week. But at the end of an hour and a half

lesson, we had reached only the twenty-sixth bar of the piece, something like that. And so we began this extremely laborious process of inching our way through this piece, with her saying, in her wonderfully high-pitched, extremely thick Viennese accent, 'No, no, dear, vat are you doing? You must play zis way, and zis is zat ...' And somehow, in this terribly difficult, shuffling, stumbling progress, we got through the first two movements of the piece in the course of eight weeks. And then I went off on vacation for a while.

But I recognized that I could play these pieces better than anything else I had played up to that point, and I began to try and work out what it actually was that made them better. What had she taught me? How had we come to this point? Then I began to realize, oh, right, it's antecedent, consequence, expectation, realization, and how they had to function in music and be related to a larger scheme. She was extraordinarily patient. Very few people have the opportunity to work with someone who will make them concentrate on every single note, and every single process. I mention this, because she was my first experience with a real artist of the German school.

The German School versus the Russian School

I began to be aware that in Los Angeles there were quite a number of these Germano-phile artists who had been rallied, initially, by the presence of Klemperer as Music Director of the LA Philharmonic, though of course he had left a long time ago. Nonetheless, there were lots of disciples left in the orchestra; players, people who had formerly been in opera houses and held very distinguished posts before the war, and who were scattered around Los Angeles. There was the circle around Thomas Mann, not to mention the circle around Schoenberg, which was a kind of mixture of musicians and writers and psycho-analysts. There was definitely a German school of musicians in Los Angeles.

And then, quite the opposite, there was the Russian school – Stravinsky, Heifetz, Piatigorsky; and Rubinstein was also part of that. Around these major figures there were of course all kinds of satellites. My teacher, Ingolf Dahl, was part of the Russian group. My piano teacher, John Crown, was likewise very friendly with Heifetz, played a lot of music with him; but he also had contacts with the German school, not only through Alice Ehlers, but through the great Adolf Koldolfsky, the violinist for whom Schoenberg had written the Piano Violin Fantasy. So I would go from lesson to lesson, or from chamber music coaching to chamber music coaching, and I would shift gears and say, 'You are now leaving the German sector and going into the Russian sector!' Culturally, Los Angeles was a little bit like Berlin after the war. There were definite sectors. You had the Brentwood UCLA territory, the German quarter; and then you had the Beverly Hills Russian sector. And there was of course so much to be learned from these different groups. I'm so lucky that I didn't have a teacher who expected me to swear loyalty to one group. There were some who did, who'd be very upset if you had anything to do with those in the other camp.

John Crown

After Alice Ehlers, my piano teacher was John Crown, who had been Moritz Rosenthal's pupil. Rosenthal was Liszt's pupil, Liszt studied with Czerny, Czerny studied with Beethoven, and so through John Crown I had a direct line to Beethoven. John was a masterful, romantic pianist whose nerves had been shot somehow or another; he wasn't able to play well in public, he just got too nervous. But he played in the studio and chamber music situation in a generous, leonine, romantic style. Impressive, wonderful sound. Wonderful approach to Liszt and Chopin and these things. And the foundation of his teaching was Germanic.

John Crown and Etta Dahl, 1965

Ingolf Dahl

Ingolf Dahl, another of my teachers, had a background in German and Swiss opera houses, but he had become thoroughly American in his viewpoint towards music. He was also very involved with jazz, and had assisted Stravinsky for many, many years as a kind of musical amanuensis, before Robert Craft came on the scene. Ingolf had been the one who had made piano arrangements, corrected orchestration and really assisted Stravinsky with the ongoing musical process of those years, the forties.

Contrasting with that, there was Piatigorsky's incredible, expansive generosity as a teacher and as a personality; the broadness of his accent, the combination of the nearly unintelligible pronunciation of extremely specific and expressive words that would challenge the vocabulary of any very well-read person. In contrast again, there was the clipped and oddly lisping and accented speech of Heifetz; very, very few words said, and in a rather halting way, but he had incredible organization as a performer.

These were all very interesting influences. I could be in a class of Schenkerian analysis, or an analysis of serial procedures in the Berg Violin Concerto, or examining the concepts of thematic augmentation or diminution in Schumann, or whatever – this whole intellectual, Germanic world round the university – and then I could suddenly be with Heifetz, playing a piece by Schumann, and I would start to say, 'Well, the augmentation of the phrase here might suggest ...' and he would say, 'Aah, just forget those words. Don't bother with them. All you must know is at any given moment in a piece what must sound.' This was, of course, a different way of describing the same process. Any system of analysis is just a way of seeing and prioritizing things. Heifetz determined these same priorities using his own methods based on his killer and patrician instincts. To this day I rely on this mixture of intellect and instinct to answer to fundamental question of each bar in a piece – what must sound?

ES: *It seems a remarkable circle of contrasting influences.*
MTT: It was. And I really got into that whole circle because I went to a concert of the Young Musicians Foundation Orchestra. They played a brass piece by Ingolf Dahl called *Music for Brass Instruments*. I heard this piece and I absolutely loved it, as I still do. I think it's a very expressive and important statement of American neo-classical writing; but it's a bit jazzier than that, with a Baroque feel ... It is what it is, it's Ingolf's style at its best. I loved the piece so much; and the composer came out and took a bow, and I thought, 'This is someone I want to study with.' I must have been around

With Jascha Heifetz, c.1963

fifteen at this time. Ingolf was teaching at USC, and I was through the preparatory school at USC and had already begun to study with the senior faculty. I was working with John Crown, the head of the piano department, but I had to make a decision about where I wanted to go to school. USC attracted me because of the strength of its faculty, and really more than anything else because of Ingolf Dahl, whose music and musical discipline made such an impression upon me. One day I saw him rehearse something, and again I thought, 'This is someone with whom I could study.'

At USC

I enrolled at USC, to be told that Dahl only taught graduate students. But on the first day of registration I was talking to John Crown in the piano faculty, and Ingolf came in and said, 'Oh, by the way, John, I am conducting the orchestra and need someone to play celeste.' And John said, 'What's the piece at the first concert?' Ingolf said, 'Webern, *Six Pieces* for orchestra.' I said, 'Me, please.' John said, 'Well, Ingolf, he's just come in, but he's a pupil of mine.' And Ingolf turned to me and said, 'Do you know Webern's *Six Pieces* for orchestra?' I said, 'I wouldn't be so bold as to say I know it. I do know how it goes. I've heard it many times on record and I love the piece.' And that was a good enough answer. So I became the orchestral pianist, and that was my first association with Ingolf.

Then, little by little, I did manage to begin studying with him in my second or third year at the university. I learned a lot by watching him in rehearsals, and also by attending some concerts with him. At one of the very first concerts we listened to a trio by Pergolesi, and at the end of the first movement he turned to me and said, 'Did you like that?' I said, 'Yes.' He

With Ingolf Dahl, c.1965

said, 'Really? What form was it in?' I said, 'Well, I was just listening to it, just to enjoy it, I didn't really, er, I wasn't paying attention.' He said, 'You weren't paying attention? Well, why weren't you? You were listening to this piece, and you didn't make any note of what its shape was?' I said, 'Well, I mean, that's like form and analysis, I wasn't trying to analyze it, I was just trying to enjoy it.' He said, 'Enjoyment of music is inseparable from analysis. Why would you want to turn off a whole portion of your brain? Western music is a curious thing, in that if you compare it with other types of music, you find music which has more interesting melody, more interesting sonorities, much more complicated rhythmic development – all these little things are much greater in other musical cultures. But the thing that Western music has is this relationship of content to form, to harmony; the idea of form and order and structure that permeates everything. The form, the projection of the form, is the supreme goal of the performer. And you must not think form is an academic thing. The form is the most expressive element in the piece. If that is expressed, that is the true message of the piece.' I was sitting beside him, all of eighteen years old. 'That's one to remember,' I thought to myself.

Ingolf had a very great influence on me at that time. Thereafter he kept me there in that environment of people, working on that approach to music; and that's why when, many years later, I met Leonard Bernstein I had so many things in common with him; we shared the same perspective of looking at the design of music as all one big expressive thing, wherein every element was expressive. You couldn't separate out one part and say that's just technique, or that's just analysis, or form, it was all one thing.

But it is true that Ingolf performed like a composer, in a somewhat chunky, blocky kind of style. He had great articulation and verve and fantasy in his playing as well. Incredible energy, God knows. It was great having him to provide this big overview of things, and then having people like Piatigorsky and John Crown, who were more elegant, carnivorous performers, as a counterbalance. They understood the special and dangerous thrill of performing. When I was around nineteen I got my first standing ovation. John Crown looked at me the next morning and said, 'Oh, tasted blood now, have we. There will be no turning back now.'

Piatigorsky too understood the curious paradoxes of a performer's life. He used to say, in his thick Russian accent, 'You know, life of performer is terrible thing. You play Brahms sonata. Brahms is grreat, sonata is grreat, and you? You maybe are like insect crawling around somehow on grreat sonata, trying to make clear what is. So you play Brahms sonata for audience. Audience applaud, but they applaud for Brahms. No matter what you

Gregor Piatigorsky

do, you're not as good as sonata. On the other hand, sometimes you look around some place, music shop, piano bench. Somewhere you find a little piece of crap. A song, ditty, something like that. And you take that piece of crap, and you dress it up. Here you put *flageolet*, and here you put *portamento*, here you put little *tremolo*, *glissando*, a *pizzicato*, vibrato, little bit choreography, this and that, you know, and then you play that piece for public. Audience goes crrrazy. Absolutely crrraaazy. And you feel great because the audience applauds for *you*. After all, composition is just little piece of crap.'

Piatogorsky made me play everything. I remember I once came in, outraged at having been assigned to play the Rachmaninov sonata, because I was only playing at that time late Beethoven and Bach, and Schoenberg. I said, 'I don't want to play this Rachmaninov thing, and I certainly don't want to play this vulgar virtuoso Valentini sonata. It's a waste of my time. I'm specializing in Bach and Schoenberg.' He looked at me and said, 'You're too talented to be a specialist. You have to play everything. Go learn.' I'm so grateful to him, because I could easily have gone off in that kind of rectangular, dark-gray world of music. But he and John Crown wouldn't permit it.

So this took me up to my mid-twenties, and to my experiences in Boston. But then – and the way things happen is such a supreme accident – Friedelind Wagner asked me to come to Bayreuth.

Screaming at Bayreuth

I went, and I was in the master classes that she had there. That summer one of the members of the coaching staff got ill, so they suddenly had to have a pianist coach come in, at a day's notice, and I got the job, playing stage rehearsals, some with Karl Böhm and Pierre Boulez. But I was definitely the low man on the totem pole there. I had 'Nibelungen Dienst'. A few times a week I had to go in and rehearse the Nibelungs. This meant being down in deepest crypt of the Festspielhaus. I gathered together the Nibelungs who were all dancers of the company and had to train them to scream on cue. I played the preceeding orchestra parts on the piano and then yelled at them '*Ein, zwei, drei*, SCHREI!' and they gave this great scream. It was one of the silliest things I have ever done. It was an absolutely freezing summer in Bayreuth, and the theatre was terribly cold. The coaching staff had two cognacs and two espressos first thing in the morning before we went into rehearsal at eight o'clock. There was nothing but Wagner and freezing basement rehearsal halls. I couldn't take it any more. I just had to get out of there.

So Friedelind and I went to Salzburg. My first trip to Salzburg. I remember it was 1966, because it was Wieland's last year, and I played for some stage rehearsals he did in Baayreuth, which was a real inspiration. It's strange that I've never gone back to Wagner, because I really love it so much. Maybe I will some day. Who knows? Anyway, I went to Salzburg, and that summer they were doing *The Bassarids* by Henze, and Friedelind said, 'Oh, there's a dress rehearsal. You must go.' So we walked in.

Salzman in Salzburg

And suddenly there I was, sitting in darkness in the Salzburg Festspielhaus, and the music began. Although I like Henze's music, I was thinking, 'What am I doing here? I've been trying to escape from opera, from the German language, and suddenly here I am, stuck back in an opera house again. I must get out.' So, after about two minutes, I just got up and walked out. And as I walked out I saw somebody else walking out, and I went over and talked to this fellow, and it turned out he was an American composer, Eric Salzman.

Invitation to Tanglewood

Later Eric showed me a piece he had written called *The Owl and the Cuckoo*, for soprano and chamber ensemble, and I agreed that I would do it at a Monday Evening Concert the next season. The piece was programmed, but as we began rehearsing in Los Angeles it became clear that the guitar part was much too difficult for anyone to play. Eric said, 'Oh, I have a guitarist in New York who can play it. We can bring him in.' I said, 'No, we don't bring people from New York just to play a part. We could only bring him in if he were a composer, that's the policy.' And Eric said, 'Well, he is a composer, we could do a piece of his.' So we brought him in, and that composer's name was Stanley Silverman. I did his piece for guitar and chamber ensemble, PLANH, which I liked very much, and I liked him very much, and we got on fine. Then he said, 'Oh, by the way, I've been commissioned to write an opera for Tanglewood next summer. Would you come and conduct it? You must come and conduct it.' So that is how I got the invitation to go to Tanglewood.

It was complicated, because Stravinsky was supposed to be teaching at Harvard that summer, and I had agreed to work with him there. It was all kind of up in the air, but finally, at the last moment, in a kind of cliff-hanger, I did go to Tanglewood, and I did do Stanley Silverman's opera, and as a result of that I won the Koussevitzky Prize, and as a result of the Koussevitzky Prize I got the job as conductor of the Boston Symphony, and then Steinberg got ill and I took over that concert in Philharmonic Hall, and so and so and so, on to the whole of the rest of my career.

So, you see, if I hadn't walked out of that performance in Salzburg none of this could ever have happened! I only met Henze recently, and I said, 'Hans, I really have to thank you for my career. Really it's thanks to you that it all happened. He looked at me very perplexed and said, 'What are you talking about?' I told him the story, and he couldn't stop laughing.

So you see, you just don't know at any moment in your life what is really happening.

Boris Thomashefsky, sheet music, 1916

MTT: Because of my family, I am closest to the Russian musical tradition. My father's family came from Russia and spoke some of the language around the house. I grew up hearing it, and still speak a little baby Russian. But still, I absorbed the sound of the words, the basic expressions, the poly-syllabic constructions, the extended diphthonging noises that come from the language. And you can recognize that same style of sound production in the way the music is traditionally interpreted, the way the phrases go, the way great Russian artists like Piatigorsky and Heifetz articulated the music. Above all, the way Chaliapin and others of that kind sang this music, the way Stravinsky sang his own music. This is the foundation of the way I approach the music.

Russian Roots

ES: *What exactly was the Russian part of your family?*
MTT: My family name was Thomashefsky, and they all came from various parts of the Ukraine, around Kiev and Odessa. They had probably lived in Russia for several hundred years. They may very well have been further west before that, even though they took great pains to transliterate the name Thomashefsky in a Russian way. Artur Rubinstein told me that any-body who has the name Thomashefsky probably, at some time or another, had to come from the village of Thomashov, which is one side or the other of the Polish border depending on the year. They were a long line of singers and cantors. One of them was the famous Tolnah Cantor that Tchaikovsky is said to have travelled to hear. My grandfather, Boris, actually got his start by being a boy soprano soloist in the famous choir of Berditchev, which was the centre of Jewish liturgical music in Russia. One day, during a high hol-iday service, one of Boris's solos got applause. Belzer, the choir's director, was horrified. Although Boris was severely punished for his 'disturbance' of the service, overnight he had become (at least in Berditchev) famous. He came to the attention of a Mr Wolff, an American businessman, who brought him and his whole family to New York. There, Boris became the soloist at the Henry Street Synagogue on the Lower East Side of Manhattan. Following the trail of applause, Boris began singing popular music as well, and when still a young teenager produced and starred in the first perfor-mance of Yiddish theatre in America. With his wife Bessie he toured the provinces, building up his craft and repertoire. They returned triumphant-ly to New York, establishing their own theatre and publishing company. They were mega-stars. At the height of their careers, around 1910, their theatre presented a repertoire ranging from classics to avant-garde and intro-

Bessie Thomashefsky, theatre poster

duced countless authors, composers, actors and singers to the American public. Much of America's theatrical, musical and film tradition can be traced back to their work. Only recently I was impressed again with their fame and influence when I uncovered a front page article from the *New York Times* describing my grandfather's funeral in 1938. Thirty thousand mourners attended.

Even today I have flashbacks to my grandparents. At moments backstage, particularly on the road, being in some draughty theatre or hearing a certain creak of a dressing-room door or a blast of icy air coming in from an alley with an oily sort of smell – sights and smells and feelings of theatre –

I have flashbacks. 'Oh sure, this is something my grandparents went through' – almost as if this is their actual experience. And I'm also very in touch with them as adventurous spirits, because they were people playing tragedy, comedy, music hall, avant-garde theatre, workers' theatre, radical theatre, cabaret – all of these things. It confused people a great deal. How to classify them? What sort of artists were they? And of course I recognize that many people have exactly the same confusion about me, and what my work is. What am I really doing? Am I doing Morton Feldman or Debussy or Mahler or Gershwin or Berio or Tchaikovsky or Colin Matthews? Or what? As for me, I'd say, of course, I'm still a musical explorer.

So I was surrounded by tales about Russia. My grandmother used to describe how on market day in Kiev you could stand on the street and it was impossible to converse with someone standing right next to you because so many bells were ringing ... so many churches, so many bells. And I was told lots of stories about the old days in Russia in the little towns and hamlets in which they lived, and the big journeys they took from time to time to go and see a miracle rabbi to help cure them. It's all part of the heritage. And of course I heard a great deal of Russian music around the house.

ES: *What do you remember?*
MTT: Well, I remember that my grandmother used to sing all of the tunes from *Petrushka*. I first learned those tunes because my grandmother used to sing them, doing children's games with me, like the end of *Petrushka*, the amazing trumpet passage. I would have to sing it as a forfeit when we played a particular card game. We would play a kind of combination of solitaire and building a house of cards, so that as you picked a card up you were then able to take it out and begin constructing a house of cards. If you knocked over the house of cards, the forfeit was that you had to go under the table, stand on one foot and crow like a rooster. And the way you crowed like a rooster was exactly what the trumpets play at the end of *Petrushka*. It was fun.

Also, a lot of Russian actors came to the house. There was a man called Lonya Snegov, who had been in the Jewish company with Stanislavsky in Moscow. He was a great friend of Chaliapin. Snegov was always wanting me to play through the score of an opera called *Tsar Maximilian* by Andrei Pashchenko, based on the confrontation between Maximilian and Benito Juarez. Imagine – a Russian grand opera set in Mexico! Chaliapin wanted to do it.

Folk Tunes and Stravinsky

Because of my grandmother's singing of *Petrushka*, and because of seeing Stravinsky perform a lot of his pieces from the time I was ten years old or so, my introduction to Russian music was largely through folkloric recognition. Recognizing that so much of the music in Stravinsky was folk tunes or phrases shaped in the manner of folk tunes gave me an approach to all of his music. It was not an analytical, avant-garde approach but an extremely coloristic, folkloric and swinging one. I recognized that Stravinsky's use of dissonance in those pieces was an evocation of joy. It was the recreation of the experience of hearing music played by instruments which had been built in a particular village. They were all out of tune with one another and produced wonderful squeaky noises, but gave the music irresistible verve and character.

St Petersburg Group

And then from Stravinsky I worked back to Mussorgsky and Rimsky-Korsakov. I recognized the similar phrase shapes in those composers' dark, folk-declamatory style. That music has an almost cartoon-character quality. You sense in both Rimsky and Mussorgsky the personalities of the old wood carvers or monk chroniclers who were so often the heroes of their operas. They set their characters on the stage to sing/speak their lines and then go. Because their music has such a strong folk-song basis, there is a feeling that even a little piece is a part of a long Bardic tale like the lay of Prince Igor's campaign. You have the feeling that although you, the listener, begin hearing it at this moment in time, but actually someone has been singing countless verses before the first one you hear.

The culmination of my interest in this whole Russian group was the festival we did in London called 'Flight of the *Firebird*: Rimsky-Korsakov in St Petersburg.' It focused our attention on the characteristic turns of phrase, the leading of the fourths, the transposition of melodies to keys a sixth away, the glittering use of percussion, the very fast figuration ... a whole range of exotic influences that are present in this music. Later, this obsession with exoticism was to have a major effect on the musical language of the twentieth century. It is clear that the St Petersburg composers were all swept away by the idea of surfaces and texture and coloration. Rimsky in particular introduced extraordinary new sounds into the orchestra, such as the soprano timpani, or panpipes tuned to an octatonic scale. All these things are used in his remarkable opera, *Mlada*. It's one of my most favourite pieces, and the source, really, of Stravinsky's *Firebird*, Prokofiev's

Love for Three Oranges, Ravel's *Daphnis et Chloë*, to name but a few.

Lots of the impetus for writing this kind of music came from the architect-writer-poet Vladimir Stasov, who'd done research into ancient Russian texts and archaeology. He gave them the idea of writing pieces based on legends, starting them on the route that went through Rimsky's pagan operas to the *Sacre*. They used these stark ancient, heroic epic tales, leading towards the kind of thing that Eisenstein was to do in his movies. This took them away from the idea of Romantic lyrical expression that was being pursued by Tchaikovsky, Schumann and Brahms. It took them towards a much more hard-edged position. In fact you can trace back a lot of the hard-edge aspect of twentieth-century music to this group of the Russian school, who abandoned the idea of music as a kind of mirror of the soul, and instead wrote music to proclaim these ancient mythologies. The hardness of the chords, the exoticism of the instruments, the planes and the organization of the music led finally towards an even tougher, gleaming, mask-like expression. This music was to have an enormous effect on twentieth-century music, especially in France.

Tchaikovsky and the Moscow Group

ES: *What about Tchaikovsky?*

MTT: Tchaikovsky and the Muscovites went in the opposite direction. Of course at first Tchaikovsky was really under the sway of Balakirev, as was everybody else.

ES: *Why was that, do you think?*

MTT: Well, when you hear a piece like Balakirev's Overture tone poem 'Russia', you say, 'Oh yes, here are all the familiar Russian ideas, the melody in the bass, then an empty chord appearing beneath it, then the tune in long notes with *pizzicato* underscoring; then imitations of carillons; and then barbaric Tartar camp music,' and so on. But one forgets this overture was written long before any of the operas, ballets or tone poems by Rimsky *et al.* – a good twenty years before. Balakirev was an original. It's true Glinka had touched on some of this language in his operas. But Balakirev was writing an instrumental piece which seemed to display a landscape – in fact a kind of psychological landscape of the Russian soul. It was so influential that all these young guys – Rimsky, Mussorgsky, Tchaikovsky even – were all hanging around Balakirev deferring to his judgement. But because he was so dogmatic, they ultimately resisted him in one way or another, particularly Tchaikovsky, who went in an entirely different direction.

Tchaikovsky knew that what he had to write about was his own personal melancholy; and the note of lyrical sadness that is in all of Tchaikovsky's music is so extraordinary. The very first pages of his First Symphony, in G minor, 'Winter Daydreams' – a distillation of several student works he had already written – present a G minor triad burbling along over which a beautiful limpid woodwind tune is spun. The simplicity expresses such a sense of loneliness and sadness. There's no outcry, it's just there, very simply stated, almost in the Italian Bel Canto manner.

It's interesting to compare the opening of Tchaikovsky's First Symphony and the opening of Mahler's Fourth. Mahler repeats a B minor chord frosted by sleigh bells over which another little singsong tune floats. Only in Mahler's case the tune dawdles around the corner from B minor to G major, becoming quite jolly, actually. Both pieces present different perspectives for contemplating a wintry soul. Tchaikovsky clearly experienced so much as a child. Think of the music he wrote for those little entertainments for his cousins when they were on vacation in the summer. Many of those tunes went into later pieces – *Swan Lake* particularly. The descending scale lines are especially characteristic. So many great melodies that Tchaikovsky wrote were based on descending scales.

I guess the most obvious one is the *pas de deux* from the *Nutcracker*, which is the most spectacular use of an unadorned descending major scale that there has ever been. But the *Swan Lake* ballet opens with a B minor oboe tune which also outlines a descending scale. And of course in the *Pathétique* Symphony, little by little, the idea of a descending scale is introduced, also in the key of B minor. In the first movement's Andante and in the development section of that movement there are always long chains of scales. They occur in other guises in other movements, but when you finally come to the last movement, he takes up the same descending B minor scale that opened *Swan Lake* – but now so many years later in his life. It's a movement that, to my mind, suggests that he was wondering, 'What was this all about? What purpose could there have been to any of this?'

Tchaikovsky's Personality in His Music

ES: *Do you think the man and the music are inseparable?*
MTT: Well, there's a tremendous controversy about it nowadays. It's quite fashionable for some musicologists to say, 'Composers just write music. Their personal lives have no influence upon their writings.' But I don't think anyone seriously believes that. Maybe specific events cannot be traced accurately in one composition or another, but certainly Tchaikovsky,

because of his homosexuality and temperament, felt an outsider. I think one can hear this loneliness right through much of his music. It tends to come forth either in a very removed, quietly fatalistic mood, or at other moments as tremendous rage and yearning.

Tchaikovsky gives a clue to that in the programmes of the Fourth and Fifth Symphonies, the little bit we know of them. In the Fourth Symphony, a great, defiant fanfare of fate recurs in every movement bringing everything to a halt, sullying the mood. Finally, in the last movement, it bursts in in the midst of the fair scene, stomping the music into silence. Then, at first very tentatively, the fair music resumes. Even though it's pretty much a recapitulation of the music one's already heard, the effect is so different. I remember Stokowski telling me, 'When you bring back this music of the fair after the fate theme has come in, it must now have an air of utter madness and desperation. Now you know that it is your fate to be struck down, to be accursed ... So fine, go back to the fair, and this time go totally crazy, take every risk, stop at nothing, after all, what's the difference?' This is not unlike the sentiment expressed by Prince in his song '1999', where he says, 'Two thousand zero zero, over now, out of time, so tonight I'm going to party like it's 1999' * – it's that same sentiment.

But then, tellingly, in the Fifth Symphony Tchaikovsky says, in the fragments of the programme that remain, something like, 'Day after day dragged down, exhausted, depressed, not knowing what to do about X.' What he offers in the Fourth Symphony are all these big, dramatic, defiant conflicts; but later in his life he's saying, 'If it only were something as clear-cut as that, if it only were something that one faced on a battlefield – but no, what one faces in life is the feeling of being slowly submerged, a little bit more each day. You can't quite grapple with the issues; they gradually wear you away, wear society away, wear idealism and innocence and everything else away.' This is a concept to which any person can relate. It's something that he felt, that came out of his own most personal life. Now we have, socially and politically, an era when, for the first time, we are trying to say, 'What really are we to think about all of this?'

ES: *And is there an answer to that question?*
MTT: For a long time the fact that Tchaikovsky was a homosexual was something that was whispered, or perhaps alluded to in a programme note. And then we went through a time when, my God, you couldn't escape it.

The very first thing that anybody said was that. And now you read in some programmes that he committed suicide. I believe that it is not at all established that he committed suicide. There's a suggestion he may have, but there's not really any definite evidence to prove it. And it diverts us from the real question, which is to search into the music to see what is being expressed. The fact that Tchaikovsky ended the Fifth Symphony triumphantly and joyously is a source for hopeful contemplation. It is the job of the performer, the interpreter, constantly to listen to the music and recognize what it is expressing. One must notice the turns in the phrase – now hope, now joy, now resignation, now regret.

Which reminds me of an experience I had with the Israel Philharmonic. I said to the concertmaster of the orchestra, 'Here the phrase begins hopefully, reaches a point, and turns back regretfully. It begins hopefully, and it ends regretfully. Do you think you could play the phrase that way?' He shrugged at me and said, 'I play *every* phrase that way.'

The Problem with Tchaikovsky

ES: *Some conductors have a problem with Tchaikovsky. Do you have any specific difficulties?*

MTT: One should think of Tchaikovsky as the Verdi of Russian music. He presents the same kinds of interpretive problems as Verdi. It's very easy to go and see a performance of a Verdi opera which is just noisy band music, postures being struck, and emotional and vocal bathos. Or it can be an immensely profound, deeply moving experience. It depends entirely on how much the performers really believe in what they're doing, and whether they are able to go out on to the edge to do it. As a performer it's as if you sometimes stand with the public on the edge of a frozen pond. You have to take them by the hand and lead them out on to the pond to where it says 'Danger – thin ice'. You ignore the sign and go further and further, past all the danger signs until you know there's only one molecule of ice beneath your feet. You take them all the way out there, and you say, 'Now look around you. You see, this is what it's like to be out here.' And then, with no commotion or fuss, you turn around and you take them all safely back to the shore.

This is what it's like to perform one of these great Tchaikovsky or Verdi pieces. You have to believe the whole way, you have to take the audience the whole way, and bring them back.

ES: *Why has he such a bad reputation in some quarters?*

MTT: Some people find undisguised expression embarrassing and over the top. When orchestras first rehearse these pieces of Tchaikovsky there are all kinds of shenanigans. You have to get past that. You have to get past all the funny lyrics, the bawdy jokes, people making funny noises during the cymbal crashes, people playing the big tune in the opening of Manfred and licking their fingers and sliding all over the finger board in the most outrageous style ... You have to go through all of that, which is only an expression of people's embarrassment, and then begin to say, 'Can you really do it now that all the joking is aside? Can you actually find a way to do this which is deeply convincing and heartfelt? Are you willing to do it?'

Phrasing

It does come down to one's own willingness to do it. It's so special. It involves above all the supreme art for instrumentalists, the art of repeating the same note. If a singer repeats the same note she has the advantage of being able to put a new syllable on it, so it can automatically give an expressive direction to the phrase. Say she has a phrase of three notes, in which the first two are the same and the third note resolves one step lower. She sings, 'I love you.' The natural expression of the words causes her to accent the second note, the 'love' note, and there's a beautiful phrase. But an instrumentalist who has only his bow, his reed or his fingers, must arrive at the effect of the missing text through a particular style of playing. In the Russian style of playing a great deal of it comes from the way the *vibrato* is produced.

In slow motion here is what would have to happen if a violinist had to play this 'I love you' phrase. He would probably start it on an up-bow. That would be the 'I' part. Then he would have to begin vibrating very slightly with the left hand, even before the bow got near the string. The bow would have to be turned so that not all of the hairs were in contact with the string; then it would have to be put into motion, and as it began to graze the string, the string would slowly be brought into vibration. And as that happened, the *vibrato* would be slightly intensified and then for an instant nearly stopped. Then he would play a down bow, which is where the 'love' part of the phrase would be. As the bow came down he would start first at a slower speed of *vibrato* and gradually accelerate, and at the same time the left hand would come to its greatest focus of *vibrato*, probably reaching a pinnacle about a quaver after the beat. Whereupon he would relax the intensity of the vibrato, the sound, into the 'you' portion of the phrase.

I have just analyzed this one simple little move, and you can't approach a piece of music thinking of every single moment this way, or you'd make yourself quite crazy. But it's by analyzing certain aspects of style that you can arrive at principles which you can apply to everything. Now, what makes orchestral playing so special and so challenging is that every person's reaction time is different. The speed at which people start an up-bow is different. The speeds of *vibrato* are different. Where one quaver after the beat actually is, the sense of time, is a little bit different. Yet to create this kind of very personal *cantabile* singing effect, which is really required in a composer like Tchaikovsky, the players must synchronize their reaction times and their sense of tonal colour and projection at a very rapid and active level, even while the music they're producing, and the illusion they're trying for, is quite slow and sustained.

We're back to what I always come back to: the Parthenon aspects of music. The audience hears a very slow, sustained phrase, an 'I love you', but actually many, many operations have gone into creating it, all linked together and triggering one another at a much faster rate. The rate, in fact, is closer to the speed of thought, because as you say, 'I love you' in your mind, there are all sorts of other associations and meanings and resonances present. There are little thrills and echoes, and delight at past shared moments, and expectations of the future, and little gasps of disappointment at the things that perhaps haven't worked out as you wanted. All that is there in that one statement, and all of that can be there in the richness of the sound, as it's produced. It is such a challenge for a soloist to imagine all of that, to see it in the music, and ask, 'What does this really mean to me? What do I think these notes really mean? What do I have to say about them?'

The process is like psycho-analysis or self-analysis. You study a piece of music this way and arrive at a sense of honesty where you can say, 'I am completely at one with what I am saying about this piece – this piece really is me, I really am this piece'. So, then you can imagine how much more difficult it is when you are asking sixteen or eighteen members of a violin section to come to a unified concept. They are all different people, they all feel something different, they all think something different, and here I am saying, 'Well, let's try and do it this way,' trying to get it to meld together. It's a very, very subtle and interesting interplay of willpowers, of who will give in, who will not, and a very gradual coming together. Quite a subtle process, which must go on over time; people must trust one another for the music to begin flowing in this wonderfully relaxed way, but they must be ready to take a quick breath, a quick nuance, a quick change of direction.

Performing Tchaikovsky's Sixth Symphony

ES: *Is this particularly difficult in a work like the Sixth Symphony, or is it true of Tchaikovsky as a whole? Are there any other examples you can think of where the problems are as great?*

MTT: Well, yes, there are, but in Tchaikovsky's Sixth it's particularly difficult because the opening is very self-consciously sad. The opening of the whole piece is just a dark, funereal, desperate, depressed beginning. Then you have this wistful, sort of feverish Allegro. It's extraordinary, because the notes are rapid, but the effect must not be *agitato*. It has to be one of flickering, luminescent points of light, and only gradually accumulate into this great, hulking Allegro. And after all the *agitato* — which I always like to think of as gossip, it sounds like Russian ladies gossiping — the music becomes grand, and then fades off.

And next you have this other theme, the first of these descending scale themes, which is a theme of hopefulness, or forgiveness, or comfort. If it's just played quietly, it sounds colourless and boring. If it's played too expressively, it sounds mawkish. To be able to play it quietly, but with this little ongoing leading sense of intensity and care, is something very special. At that moment, everyone on stage must actually feel that they care about presenting this message to the audience. If it's hard to care about a whole audi-

With Artur Rubenstein, c.1971

ence, you can think of some person, or some situation in your life – it really does help. To say this is revolutionary now, because it's not at all fashionable to think in this way, and hasn't been for a while. However, in this sort of music, having a sense of an image, a subtext, or someone or some part of yourself can be inspiring.

I remember first coming into the orchestral life, to the Boston Symphony Orchestra, which had had such a tradition of working with Koussevitzky and Munch, who had both talked a lot in poetic terms. At that point some members of the orchestra were saying, 'Well, let's not have any more of this talk of music being like sunrises, or 'mysterioso', or anything like that. Let's just say, it's in the upper part of the bow and it's on the string.' This completely technical approach to shaping music was all the rage, and it fitted in very nicely with the analytical temperament of the times. Nonetheless, I remember the best playing I heard the Boston Symphony do at that time was a concert with Rubinstein. I accompanied him in Brahms's Second Piano Concerto. At one point in the last movement, he suddenly said, 'What is this? I don't hear paprika, I don't hear goulash, I don't hear goose-fat. This is Hungarian piece.' And he looked over at the fiddles, and he played this sort of cabaret phrase from the last movement, and said, 'When you play this, my dears, you must be thinking, "Oh, Hungary, it's you I'm lovink," ' and, right away the whole orchestra began to play in the most ample and expansive and generous kind of way.

Sound is analogous, somehow, to a certain emotional intensity that exists in the voice, and to try and ignore that in a composer like Tchaikovsky is a great mistake. I've even had battles with Russian colleagues in these last years about it. One would come to perform a Tchaikovsky piano concerto, or whatever, and say, 'Oh well, let's just play it coolly and straightforwardly.' And Rachmaninov the same. No! This is just copping out. You have to be willing to deal with the emotional message of the piece, and to set it forth, with discipline, of course. It is easier when it's a loud, impassioned, desperate message. It's much more personal, much more revealing, when it's something quiet and expressive.

ES: *After the performance of the Sixth last night, you said you felt frustrated in some way because it was only half there. I'm interested in the players' feelings – what did they feel? Have you spoken to many of them?*
MTT: They were very happy about many things. And of the things I drew their attention to, they said, 'Oh well ...'

Look, if anything goes wrong in a performance, if there's anything that I'm not happy with, I am to blame. That's what I go home with. That's what I'm up all night with. I never think some player didn't do something right, or some section didn't do something right. It's always my fault. I didn't prepare it correctly. I didn't rehearse it correctly. I didn't show it correctly. Whatever. That's just the way I've been raised. Then I try to imagine how it can be better next time. Last night's performance was a first step toward bringing people round to the idea of trying to play the piece as it really needs to be played. All the big things were already there, and there was some extraordinary quiet solo playing from Andrew Marriner, the first clarinet, and a great trombone and tuba choral.

ES: *In practice, is playing Tchaikovsky so very different from other Russian composers, Rimsky-Korsakov, for example?*
MTT: It's an entirely different thing, playing Rimsky. Rimsky is more Russian, more primitive. Tchaikovsky is more elegant, more Italianate. But both composers' works define the best of Russian fiddle playing.

Russian Fiddle Playing

It's so extraordinary, isn't it, that in this age we live in, with mechanical instruments and moon probes and computers, there is still nothing which can reproduce the particular sense of communication that comes from human fingers vibrating at their own particular individual speed on a strand of metal-wound sheep gut stretched over some pieces of wood and activated by the tail of a horse!

Russian fiddle playing, as exemplified by Auer and his school, was based on the idea of positions on the fiddle. The hand took various positions on the different strings, and, having set your hand in that particular position, a number of notes were accessible with the fingers that were there. You practised and approached the instrument so that you could move very easily from one position to another. This encouraged the player to get the maximum number of colours out of the instrument. This is because the same note can be played on many different strings of the violin – but the impression of the note is entirely different, depending on the string on which it is played. The strings are analogous to voices, they're like soprano, alto, tenor, bass. The same note can have a very easy middle-of-the-voice sound on one string, but it could to have a much higher, breathier sound if played two strings lower. And of course you can also play the notes in harmonics; there are many, many possibilities about the colouration of the fiddle. Old-style playing encouraged different colouration. Modern playing uses another system called extension, which tries to keep the colours as even as possible.

This is a kind of technique which is very good for Stravinsky, and some people think it's very good for Mozart or Bach.

But what we're beginning to feel now is the lack of colour, so that we need to go back more to the old style of playing for all Brahms, Tchaikovsky, and the rest of the Romantic repertoire. We need to have the facility to evoke those colours. When you look at parts that were used by orchestras of the nineteenth century, and were marked by great concert masters, the fingerings that you see, the suggestion of where these notes should be played, are quite extraordinary by today's standards. And it's also very interesting to note that the bowings, by and large, have gone through a complete reversal. In all sorts of music by Strauss and Tchaikovsky played by the great orchestras at the turn of the century, a great number of passages which they played down-bow are now commonly played up-bow. It is very interesting, because the down-bow in those days was the style of down-bow I mentioned before, where the bow is moving and little by little it grazes the string and then draws out this sound. Twentieth-century music and twentieth-century life has produced a down-bow which is used with an aggressive accent like a tennis serve. If people are trying to avoid making an accent, they'll say, 'Well, let's do it on the up-bow, it can be gentler.' But it's a different sound.

This used to be a great frustration when I was a young man talking with Heifetz and Piatigorsky. I was trying to get ideas about bowing from them, and one day I asked Piatigorsky, 'How would you start the Tchaikovsky *Pathétique* cello solo? You've played this millions of times in the Berlin Philharmonic and the Bolshoi.' He said, 'Oh ja, I played.' 'Well, how did you play it?' 'Oh, I don't remember.' Finally I said, 'Well, look, do you start up- or down-bow?' He just said, 'Up-bow and down-bow, same thing. No difference between up-bow and down-bow. Depends only what you want to do with bow.' They had a much more poetic approach to those things.

One great concert master said to me, 'Look, I always presume that at any concert maybe forty per cent of the section is actually conscious of what's going on. And if you can create a bowing so that the music comes out the right way even if the musicians aren't awake, that's a definition of a good bowing. That'll be the right sort of sound, it'll be the right sort of attack, according to where people are playing on the bow, whether they are thinking or not.' This is completely opposite to the old-timers, who said, 'Here is a bowing with which you can achieve a miraculous effect, if you think about it. Of course, if you don't think about it, it's a catastrophe.

Rimsky-Korsakov and *Sheherazade*

Anyway, going back to our conversation about Rimsky. Rimsky really requires this sort of colouristic approach to playing. The whole nature of Rimsky's music is much more one of improvisation, and much closer to the world of the exotic gypsy, the cabaret performer. And to play something like the third movement of *Sheherazade* nowadays, I think you almost have to begin by overdoing it; that is, by putting in *portamenti*, getting everyone to do them in the most libidinous fashion and then, having established that, pulling it back to a more innocent presentation of the same sort of ideas. That's actually something Leonard Bernstein suggested to me. I was working on *Sheherazade* with the New World Symphony, and we had really incredible *portamenti* happening. He said, 'It's all great, but it's just too carnal. They can do the same thing, but be innocent.' And it really worked. But this style has become so remote from us, that to try to approach it little by little doesn't work. It's easier to overstate it, and then pull it back to where it needs to be.

Sheherazade is such a fantastic masterpiece, but you have to really ride the front edge of the music the whole time. You have to sustain your belief in it every single minute. In this kind of Russian music – and a lot of Italian music, as well as in certain aspects of French music – the necessity is there for a performance to keep the line, to keep the front edge. It's like storytelling. In certain German music it's not so necessary – the design of the music seems to take care of itself more. Does that mean that any of these musics are any less profound or important? No, I don't think so. It's a different side of human expression. Besides which, so many of the performance problems that you get in Tchaikovsky you also find in Brahms, for example. Brahms again is a composer who writes music like the phrase in the *Pathétique* Symphony we mentioned, where great tenderness is necessary. You're trying to say something which is very sentimental and very subtle. If you don't say it enough, it's boring. And if you say it too much, it's mawkish. Trying to find a balance is a real art.

My experiences with Russian music started with Stravinsky, but in recent years I have come more and more to appreciate the roots of the Russian musical tradition and to recognize their echoes in all Russian twentieth-century music.

Stravinsky in Los Angeles

Early Recollections

ES: *What are your early recollections of Stravinsky?*
MTT: Stravinsky was perhaps my favourite composer in the earliest years of my life. I can't remember a time before I knew *Petrushka* and *Sacre* and *The Firebird*, largely because my grandmother used to sing all the tunes that came from *Petrushka* and even some from the *The Firebird*. *Sacre* was a record that I loved so much that I played right through it. When I say 'played through it' I mean literally that. In those days it was 78 rpm records. Lots of them had been made during the war when there were shortages of acetate or resin. The records were moulded around a disc of felt, or some kind of cottonwool or something. So, if you played a record enough times you finally got to the point where you played through the shellac, and started to have wispy threads spinning out of the gramophone. I played through all the Stravinsky records we owned.

My parents were active concert-goers, and we went to concerts of new music in Los Angeles, and especially concerts at the LA Festival, which presented large pieces a few times a year, particularly by Stravinsky.

I have early memories of seeing him conduct some small pieces, and seeing this very thin, gangly man coming out and making music that sounded quite unusual. But what I can remember absolutely clearly is seeing him conduct *Rossignol*, complete, when I was around ten or so. It made such an impression upon me to hear that whole score. From then on I insisted on going to every Stravinsky concert possible. He'd perform new smallish pieces at Monday Evening Concerts, and, then at the festival concerts I mentioned, you'd hear larger works. I was impressed by his angular, yet courtly stage presence, and by his precise way of speaking.

I was aware that there was a controversy about the sort of music he was composing at that time, which was already quite severe compared to the big hits of his musical past that the audience unquestionably revered. I began to become aware that there was a circle of musicians around him in Los Angeles, and that my teacher to be, Ingolf Dahl, was one of them.

With Igor Stravinsky, c.1965 (© Arnold Newman, 1994)

Stravinsky was quite friendly with many musicians in Los Angeles at that
time – musicians like Sol Babitz, the violinist and pioneer in Baroque original instrument performance. Stravinsky also rubbed shoulders easily with
studio musicians and composers, particularly at the informal gatherings following Monday Evening Concerts. As you entered the room you were aware
of all kinds of Bohemian and artistic types circulating and conversing. Off
in one corner there was always a tangle of people, much more densely compressed than anywhere else in the room. At the centre of this was Aldous
Huxley holding forth on some arcane topic that had momentarily interested

him. I was once introduced to Huxley. He talked to me of the sex life of the lobster.

Stravinsky as Audience

It all began to come much more into focus when I myself became a performer at Monday Evening Concerts. I was on programmes with my teacher, Ingolf Dahl. Stravinsky sometimes came to a rehearsal or a performance. He always sat in the front row at the rehearsals with his scores, listening and commenting. At the performances he sometimes sat just off-stage, not in sight of the audience, but looking through a filmy curtain between the stage and the back-stage area.

In particular, I remember the night *The Owl and the Pussycat* was premièred, which Ingolf played. There had been so much *Sturm und Drang* going on, because the soprano who was supposed to have done it had trouble learning the intervals and at the last minute somebody else had to come in and do it. Everything began to calm down. That night I was playing Beethoven's op. 111 Sonata, and I actually had a facsimile of the manuscript. I sat back-stage with the old man, and had tea with him in fact. I used to take a thermos bottle full of lemon tea to all my performances in those days – it was part of my ritual – and I offered him some tea, and being a good Russian he of course accepted, and we sat back there sipping. I said, 'Well, Maestro, I have the manuscript of the op. 111 Sonata if you care to follow it, although it's quite difficult because it's so messy.' He said he would follow it. Then I played the Sonata, and came off; we still had time before the next piece, and he talked to me about it. He said, 'It's so extraordinary, you know, it's all acoustics. Everything is vibrating. The low notes vibrating with the top notes on the piano. Beethoven is relishing the sheer acoustic phenomenon of the instrument. How curious that a composer who was completely deaf at this time should have been so obsessed with resonance and the question of acoustics.' Then he told me that he really preferred the string quartets to the late piano sonatas, because he liked their more angular and independent lines. But he was very happy with my performance.

ES: *How old were you?*
MTT: Nineteen? But I should backtrack.

First Meeting with Stravinsky

I think the first time that I actually said a couple of words to him was when we were recording, or attempting to record, the *Huxley Variations* in a recording session in the American Legion Auditorium in Hollywood which was used for recordings. There was an orchestra called the Columbia Symphony, which was actually a bunch of pick-up musicians, good sight-readers from all over LA, with a few student types like myself thrown in. Under the guidance of Bob Craft they were all assembled by a veteran Hollywood contractor, Phil Kagan. Phil had the ingenuous habit of making a tremendous amount of noise with a pocket full of change. As he was talking he would rattle these coins, sometimes even during the actual takes; you can hear it on some of those Stravinsky recordings.

So I was on this date, waiting for the Maestro along with a bunch of tough LA studio musicians sitting around jawing about their real estate investments and stock market portfolios, and all that. The second that Stravinsky appeared, the whole lot of them leaped to their feet. They were absolutely quiet and respectful. Stravinsky came in with a big towel around his neck, and we began recording his piece. It was so extraordinary, because even though it was the *Huxley Variations* – you know, a complicated, abstract, serial piece – he actually sang it to us. He never said any number, he never referred to any abstract question of structure, or whatever else may have been involved with the piece. He just said, 'My dears, music must go tee ta ta ta ta ta taa,' with a sort of bizarre *solfège* of grunts and sighs and whistles and chattering noises that he made with his teeth. It was all rather whispery, but quite clear, and it was accompanied by a series of strangely arrested simian gestures, which perfectly expressed the tension and release of each phrase. I was most impressed by him; how clear his musical intentions were, and the sort of energy he had. He was like an old bird of prey, a bit feeble but still dangerous. He'd look at us with his hooded eyes as if he were ready to strike at any moment. But his way of speaking and working was very courtly, still very much in the manner of the Kirov Theatre. He addressed us as, 'My dears', 'My gentlemen'. He was utterly charming.

He had to rest between the takes, but we were all very patient. I don't think the work was actually finished on that day, nor was it a few days later when we were supposed to do part of *Agon*. It was difficult for him to carry things through, and, like as not, Bob Craft would come in and finish off these projects. But still, when Stravinsky himself conducted, there was an electrifying sense of what he wanted. The same was true with *Requiem Canticles*, a year or two later, at the Los Angeles Art Museum. He conducted part of the rehearsal, and again there was an almost terrible sense of excitement at hearing these notes for the first time. Hearing his way of speaking or inflecting the phrases gave them so much character. It was still so connected to the whole Russian tradition of music, a many-vowelled, polysyllabic, multi-diphthonged sort of a style, going beyond the rhythmic complexities to an unerring instinct for gesture.

The Monteverdi Vespers

Sometime after that recording session, I was asked to play continuo in a performance of the Monteverdi Vespers that Bob Craft was conducting. It was one of the first modern recordings of the work. At that time I'd never heard the Monteverdi Vespers. I was vaguely aware there was something called the Vespers of 1610, that's all. I was told there was going to be a continuo rehearsal, and that I should be there. I was to play harpsichord and was assured I would be able to sight read the part with no difficulty. I went to the rehearsal, and we began going through it. While the music was simple,it was almost impossible for me to keep my place because it was so beautiful. I had the greatest difficulty in concentrating. The freshness and surprise of each new chord was such that I was scarcely able to go on to the next one. Then I noticed there was someone looking over my shoulder, and I turned around and it was Stravinsky. So then, of course, I was really so nervous I could scarcely play anything. But that was the first time that I spoke more than a couple of words to him.

Bob Craft

Then a few times I was up at Stravinsky's house for rehearsals, and I got a little glimpse into his world there, of composing in the morning, and then lunch, and then playing cards, and this whole very gentle life that he was leading up there above Sunset Boulevard. So much has been written in recent times criticizing Bob Craft as a kind of *éminence grise* whose mission was really to separate Stravinsky from the rest of the world, the rest of civilization. I can't say that I entirely agree with it. Yes, it's true that Bob wanted Stravinsky to converse and spend time primarily with other geniuses, partially because Bob felt that this company would stimulate Stravinsky. Bob's devotion to Stravinsky was incredible, and he very much wanted to extend Stravinsky's composing life as long as possible. Introducing him to serial music and to new ideas was a way of keeping his interest at a peak.

Even more touching, I thought, was Bob's playing the piano with

Stravinsky. When Stravinsky had one of his strokes, and was really in a great depression and slowed to nothing, Bob began playing four-hand piano music with him, actually for a period of weeks. And then one day, when Stravinsky was just sitting in the audience at one of these rehearsals, we noticed that his fingers were moving in the air, as if he were playing the piano. Shortly after that he began composing again ... Bob had correctly understood that a lot of Stravinsky's way of making music had come through ideas that he felt in his fingers, perhaps even before he perceived them in his mind – and this was a way of getting him back into action again. It worked very well.

The Rite of Spring

Ralph Grierson and I had the chance to make the first recording of Stravinsky's four-hand version of the *Rite of Spring*. I had communication with Stravinsky at that time about questions of text and doubling, and so forth. He had an unerring sense of tempo. He said 'The Glorification of the Chosen One' was meant to be a very fast dance; and the 'Danse Sacral' was meant to be driving but deliberate. He discussed the manner of articulation of the phrases, and the way he sang the phrases was so *rubato*, so full of character. He always sang in a way so that there was a little bump, a quick, expressive accent at the beginning of each grace-note figure, whether or not it was under a slur. These things were very suggestive of how the piece was meant to go.

I think that it was from the sound of his voice, and from my memories of my grandmother's voice, that my idea of a folkloric presentation of the music began to develop. All of those grace notes are suggestive of the breaking in the voice in folkloric singing. You see, with the *Rite of Spring*, the most important thing to catch on to is that it's a happy piece of music. It's totally ecstatic – abandoned, wild. After all, it is a fertility rite. The *Rite of Spring* is a fabulous party. Once a year, people get together and have this incredible rave and, oh, and isn't it too bad when they are sweeping up the next morning and they find this girl dead? She had such a good time, poor thing, that she killed herself. It's a familiar story. It's not a tale of grim ritual or vengeance, but of people having such a good time they just can't stand it!

There seems to be an element of mystery in the *Rite of Spring*, part of which is the contemplation of the primordial origins of things – a little bit like Gauguin's painting 'Where do we come from, who are we, where are we going?' At the beginning of this party, everyone knows that someone is

With Ralph Grierson, 1968

going to die, but no one knows who it is. That's the mysterious and slightly apprehensive aspect of the piece. In some of the very soft music there is that shivery sense of, 'Oh gosh, is it me?' That's what is so great about Pina Bausch's version of *The Rite of Spring*. She has so successfully created that atmosphere of people wondering if it's them or not. But once it's decided who it is, well then, the ecstatic events proceed.

ES: *Yes, that throws a very different light on the piece.*

Russian Village Orchestra Sound

MTT: The thing about all those early Stravinsky pieces is that dissonance was used not to suggest pain, suffering or aggression. Primitive people make music with whatever is to hand. Nothing is in tune with anything else, but there is a joyous, and very often a sparkling, glittering quality to that sort of music. Stravinsky was trying to get that kind of feeling with what was to hand, which for him was a traditional orchestra.

ES: *Some of those sonorities are extraordinary. They do sound primitive ...*

MTT: That's why when he wrote *Les Noces* he found what he had really been looking for throughout all the earlier pieces. *Les Noces* is certainly the masterpiece of that first period. All the exotic lushness of St Petersburg has been pared down to lean lines of voices, piano and percussion. The piece ends with gleaming dissonances of vibrating metal hanging in the air that both symbolize the excitement and conflict of those days in Russia, and still sound as fresh in London or San Francisco today.

The Sixties in LA

During the sixties the Sunset Strip in LA was the centre of all kinds of psychedelic sub-cultures. People were swaying their way up and down the street in various states of euphoria on the lookout for celebrities. As the Stravinskys drove down the hill from their house on Whetherly Drive they were often amused to find teeny-boppers peering into their Lincoln hoping for a glimpse of Jim Morrison.

I remember another night going to dinner with Aaron Copland and Lawrence Morton at a small restaurant on the Strip. When we left the restaurant there was an amazing crowd of purple suede-fringed flower-power children who were elated to recognize the creator of one of America's great musical mythologies. 'Man, I'm gassed, the cat is Aaron Copland,' said one.

ES: *What was the most characteristic thing about Stravinsky as you knew him?*
MTT: I think the thing that was most remarkable about Stravinsky was his incredible curiosity. He was so interested in new things. New music, of course, but also old music which he didn't know. A new composer from the past, a new sonority, a new instrument, anything. He was so interested whatever it was. So interested in geography, so interested in new words, so interested in going to see terrible Hollywood movies which showed landscapes in parts of the world that he had never seen. I remember he went to see *Khartoum* four or five times, saying it was a horrible movie, but it was so interesting to look at the backgrounds, to see all these geological formations and colours of rock.

Every room of his house had several dictionaries and atlases in it. As my mother would have said, he believed in seizing the moment of excited curiosity about any new thing that came up. 'Let's look it up, let's check this and see what it's about.' A great part of that of course was that he and Bob were always looking for something to stump Aldous Huxley, who was part of that Monday Evening Concert circle as well. When they discovered

Carlo Gesualdo, they were so excited because they thought they would finally stump Huxley. They casually announced that they were going to do some madrigals by Gesualdo at a Monday Evening Concert. And Huxley said, 'Oh yes, Gesualdo, Prince of Venosa, he murdered his wife. He wrote in the most interesting shorthand Latin; I remember I translated a couple of documents of his at one point during my studies of arcane Latin shorthand ...' I think they gave up at that point.

I vividly remember Stravinsky's sense of delight with the music of Schütz. We were doing the Schütz Christmas story, and he was just thrilled by it. He would sing little bits of the choruses under his breath, greeting each person with a little excerpt of Schütz. This liveliness and curiosity from someone his age and in his position was so different from what one might have expected. He might have been preoccupied only with his world view and what was contained within it, but, quite to the contrary, he was always interested in discovering something new. He hated the idea of repetition of the familiar, particularly in music. At one time he was obsessed with Beethoven's string quartets, and nothing but Beethoven's string quartets. So Lawrence Morton and I got some recordings and scores of Schubert's string quartets, and sent them up to the house. It didn't work out so well, because every time there was a repeat in the music Stravinsky took the Schubert scores, threw them on the ground and cursed in Russian. He just couldn't stand the idea of anything being exactly repeated at that time.

ES: *That's an interesting insight into the way his mind worked. It might account, too, for the differences in his recordings of his work.*
MTT: Absolutely. Central to his nature was the idea that if you have done something once in one way, you should do it in quite the opposite way the next, even in his music. You can see that from the positioning of his major and minor triads within the same chord. He and Ravel had a discourse about that, with Ravel saying, 'Well, the best way to place these triads is in this particular sort of arrangement,' and Stravinsky saying, 'Well, in that case, next time I'm going to do exactly the contrary.' I'm sure that growing up around someone like that had a great influence on me, and in a community he so influenced. It has pressed me to be on the lookout for something new, something that is contrary to what is expected. I remember Stravinsky's words, 'Nothing is as boring as the recent past.' Getting beyond the fashion of the moment, and seeing what may be next, is what I try to do.

Stravinsky's Later Works

ES: *How do you think people rate Stravinsky's later works?*

MTT: Perhaps because I heard Stravinsky himself perform so much of his late work, I find his music very personal, and strongly related to all the music that went before. I know other composers, like Oliver Knussen and Charles Wuorinen, who feel that way as well. Ollie and I have entertained many a party by singing Stravinsky's *Huxley Variations*. We can sing it with no problem from beginning to end because it is such a straightforward, gestural work.

Stravinsky's later work is undervalued by the public. That's a great pity, for the music, though spare, is so beautiful. It requires only a sympathetic performance to let its best qualities shine. It must be performed with clarity, simplicity, but also, especially in the vocal works, with beauty of sound. It helps for it to be heard in a warmer acoustic than the usual dry-as-bones studio recordings. A piece like *Canticum Sacrum* has such majesty and depth of expression. It's one my favourites.

Agon, is great fun for me to hear, because it is a kind of (snapshot) of those Los Angeles years. If you listen to the movements of *Agon*, you say, 'Well, here is a piece that sounds a little bit like madrigals, and here is a

With Oliver Knussen, 1992

piece that sounds a little bit like Schütz, and here's a piece that sounds like Webern, and here's a piece that sounds like Boulez, and here's a piece that sounds like early Baroque dances, and here's a piece that sounds like Ives.' Of course Stravinsky was hearing all those pieces performed at Monday Evening Concerts. He was picking up ideas and reducing them to exactly what was necessary for his purpose – a lute-like harp phrase, a brittle flourish of mandolin, a stroke of castanets, a four-part brass canon. He used these bits to make a kind of brochure of highlights of the Monday Evening season in the form of a serial ballet. *Agon* is a very entertaining souvenir of the sort of musical curiosity, power of invention and sense of humour Stravinsky still possessed even as an old man.

Bernstein

With Leonard Bernstein at the Charles Ives Centenary, Danburry, Connecticut, 1974

Thoughts Prompted by Last Night's Bernstein Concert

ES: *What were your feelings after last night's Bernstein memorial concert?*
MTT: I felt so sad and happy. Sad, because Lenny is gone, but so happy to feel the power of his spirit in his music, especially the later music from *A Quiet Place* and *Arias and Barcarolles*. I wanted so much for the audience to understand that Lenny was moving in a new musical direction and that he wanted to take us along with him in to a more adventurous musical language. Of course, all of his music is filled with references to his, and the whole world's, musical past, but he has a unique way of presenting even the most familiar material, and then seeing whether it will hold its own against an all-out attack of compositional techniques.

I am very happy with the *Suite from a Quiet Place* that Sid Ramin, Michael Barret and I have extracted from the opera. It is quite like the typical evenings with Lenny that we all remember. The shape of the suite is as follows. Introduction: a sense of mystery grows on you as you walk the Gothic corridors to his flat in the Dakota. Then comes a shouted greeting, and an overwhelming bear hug leading to the Allegro: a flurry of random and ever-more aggressive questioning. 'How the hell are you? Did you hear about my Viennese medal? Can you believe the way they've messed up Cambodia? Why haven't you called me?' Then a crash into utter despair, the Adagio: 'Hopeless, it's all hopeless. This time it's for keeps. Man's greed, destruction, no way out. Hopeless.' And then the Allegretto (with bounce): 'By the way, did you ever hear that jive fox-trot Spivey used to sing in her night club in the 1930s? (singing) "Hopeless, I'm hopelessly falling for youuuuuu." ' And finally the Adagio: 'It's so late. I've still so much to do. Let's all pray that somehow our better natures will see us through. Amen, adieu.'

Quiet Place and *Aria*s *and Barcarolle*s both show LB as a masterful musical conjurer. He is so amazing in transforming tone rows from angry ostinatos to scat riffs, bluesy ballads or Mahlerian adagios. The music is so clever, yet engaging and satisfying to follow. He was so happy that in these last two works he had really conquered serial writing and that he achieved it, not by excruciating study, but by applying his brilliant sense of gamemanship. If Lenny had wanted to write 'brainy' really difficult music he certainly could have. With his mastery of mental jotto and acrostics, he could have out puzzled us all. But the essence of music and life for him was communication. His work poses questions and conundrums but also offers solutions.

ES: *To some extent all his pieces end with a kind of catharsis, a feeling of consolation, reconciliation, optimism. Was he really an eternal optimist?*

With Frederica von Stade, recording *On the Town*, 1993

MTT: Well, he was a patient and extremely hopeful pessimist, or perhaps he was an extremely pessimistic optimist – I'm not sure how you would express it. He could be very depressed about the state of the world and won der how things could ever get better. Yet he gave so much time to music students, his family and friends. He really was extremely generous with his time. His attention towards so many generations of musicians was quite extraordinary. So many people felt that he was their friend. I think that with each new friendship, as with each new composition, he was hoping to reaffirm his own ideals and optimism.

ES: *His music is, all of it, incredibly communicative, I think.*
MTT: What's interesting about his music is that one senses him; the more you are aware of his personality, the better it is. It's so important that he wasted very little of his time and his life trying to be original. So many very talented musicians don't see it that way, but they're really wasting a lot of time trying to come up with something that nobody else has done – instead of just saying, 'Well, this is what I have to say. This is what is vital for me to communicate. Let someone else decide whether it's new, original or important.' They will anyway.

Getting to Know Bernstein

ES: *When did you first meet him?*

MTT: Just after I had won the Koussevitzky prize in Tanglewood, in 1968. I had done several things at Tanglewood which were considered to be musically strong – I guess there was a certain brashness to them. I was playing the piano, writing choral pieces, and conducting. This reminded people of somebody else who used to be around there years ago, and it was arranged that after the closing exercises at Tanglewood I would go to New York about a week or so later and meet Lenny – which was quite an awesome thought.

We went up to his place on Park Avenue. He lived at the corner of 79th Street and Park Avenue, a very nice place, and we met in the late afternoon. He said, 'Well, play something on the piano.' So I played some Bach, and some Haydn, and Copland and Stravinsky, and so on – a kind of a catalogue of pieces. Pretty soon we were both playing the piano and he was asking me, 'Oh, do you know this, do you know that, do you like this, do you like that?' Finally he said to me, 'So what really is your most favourite musical moment? If you could only keep one moment in all of music, what would it be? I went to the piano and played the oscillating minor thirds and then the lonely oboe solo in the last movement of Mahler's *Das Lied von der Erde*. That was a very important moment for both of us. That music was so much the centre of what he loved the most. It's so simple, and yet the ambiguity is so vast. So much is suggested by just those few notes, because so much is left out. It's like a great poem. There is so much left out, and what you fill in around it is so meaningful.

Over the next few years, whenever we met, it was always a sharing of new music. He was obviously so busy at that time with the New York Philharmonic, and also trying to compose. I had a lot to do too, but I was a much younger musician and had more time. Sure, I was studying like crazy, but also I was listening to all kinds of music, including avant-garde, rhythm and blues, rock and roll, and especially folk and ethnic music. I went to off-the-track music shops and bought obscure blues and rockabilly records that had had no commercial release and tapes that people had brought back from Sumatra.

ES: *How old were you then?*

MTT: I don't know – early twenties. So that was really fun. I would save these musical treasures. Then when we met I would play them for him. Most were things he hadn't heard before. I know he enjoyed it, and I so much enjoyed the collecting.

Sometimes, though, he would really surprise me. I played an obscure piece of gagaku music for him, and he said, 'Oh yes, *Ryu*! I was there at the Imperial Palace when they played that one day, and I was sitting next to them as they did it. It was really tremendous fun.' Of course he was constantly querying me about the repertoire. He was always testing me. 'Do you know this, do you know that? What key is this in? Where does Beethoven first use this theme?' and so on. Sometimes I knew the answer, sometimes I didn't; and if I didn't, he'd say, 'Oh, you have to get to know this, we have to go through this together, I have to show you this. Get the score down from the shelf.' There was a wonderful excitement about it.

The 'Do You Know This' Apotheosis Dinner

I think the climax of it all was reached one night at the Pyrenees restaurant, a kind of country inn forty-five minutes' drive from Tanglewood. It was a nice, quiet, fairly swank place. One night I was there with Lenny and Aaron Copland. I had known Aaron in California, since I had played his Piano Variations and the Piano Fantasy to him when I was about eighteen years old. We were talking about Aaron's *Inscape*, which Lenny was contemplating re-orchestrating. Suddenly Lenny got on to a, 'Do you know this, do you know that?' He said, 'I bet there's one thing you don't know; I know you don't *know* this.' And he started singing,

'Young Strefan is the kind of lout
We do not care a fig about!
We cannot say what evils may result in consequence
But lordly vengeance will pursue
A dire revenge will fall on you
If you besiege our high prestige
Or offer us offence.'

I immediately sang in response:

'Our lordly style you shall not quench
With base *canaille*! (That word is French) ...'

He sang back:

'Distinction ebbs

Before a herd of vulgar plebs!
(A Latin word) ...'

I sang,

'Twould fill with joy and madness stark
The hoi polloi!
(A Greek remark) ...'

And then both of us together sang out,

'A Latin word
A Greek remark
And one that's French'

Of course I did know *Iolanthe* and most of Gilbert and Sullivan, because I'd seen the D'Oyly Carte company on tour in Los Angeles many times, and when I was ten years old my parents had bought me those classic recordings with Martin Greene and Peter Pratt. I had memorized them, and used to sing them with a couple of friends of mine in the fourth or fifth grade, riding our bicycles to school. Not the typical Los Angeles experience.

So, this was all terribly amusing to Lenny and me. We kept saying, 'Ah, what about this scene, and this scene?' Finally having to confess that we really didn't know *The Gondoliers*, either of us, that well, but who does? And all through this Aaron was very agitated. He kept saying, 'Fellers, fellers, everyone's looking at us, be quiet.' We *were* getting rather loud. Then Lenny shrieked, 'Tresses tresses of my hair?' – the opening soprano solo from *Les Noces*. So that was amusing to Aaron, because he of course had recorded *Les Noces* with Stravinsky and knew it backwards anyway. *Les Noces* is one of my favourite pieces. Lenny adored it as well. With no consultation we threw ourselves into it Using a couple of knives and forks and the glasses and plates around the table we started banging out a few notes and bits of the opening tableau. Then we really got carried away. We started actually to perform the piece, using whatever happened to be on the table and singing riotously. Aaron's nerve broke first. He got deeply embarrassed. He pleaded with us, 'Fellers, fellers, I can't stand it. The whole restaurant's looking at us,' and of course they were. But the more he tried to shush us, the louder we got.

ES: *That says a lot about the three of you.*

MTT: We made quite a commotion. We went through a great deal of *Les Noces*, ending with the big chorus, those great unison chords, screaming away. We got quite a respectable hand at the end of it all. That night seemed to be the zenith of the 'Do you know this, do you know that?' trials. Lenny never stopped testing me, but his questions grew more subtle. In fact, asking questions was one of his greatest methods of teaching.

ES: *It's interesting, going back to the Gilbert and Sullivan for a moment, how few people realize how significant those pieces are in the history of American musical theatre.*

MTT: Oh, colossally.

ES: *When I hear your recording of Gershwin's* Of Thee I Sing *I'm just astounded by how much Gilbert and Sullivan there is in it.*

MTT: Well, sure. Broadway is really a combination of Gilbert and Sullivan, Yiddish theatre and jazz and other black music. What Lenny and I enjoyed doing so much was bouncing back and forth between all those worlds and laughing at their curious similarity to some of the most revered moments in clasical music. For example, we loved noticing that almost inevitably the climactic phrase of twelve tone vocal pieces is identical to the opening of Sammy Cahn's camp classic 'Be My Love'.

ES: *Were you astounded by the breadth of his interests, or did it come as no surprise?*

MTT: No, I was quite taken aback by the whole thing. I didn't have the experience of seeing him in action as a composer at that point, so I first got to know him as a conductor.

Bernstein the Conductor

The first big piece I saw him do in Tanglewood was Mahler's Second. It was impressive in its energy – a kind of big-as-all outdoors performance totally suited to the venue. He didn't have much rehearsal and I wasn't able to attend much of it because of my own rehearsals with the Berkshire Music Center. Suddenly, I received word that the Boston Symphony's assistant conductor was ill and that I had been assigned to conduct the off-stage music in the concert that very afternoon. I was told to meet LB an hour before the performance to go over the entrance. At this time the Shed at Tanglewood was very low-tech – no TV, no monitors. Conducting off-stage meant peering through cracks in the backdrop, listening to a mixture of muffled acoustic and thinly amplified sound. I was nervous. I met LB back-stage and was about to ask him my desperate questions, but he interrupted me. He said, 'You know, I've done this piece so many times before and I've always used a score. But I really think I know it. After all, if I got lost or wasn't sure what was next or how many bars till the next fanfare I could just stop and listen and give a sign when the time was right ... couldn't I? What do you think? Should I try it by heart?' I said, 'Well, sure, I guess so. Why not?'

ES: *That's like Mahler asking Klemperer – when he directed the off-stage band in the Second – if he should use the score!*
MTT: And then I thought, 'Oh my God. If he's just listening, waiting for something to happen, how will I know whether to bring in the off-stage group or not?' I started to ask him but he again interrupted by saying, 'Oh, don't worry. Just remember that on *your* advice I'm not using any score, so let's see what happens.' Of course, the performance was sensational and without a hitch. We were all on our toes, it felt slightly dangerous, yet very playful. This was a way he liked to work.

Bernstein Rehearsing

ES: *When you were observing him working on a piece like that, what were the things that stuck in your mind about how he rehearsed as a conductor?*
MTT: Well, nothing much stuck in my mind about that performance other than its energy and danger. But the following season in Boston he came and conducted Beethoven's Ninth. That was the first time I saw him rehearse something from beginning to end, and it was very impressive. That was the first time I thought, 'This guy is the real thing.' Up till then I didn't know, I had just seen him on television, doing these concerts, which were quite theatrical, and he was being very theatrical, and television made a lot of it look even more exaggerated. But seeing him rehearse Beethoven's Ninth, it was so no nonsense, it was so totally purposeful, and it started with the most fundamental things, like just how a particular *tremolo* should sound and then exactly how the inflection of the opening theme should be. He talked of what the music is about. He had the absolute courage to stand in front of the Boston Symphony Orchestra and speak for several minutes on the meaning of *Innigkeit*.

And once again there was extraordinary family feeling about it all. Jimmy Stagliano was the first horn in the Boston Symphony at that point. He was a veteran, a wonderful, air-borne horn player. He had a young student named David Ohanian, a brilliant musician and spectacular horn-player, who was around my age. Jimmy Stagliano brought him in to play fourth horn in the BSO for this concert. When they got to the fourth horn solo in the third movement, Lenny took a lot of time rehearsing that solo, really shaping it with David, lavishly praising and encouraging him. It was a wonderful experience, because I was so happy for my friend David, but also so happy for Jimmy Stagliano, for the whole orchestra. Lenny was doing that thing he did, making everybody on the stage proud of what one of their colleagues was doing, and having that feeling of this is something that we're all doing together.

ES: *Had you conducted the Boston Symphony yourself at that time?*
MTT: Yes. I am lucky that I saw him work on a lot of things from the very beginning to the end, from the foundations to the fruition. There are so many films of him teaching conducting students in front of an orchestra and all that, and those are very meaningful and important, but it wasn't quite the same as what he actually had to say when you went to him with a score that you'd studied, and sat down, and he would say, 'Okay, now, what is the very first thing we notice ...'

Schumann and Subtext Fantasies

Some of the most important pieces that I did with him in this way were Schumann's symphonies. He insisted from the very first moment that there would never be anything changed, there would be no re-touching at all. At that time it was a very daring position. You must remember that in the 1960s George Szell's recordings were looked upon as the great Schumann recordings, and they were extensively re-orchestrated, following the model of Mahler. Lenny would say, 'No, nothing can be changed, but you can be very specific about how you want everything executed.' So we discussed the phrasing of the pieces. I pointed out that the opening of the Third Symphony had many phrasing possibilities. It could be done in at least two ways. It could be in big, swinging bars of three or it could be in longer phrases that stretched across the bars. You could take a breath here or a breath there. There were so many phrasing possibilities. And he said, 'Right, well, if you have so many possibilities the only thing you have to do is become convinced of what the real phrasing is. You must decide. Therefore what you need here is a subtext.'

So he said, 'Come on, what are the words to the opening of the Schumann's Third Symphony? Make some up.' I thought for a minute and said, 'Well, maybe something like this … ', and I sang,

'*Rheine, ach du schöne schöne Rheine,*
Schönster mehr als Heinrich Heine,
Und ich schwöre ich bin deine …'

Or, in English,

'Rhine, Rhine, you beautiful Rhine,
More beautiful than Heinrich Heine,
And I swear that I am yours …'

He thought that this was absolutely hilarious. It was the middle of winter, and he went dashing out of his composer's cottage at his country house, screaming this song, running around the grounds, bursting in on his wife Felicia and the family. We suddenly went off with this fantasy. We were going to make a whole musical *à la Kismet* with the music of Brahms and Schumann. And he said, 'This will do two things, because it will make everyone know these tunes, which are so great, and it also will mean that it will force people to listen to new music in the concert hall, because they'll become so sick of hearing all this Brahms and Schumann …'

And then, after the diversion of imagining and casting this entire musical he said, 'Okay, okay, back to work. So now we have a phrase shape for the first two bars; what about the accompaniment? What about this, what about that?'

So that was my introduction to his way of working, which was a combination of tremendous attention to detail, analysis, fantasy and fun. There again was that playfulness.

ES: *Which was so strongly communicated in the young people's concerts.*
MTT: Sure. And that's something he shared very much with Adolph Green. The two of them were always fantasizing, playing with outrageous lyrics for symphonic masterpieces. That was really upsetting to some people, who said, 'Oh, now that I have heard those words I can never take the piece seriously again.' For us it was a way of breaking through the kind of armour-plate of tradition and seriousness surrounding a piece, and trying to get back to the *Ursprung*, the original welling of inspiration, the desire to communicate.

So many people said that very same thing to me, you know. Piatigorsky used to, whenever we came to play a big piece – a Brahms sonata, a

Beethoven sonata or some such piece – he would always say, 'The first thing you have to do when you play a piece by Brahms or Beethoven is take a big crayon and cross out Beethoven, cross out Brahms, and instead write Grützmacher ...' Grützmacher is the Czerny of the cello world. He's the person who wrote those endless, sawing-away sort of studies that you have to play; and your big struggle when you play a piece by Grützmacher is to try and make something that really sounds like the work of a musical carpenter into something that sounds like music, something that has imagination and communication ... It's simply a piece of music, you have to say something, you have to do something with it, and the name of a great master mustn't stand in your way.

ES: *And that was Bernstein's philosophy too?*
MTT: Oh yes. Absolutely.

Rehearsing Brahms's Fourth Symphony

One of the most daring things I ever saw Lenny do was out in California one summer, when we had the orchestra that was the prototype of the New World Symphony. He was going to do Brahms's Fourth Symphony. I prepared for him before he arrived, had a couple of rehearsals, so they weren't sight-reading.

With Leonard Bernstein at the New World Symphony, 1990

He came in on the first day, and he was outrageous. At that time he'd been told by his dentist he should wear a retainer in his mouth, a sort of prosthetic device that he put in to stop him grinding his teeth. So he had this new thing he was trying to contend with, and of course he had a cigarette, and he had worry beads, a soft drink and a fan. He came in, very jet-lagged, and said, almost sub-sonically, 'Well, all right now, we're going to work on Brahms's Fourth ...'

It was quite grotesque what he was doing with the orchestra. He was rehearsing the Fourth at perhaps one half of the proper tempo, so it was in super-slow motion. It was just barely moving along, and at each note he'd say, 'No, no, you see you have to sing into the note, just move the bow very slowly, just turn, just graze the string; now vibrate your left hand ...' He was making these surges with his voice, these very exaggerated surges, and making the orchestra do them on every single note. 'And now the violas, and now the cellos.' In the first rehearsal I think they barely made it through the development section of the first movement. And this was with every instruction being punctuated by having to stop to take the dental thing out of his mouth, puff a cigarette, take a drink, and so on. The kids in the orchestra were saying, 'Well, I guess he was great once, but this is really impossible.'

I was beside myself. I didn't know what to do. I said to him, 'Well, maybe you can just play through it, Lenny ...' He said, 'No! I know what I'm doing, I know what I'm doing, leave me alone. You're doubting what I'm doing, just leave me alone.' The next day he came in, and he continued from the development section onwards, again super-slow motion – 'Sing; now *vibrato,* now this, now that.' On through the entire Symphony over three days, in this incredible slow motion, squeezing every drop of *vibrato* and sound out of every single note. There were some lovely sounds, but nothing resembling the piece. And we were all kind of at a level of desperation and terror, because it was the day before the concert.

The next day, at the dress rehearsal he came in, and gave the upbeat to Brahms's Fourth. The orchestra again played in this kind of slow motion, undulatory way, and he stopped and said, 'No, no, that was rehearsal; now this is the dress rehearsal, this is performance; in tempo, in tempo.' The orchestra began to play, following him in tempo. The sound they produced was the most rich, gorgeous, totally conscious, ravishing performance that you've ever heard given by an orchestra of young people.

This was his big strategy. He went through the piece, he made them think about the way they were going to play. They were going to make a beautiful sound on every single note. It was in super-slow motion, and then he just said, 'Now, fine, link it up.' And there was everyone in the orchestra looking at one another. 'Where did this come from? We are suddenly hear-ing one of the greatest performances of Brahms's Fourth we ever heard, and one of the greatest orchestras we ever heard. How did it happen?'

Bernstein the Composer

ES: *Turning to Bernstein the composer, I know you were involved in the writing of his* Arias and Barcarolles, *but were you involved in the compositional process at any time before that?*

MTT: Well, he would show me a lot of things that he was doing. I was around a lot during the time of *Mass,* when he was doing it in Washington.

Mass

ES: *This is a very special piece for me. What were your feelings at that time about* Mass? *Were you caught up in the celebratory feel of it, or were you sceptical?*

MTT: Oh no. I was really swept away with the whole piece, especially because a lot of people who were in it were friends of mine from Tanglewood. He said, 'Well, let's get all these musicians, we'll have them on stage, and there'll be a marching band, and there'll be soloists ...' They were all people who'd been there that summer, and had now suddenly arrived down in Washington, and he was writing this big show with a part for everybody. That was great fun.

I was very teary-eyed during the first performance of *Mass,* I think because I knew how far out on a limb he was going in that piece. He really was wearing his heart on his sleeve, and making references to all these forms of pop music, and it was a very kind of open-ended, loose, happening-type piece. I think he knew it was bound to meet with a great deal of hostility and suspicion.

ES: *Yes, warts and all I still feel it is his most important work.*

MTT: I always told him that he had to go back to it, because there was some music missing. You see, he was desperately running out of time while com-pleting it. And what I think is missing from *Mass* is about two minutes of extremely fast, angry music at the moment where the celebrant has his breakdown. It's there in terms of the stage direction. He smashes things and so on, but the whole thing leads up to this huge chorus *crescendo* – and then there should be two really angry minutes of very fast, denunciatory music, which begins to fragment and slow down, and turn into a real mad scene ... But he just didn't have time to write that two minutes of angry music. And later on when I chided him about it, he would say, 'Well, maybe ...' And I would bring it up again, and he would say, 'Well, if you think it should go there, you should write it yourself. Enough already.' Maybe some day I will.

ES: *He wanted to do everything. But he was a composer first. Do you think he compromised himself in not allowing more of his life to be spent in writing his own music?*

MTT: I think there were definitely moments when he felt that, sure, but he also would get completely intoxicated with conducting. He'd come back from these trips to Hiroshima, Vienna, wherever, and describe these endless ovations and spiritual healings, and everything else that had happened. He enjoyed that role, he enjoyed the role of the musical celebrant, very much.

Arias and Barcarolles

ES: *He asked you to collaborate with him on* Arias and Barcarolles. *What was that like?*

MTT: Well, as I look back on it, for some reason, whenever I worked with Lenny, even for a performing project, it always seemed to turn into a compositional project, particularly if you were four-hand. Playing four-hand piano with him was extraordinary because he always wanted to re-write the pieces, or at least redistribute them. He'd always say, 'It's so silly for me to be playing this music up here. It would be much better for you to play this down there, and then I could take over that, and you could just cross over my hands here, and then we could do this – and it really would be much better.' And that was really the case when we did *Sacre* for four hands once. He just kept re-writing, re-writing, re-writing, and he was very charming, but he would also get so nervous when he had to play the piano. He was fine as long as he could keep his hands in one position, playing in one area on the piano, but if he suddenly had to move his hands an octave or two in one particular direction, the moment just before the jump there was a little explosion of panic. 'Oh my God, where am I going next ...?' And if he really didn't know where he was going next, and suddenly realized he was about to make a mistake, he would as like as not bring his hands crashing down right on top of where I was playing. If somebody was going to make a mistake, we were all going to make a mistake together. This reached its peak when I was playing something way down in the bass of the piano, ostinato figures, and he was supposed to be playing something way up at the top. One of these leaps came, and suddenly, bang, Lenny was playing right on top of where I was playing. And I turned to him and said, 'What are you

Rehearsal of the *Arias and Barcarolles*, 1988

doing here? I am playing secondo. I'm way down here in the bass, extreme bass of the piano, and you know, banging out this stuff, and you're supposed to be playing this squeaky tune up there. What are you doing down here in my part of the piano?' And he said, 'Your part of the piano? You have such an ego problem!' That was such a Lenny thing to say.

It was the with *Arias and Barcarolles*. We had already gone through the experience of re-writing Schubert, Mozart and Stravinsky, so when it came to his own music you can imagine how free he felt to change things around. *Arias and Barcarolles* started when he called me in London and said, 'I've been writing this new piece, and I want you to première it with me. It's for four-hand piano?' I said, 'Sure, when is this going to be?' And he said, 'Three weeks from now.' I said, 'Terrific. Will you send me the music?' And he said, 'No, I can't really send you the music because it's not written yet. As it's completed, you'll get it.'

Sure enough, every day or so another couple of pages arrived by fax or courier. Then I got to New York and began working on it with Lenny. It was absolutely hysterical. Whenever we played the piano four hands we laughed so much. For some reason, I guess something about Lenny knowing my association with Yiddish theatre and Piatigorsky and all these other people we had known together, he used to speak in various accents a lot, Russian, German and Jewish accents. We would be trying to play this piece, which had disjunct rhythms, and he would be loudly counting, 'Vun, vun, two! Luftpause!! Vat you do?'

The atmosphere was always such that if we made mistakes, the reaction wasn't annoyance or tension, it was hysterical laughter. We would collapse sometimes, we would hurt with laughing. And he'd say, 'What would happen if you played that two octaves lower?' Or sometimes I would play something a bit differently, and he'd say, 'Oh, you didn't play what I wrote, but it sounded better. Do that again.' They were sometimes slips, sometimes little attempts to make the piece a bit more convenient, like putting it in some other register, or another key. And then in a couple of places there were spots where it wasn't quite filled in musically, and I would improvise something, and he would say, 'Oh, what was that? Do something like that again.'

We would go on for hours and hours. When Michael Barrett and Bright Sheng came over, Lenny and I would play it, and then they would play it. Lukas Foss would come over and he'd play through it with Lenny. So there was this whole little community of people who were all on the scene, working with Lenny at making this piece happen. It was so exciting to see the piece growing every day, changing every day, and having fun improvising something in rehearsal. And then overnight he would have transformed and refined it into something special.

There was a wonderful moment when we were playing the song which he dedicated to me. It's called 'At My Wedding', and it's a song in Yiddish about a wedding at which they invite a musician to come in and play. No one's ever seen this fellow before, and he's very strange, and he comes in and starts playing the violin, and because of the way he plays, he possesses the people with his music, and the whole wedding is swept aside. These people dance and react to this music until they are just tearing their hair out and screaming, 'Have mercy, have mercy, stop!' 'Have mercy' – one of James Brown's favourite lines. So we were playing it, and I said, 'Oh Lenny, it's so beautiful, it's sort of like Mahler and Mussorgsky and you; and so dark and mysterious. Wonderful.' We played it a bit more, and I said, 'Wait a minute, this really is Mussorgsky. This is the middle of 'The Market Place at Limoges'. That is exactly what these chords are – this is *Pictures at an Exhibition*. This *is* Mussorgsky.' And he looked archly off into space, and very quietly said, 'Mussorgsky? *Pictures at an Exhibition*? Never heard of it. And anyway, as I've always told you, if you're going to steal, steal classy!' His big line.

The other thing about *Arias and Barcarolle*s, of course, is the scat singing in the last song. He didn't tell me about that, that I was also going to have to sing in this piece, until I got to New York. I found there was this new movement in which there was supposed to be not only singing, but scat jazz singing of some sort. There were no words, just a dummy lyric for the very first pattern. So we improvised all those other words which are now in the piece. I improvised a lot of them, and then it was kind of one-upmanship. Actually some of the naughtiest ones never made it into the printed version of the piece, but that was another cause for great amusement. And yet the piece itself wound up being such a touching work. It was his ultimate salute to insomnia, because so much of the music, and so many of the texts in the piece, really reflect his preoccupation with his sleepless hours.

It is so remarkable that Gershwin and Bernstein and Berg were all moving in the same direction, exploiting the curious similarities between phrases and chords in pop music, jazz and serial music. I recognize the sevenths and ninths and oddly shaped thirds that form themselves into this language. I have this theory that if Berg had lived longer his music would have become simpler, and if Gershwin had lived longer his music would have become more complex, as it already does in *Porgy and Bess* and Berg's Violin Concerto. There are moments when you could almost superimpose them and they would sound like the same composer. Clearly, in *A Quiet Place* and in *Arias and Barcarolle*s there are some very powerful Bergian references. But, more important than that, in *Arias and Barcarolle*s Lenny really has attained a kind of mastery over the row. He can have a twelve-note row, and can quite deliberately show it to you – 'here it is' – in the most non-associative, quasi-plinky-plonky way, and then suddenly you hear something that is a haunting torch song, and it takes you a long time to realize that the torch song has exactly the same row that you just heard only a moment ago. And then suddenly you're hearing this be-bop, scat music and that's the same thing again.

ES: *Genius – making music from dry theory ...*
MTT: Yes, and that's really what he had attained. That wonderful conjuring-trick style. And like Berg and Ives and people who have known how to use this technique, he also recognized that it was important for the piece to have moments of great simplicity, so that the audience can first grab on to those moments, and then, little by little, work their way from those islands of familiarity and safety into the more daunting and challenging music.

ES: *People need that.*

MTT: Absolutely. Well, that's why people like the Berg Violin Concerto, because when they first hear it there are a couple of moments that make even the most anti-contemporary music person say, 'Oh, well, that bit's good there. That's pretty.' And from that, if they are patient, over time they come to realize that everything in the piece really is that same moment. It's just presented from another angle, perhaps. More oblique, more starkly in relief. Whatever. But it's the same. That's really the level of mastery that Lenny was getting to. But it's great, isn't it, when there's a composer who realizes that people do need songs, dances and lullabies, all those things we need for daily lives? And he can write those, even in the context of a rather serious piece, so that you have the whole piece, but you also have this nugget from it which you can take home with you.

The Essential Bernstein

ES: *If you had to pick the quintessential Bernstein, could you actually home in on one piece and say, 'This is what he was about?' Would you pick a song, or what?*

MTT: 'Some Other Time' is a great song. Its simplicity, sophistication and vulnerability have made it a classic tune. Somehow I can feel its tenderness echoing in so many of Lenny's pieces, even the twelve-tone ones. I think it's his signature tune.

Part Three

Lincoln Theatre, Miami Beach, home of the New World Symphony

American Music

The New World Symphony

ES: *Before we start talking about Ives and American music proper, I want to ask you about your work with the New World Symphony. From your point of view, what is it like, working with a group of young musicians on the threshold of a professional career? How does working with them differ from working with professional orchestras?*

MTT: Well, working with a great professional orchestral is the most exciting test that one has as a conductor or as an interpreter, because you're working with people who have enormous experience, and who have, very often, thoroughly performed the music, and who have wonderful perspectives and traditions.

When you're working with an orchestra like the LSO you have great wind soloists, for example. It's a pleasure to create space for the soloists to play and to accompany them sensitively. It's a real dialogue. With the string section, you're working with a tradition that already exists, and reshaping it. Hopefully the new ideas you contribute may bring parts of that tradition into a different perspective.

You can come to a professional orchestra, one that knows a particular piece very well, the LSO with the *Rite of Spring*, or the Vienna Philharmonic with the Mozart *Requiem*, and present something quite different from what they've done before. And if you are absolutely certain about what it is you want to do, they can do it, and will do it absolutely brilliantly.

Working with the New World Symphony is rewarding because there is this excitement of seeing young musicians come to the orchestra who are very, very gifted, but who have always played in a rather circumscribed musical situation. They haven't had that much chance to play a lot of repertoire, they don't really know what they're capable of. That can be because they have been in a conservatoire where they've only played very limited repertoire, or perhaps they spent the whole year playing one concerto or two symphonies, or whatever. And suddenly they're in a situation where, yes, there is a lot of repertoire going by, but at the same time there is a chance to really immerse oneself in it fully. They realize that this is something that they really can do, and they begin to play the music not just as dots and dashes and tasks that have to be performed, but as something that they understand musically, and can be much more emotionally involved in.

I created the New World Symphony for young musicians because I realized there were a lot of wonderful young musicians who weren't sure of their next move after leaving conservatoire or college. Should they stay on and take another advanced degree in music? which is of questionable value unless you just want to have more time to work with a particular teacher. Or should they try and get into some regional orchestra, where perhaps the musical level might not be so high? Or practise their brains out and try and get into a major orchestra? Which means that they're committing themselves to five to ten years of being in a state of continuous panic as they try and learn the entire standard repertoire – a major piece every week. It is possible to do that, but it leaves one in a kind of shell-shocked state with regard to music thereafter, because you have to absorb too much, too quickly, at too high a standard. Some people never recover.

It's true that the older members of the great orchestras always say, 'Well, we didn't start in this orchestra, we started in a smaller orchestra, and then we made our way here. That gave us a greater appreciation of what sort of people we were playing with, and what sort of level we were playing at, and it gave us a sense of pride about working here. Maybe people who come straight from a conservatoire don't ever have that, because for them it's too much, too soon.' But with the New World Symphony, because of our alternation of orchestral music and chamber music, and our outreach programmes into new music (and we hope now also earlier music), it gives people a chance to find out what sort of musicians they really are; what they want to do; what is the best place for them to be in the world of music.

I feel so often that musicians are obliged to play music to satisfy other people's expectations. At first, when you're very young, you often play to satisfy your parents' expectations, and then perhaps your teacher's expectations, and then the expectations of a particular university or conservatoire. So much of that goes on, and it's all very wonderful – one learns a lot from it. But I think there must be time in one's life where for a year or two you can ask, 'Well, what is actually out there in this profession? What could I do? What sort of course could I follow? Who am I?' And that is the ideal, the principle on which this orchestra, this academy, if you like, was founded. I mark the success of the institution by seeing that in the first three and a half years some of our musicians have gone on to be members of outstanding musical ensembles in the United States; and now, increasingly, in Europe as well.

Ives's Fourth Symphony: Starship America

ES: *What can an orchestra like the New World Symphony bring to a work like Ives's Fourth Symphony? There must be huge advantages here for a group of young, enthusiastic, fearless American players.*

MTT: Absolutely. This is the second time we have done Ives's Fourth. The first time we performed it was just after the materials of the critical edition had been created, and we had all the editors of that edition down here as we read it for the first time. That was an occasion when the incredible patience and, as you said, the fearlessness and open-mindedness of the orchestra was most important, because there were so many things to be sorted out. Questions of breath and phrasing and style and balance, not to mention notes and articulations. There were still millions of anomalies present. That's the sort of thing which any orchestra, but I think particularly a professional orchestra, can find very vexing; and these young people were extraordinary in their patience, and devotion to realizing the piece, and letting the piece finally sound.

One of the young musicians in the orchestra said to me, 'It's so strange, I just don't understand the piece, because at certain moments it's so beautiful, and then suddenly it will become so quirky and aggressive, and so dense and ugly, really. It's just as if whoever wrote this wanted to vex and torment me, and I can't understand why someone who could write all these exalted, beautiful passages should suddenly write music that seems designed to torture me? Does he really want to torture me?' And I said, 'Yes, he does want to torture you. He's Charles Ives. He wants to delight and inspire you, challenge and amuse you, and yes sometimes torture you. He wants to put you through the complete range of feelings that life offers.'

But of course, particularly for this orchestra, their understanding of the piece as part of their heritage is important. It's important, in that most of them do not have any longer a connection with that heritage. But perhaps what is most alarming is that all these hymn tunes and popular tunes that Ives thought everyone would know – and therefore be able to follow his concepts clearly – these tunes have nearly passed into oblivion in such a short time. All classical music in a way rests on the language and traditions of a number of other sorts of music. Religious music, folk music, dance music, popular music, patriotic music – the majority of the population is now removed from all these traditions, which were once a very rich part of everyone's life. And the degree to which this tradition was once so meaningful, and so meaningfully represented in classical music, you can see quite clearly by all of the passages in Haydn, Mozart, Beethoven, and so on, where there's a plagal cadence, for example, where there's a reference to a particular kind of cadence, which people would recognize. 'Ah yes, that's a church sort of cadence ... Oh, the degree of the scale here evokes a certain folk-tune quality ... The quirky little dotted rhythms at the beginning of the phrase are evocative of dance music from one country or another ...'

These things were felt. The spice, the expressive punch of music, came so much from references. Sometimes very oblique, sometimes very direct, as in a composer like Mahler, who makes a point of writing passages which have a folkish quality. But even in Haydn, Mozart, Schumann, all the others, there are these references to this close-to-home, hearthside tradition in music. And this has gone. People who are born today know music from the Beatles till now, and they know a series of 'hooks', and re-processed versions perhaps of certain older tunes, but really the jazz standards are unknown to the great majority of them, let alone hymns, popular ballads of the early part of the century, marching tunes, all these things.

So it's turned out that a piece like Ives's Fourth is a way of re-discovering their own past for an orchestra of Americans. And sometimes there's a dim echo in their minds, and they say, 'Oh yes, that is something I once heard in church,' or perhaps, 'I had an old aunt who used to sing that.' But it starts to link up, they start to understand what it truly is about. That's been one of the reasons why I always begin a performance with the quotation of the actual tunes; and why in fact the very first thing that I did in rehearsal was to sit down at the piano, and play all of the hymns and all of the songs that are quoted in the piece. And I kept doing that at the start of each rehearsal. It begins to sink in.

ES: *Do you have a view of what this particular piece is? Do you think it has a particular objective? because we all have different ideas. I used the term stream of consciousness because the second movement seems to me to drift through past and present and future. Do you have a view on that?*

MTT: Maybe we should start with Ives as a larger topic. It seems absolutely plain to me that Ives is the greatest American composer. He's America's great Romantic composer. He's an extremely adventurous, bold Romantic. His desire in music is to express, very powerfully, his deeply felt emotions. He's a difficult person to understand because his use of such diverse musical materials has cast him in the role of being a kind of musical tinkerer, or

Charles Ives

experimenter, or homespun avant-gardist. I think it's important to recognize that there were certain pieces that Ives did categorize as experiments or take-off points, or whatever it is he may have called them. But his major pieces were not experiments. They were thoroughly thought-out, composed pieces, and there was a real message to all of them.

It's important to understand Ives as someone who continued the American Transcendentalist tradition to the next generation. Emerson, Hawthorne, Thoreau, Whitman, Dickinson – all these writers had such a powerful, spiritual message, but they did not, in most cases, have literary successors. Ives continued their line of thinking in the area of music. He was using music to express, very often, philosophical, meditative concepts, to express his perceptions of what was happening in time, in the United States. He had things in common with the Transcendentalists, particularly with Walt Whitman.

Ives was quite suspicious of Whitman, but he had a couple of major themes in common with him. Whitman had written so movingly about his experiences as a child, in poems like 'There Was a Child Went Forth', and all through the poem 'Sea-Drift'. You know, 'Out of the cradle endlessly rocking'. This experience of the boy on the beaches, this experience of a childhood remembrance, these boyhood remembrances, were always filled with a kind of haunted sadness about how rich and meaningful the life of this earlier time had seemed. How deeply expressive it all was, how close, how personal, and how so much of it had passed away over the course of time. People had died, whole aspects of village life and communal experience had passed out of existence, society had become more mechanized, more impersonal. The old social structures had passed out of existence, and there was a new kind of tough, mercantile, efficient, soulless, heartless quest for affluence. This deeply concerned Whitman, because he felt this was the spirit of America being lost. Indeed, he, as well as the other Transcendentalists, perceived the Civil War as the greatest disaster that America ever endured, and something which permanently turned it off its original idealistic course. And this was something that Ives, and Ruggles, felt very much as well.

One way I stumbled on to this, this powerful feeling they had about the Civil War, was when I met Ruggles and talked with him about his piece *Men and Mountains*, in which one movement is called 'Lilacs'. This is a very expressive, highly-chromatic, condensed piece. I went to see Ruggles' home in Arlington, Vermont, in what used to be a small school house. It was surrounded by lilac bushes, and, of course, I'd already figured out that those years he was writing the piece – he wrote everything with agonizing slowness – he must have been writing some of this music while he was drenched in the actual fragrance of these lilac bushes. When I spoke to him about the piece, he said something like, 'Oh yes, lilacs. So sad, such a pity, so sad, such a pity.' I wasn't quite sure what he meant, and then John Kirkpatrick explained it to me. In the later part of the nineteenth century, and in the beginning of the twentieth century, as one went around New England in the springtime, you could see on all of the hills a broken chimney and massed clump of lilac trees – and that was all that was left of the homesteads of the boys who'd gone off to fight the Civil War and never came back.

Again, there's Whitman's poem 'When Lilacs Last in the Dooryard Bloom'd'. So lilacs became the symbol of tragic, haunted regret about this wonderful time, this wonderful era of such idealism. Regret that the Civil War could have been fought only over one issue, really – money. That people could enslave other people, and do all of the things that they did. And for what? Just for money. For Whitman, the United States was the most idealistic experiment in politics for some thousands of years, and the idea that people could have abandoned this – brother could have been fighting brother and killing each other – over just money ... It was so appalling. And this is something that Ives felt very much as well.

Of course Ives also shared with Whitman this idea that the grand universal order is somehow reflected, and is present, in the most common, everyday occurrences. That in each leaf, in each bit of blacksmith's song heard over the whispering wind, whatever, in all of these signs and portents there is something of great significance, and something which does reflect the way that the universe, the cosmos, is working. Whitman sketched a prose poem on music, but didn't write it. Let me read it to you:

An opera in a dream – different singers and characters – the suggestions, associations. Some old songs? hymn? Rock me to sleep mother? Rock'd in the cradle of the deep? – With its memories, associations – or where I last heard it, in Hospital? some typical appropriate? tune, or? hymn – or? something played by the band (? some dirge or? hymn – march) Calling up the whole dead of the war. The march in last act of La Gaza Ladra. One stanza must describe a strong triumphal instrumental and vocal chorus as of triumphant man – triumphant over temptation and all weakness.

Whitman never wrote this poem, but Ives did, in the form of music, particularly the Fourth Symphony. Many of Ives's pieces are realizations of this kind of ideal in music. I don't know if Ives ever saw this sketch of Whitman's, I would doubt it. But these concerns are all present in Ives. When Ives is using quotations, he uses them to evoke a particular time or place; but in the way he re-harmonizes these things, and the way he fragments them, he puts them into this lost, bygone, tragically removed period. And then, in the way he goes from just two or three notes of a hymn off into something which is original, that suggests the mind playing with a particular part of the phrase, and somehow going off into a reverie. Then perhaps coming back, no longer with the same hymn tune but with another tune.

It's very subtle the way he weaves in and out of this. His combination of very simple music and extremely complicated sound collages reminds me of the lines from Whitman's *Song of Myself*:

I hear all sounds running together, combined, fused or following
Sounds of the city and sounds out of the city, sounds of the day and night

The most amazing thing about Ives is his freedom. He wrote a great deal of music in a short time, but he never wrote music in a particular system, it was all very freely composed. I mean, there certainly was order and design, but he didn't, as so many other composers did, say, 'I must come up with some system, some stylistic approach which will make the process of choosing simpler.' Ives never did that. It was all originally thought up. What's remarkable is the range of his work, which anticipated nearly the whole rest of American musical history. There are moments in Ives, in *Thanksgiving*, for example, the last movement of the *Holidays* Symphony, when you can say, 'Ah, this is Copland,' or, 'Oh, this is Gershwin,' or, 'Oh, this is Carter' – or Sessions, or minimalism ... It's all there, but just touched on, as part of the pungent and interesting colouration that he is searching for in setting forth his larger emotional message.

Then of course there is a quite contrary, trickster aspect of Ives's personality. He does love parody. He does love the preposterous. He loves introducing irresolvable conflicts into the music, like rhythm going against the other, or one sonority, one tonality against the other. For instance, in the Fourth Symphony, he very amusingly uses a system of priorities to guide the performers in what is the correct balance in the piece. Instead of using *hauptstimme* or *nebenstimme* (main theme or subordinate theme) as Schoenberg did, he puts instead a small letter of the alphabet at the beginning of each passage – a, b, c, d, e, f, g, etc. 'A' is meant to indicate the most important line, and later letters in the alphabet show those less important. However, there are passages where the solo piano plays a kind of fragmented waltz, and they're not marked. The clarinets are playing along with it, and they're marked 'b', except the high notes they're meant to shriek, which are supposed to be 'a'. Then you have all the cellos, basses and percussion slamming out enormous, mechanical noises out of phase with each other, and they're marked something like 'c' or 'd'. Then there is a furious trombone line which is marked 'e'. All this stuff is *fortissimo*! And while all this is going on, there is a triangle playing *pianissimo,* and *that's* marked 'a'! He loves to send up the performers in this way.

Ives wrote six symphonies; completed five of them. The symphony he was working on after the Fourth, the 'Universe' Symphony, was left in sketch form. The first three movements of the Fourth Symphony were brought pretty much to completion. Ives was still working on the last movement. He had never completely resolved it. So, it is a big project.

ES: *How do you think he conceived the Fourth?*
MTT: It's conceived as layers of music, as streams of music which are going on simultaneously, but which were originally composed as freely occurring in space. When you look at the original score, you see that there is one group of people playing a very quirky and highly accented 5/8 music, full of syncopations and stops and starts, and that's at one tempo and dynamic, and at the same time another group is playing very luminous chorale music in 3/2, at a different tempo. A third group is playing a kind of two-step in 4/4 – and all these musics are going on at once.

ES: *How on earth do you co-ordinate them?*
MTT: That's always been the major performing problem of the piece. If you have different groups of players conducted by different conductors, then there's a problem, because they do all have to work out by one time or another. It's difficult to rehearse like that. Or you can notate these different musics in terms of a central metrical pulse, in which case you sometimes get very, very complicated syncopated-looking things on the page which, as you sort them out, become something really rather simple. The edition we've made now is a compromise between those two things. It's a way of repre senting the music so the players can get the swing of it. And the swing of it, the feel of it, is the main point. Performing Ives's music is not so much about a particular note being exactly at a certain place at a certain time. It's more about the swing of that particular line making sense within itself, and being just about at the right place with respect to the other lines. If each group within the orchestra has its own integrity and its own feel very well in hand, the music will sound well.

Now, as to the piece itself. The Fourth is meant to answer a question. And the question is, 'What is the meaning of existence?' Right at the very front of the piece there is a bold and craggy theme in the double basses and the piano, quite aggressive, which is the most lengthy bit of original musical material in the symphony; and this question thunders out very defi- antly – 'What is the meaning of existence?' Or perhaps, as Whitman or Ruggles or even Ives himself might have said, 'What the hell is it all supposed to mean, anyway?' And then comes a series of answers. In the first movement, just after the main theme is introduced, you have a group which

Second Movement of Ives's Fourth Symphony

Ives called the 'Star of Bethlehem'. You can think of it as the Star of Bethlehem, or Haley's Comet ...

ES: *He actually called it that ...?*
MTT: Yes. It's a group called the Star Group, which you can think of as either the Star of Bethlehem or Haley's Comet. And this is a group of musicians, violins and harps who are meant to play someplace suspended above the stage. They play the first hymn tune in the piece, 'Nearer, My God, to Thee', which is, as you probably know, the hymn tune that the musicians on the *Titanic* were playing when they went down. A hymn of great significance, because of its words: 'Nearer, my God, to Thee, nearer, nearer to Thee, still all my soul shall be, nearer my God to Thee.' It's almost a mantra-like repetition of a Transcendentalist's ideal, to be nearer, to be at one with God.

And then this moves into a beautiful cello solo, which sounds quite unusual but in fact is the verse of another hymn, 'In the Sweet By and By'. And this bit of tune is quoted more than anything else in the whole symphony: 'There's a land that is fairer than day ...' So this bit of music and its accompanying words are quoted more than anything else in the symphony: 'There's a land that is fairer than day, and by faith we can see it ...' But it's really a stretch to recognize it, because it is so elongated, and it's accompanied by quintuplets in an entirely different key, and it swirls and loses its direction.

Then he introduces another theme; the chorus sings another hymn, 'Watchman tell us of the night, what the signs of promise are.' So the first movement is really an answer, saying, 'The meaning of existence? Well, we don't know, but there's a light in the sky. What it means remains to be seen.' That's the first movement, ending with this haunting 'Nearer, My God, to Thee' – just the Star of Bethlehem group, all by itself up there.

The second movement offers another answer to the meaning of existence. 'Well, it's all the things that appear to be.' The second movement is saying this is Maya, the material world. It is also the movement that Ives called a comedy, in the sense that some of Hawthorne's pieces, grotesque crowd-scene pieces, were identified as being comedy pieces. And it makes reference to everything that's happening in America, particularly the onslaught of mechanization, the noisy aspect of modern civilization.

ES: *Like that noisy jet overhead!*
MTT: It then introduces an ensemble of instruments playing in quarter tones. So after this very noisy, improvised, extraordinarily textured begin-

ning that the piece has, there then comes a harmonization of the hymn, 'Jesus, Lover of My Soul', in quarter tones. It turns into a phrase of 'Be it ever so humble, there is no place like home', all in quarter tones, so it has this very warped, melancholy aspect to it. And then a remarkable passage actually based on the idea of the celestial railroad; it's a passage that does invoke an old steam train starting up, with all its fits and starts and funny noises. The train gets going, and then we're just in a flurry for the rest of the movement, which is a quodlibet, quoting the most diverse materials. Quotes all manner of licks, as we would say, from ragtime to the noises of foundries and workplaces, the odd hiccups of mechanical instruments and early mechanical player pianos. Then of course there's the overwhelming presence of marching bands, sometimes many at once, playing all kinds of music. March music superimposed over ragtime, with insane violin virtuoso stunts, stirring up a great racket, which suddenly clear out and leave you with patches of the most sentimental music, which Ives introduced as a parody of high-toned music.

The whole movement really is a parody. It's a parody of the hustle and bustle and overkill of noise in modern society, and a parody of the sort of music that is played at ladies' teas, when they have pink lemonade and listen to salon music. The salon music is made out of a hymn tune called 'Beulah Land'; it's a very Mahler-like shape, but preposterously harmonized and so over the top. Instruments at the back of the orchestra, which Ives called shadow instruments, continue to play in their own odd meandering way, having nothing to do with the shape of the hymn tune in the foreground. It's just a big stewpot of everything in musical society at that time. There's even one section which is meant to sound like really serious music, latter-day Schumann type of thing. But the attitude he has towards all this music is, well, it's just part of human comedy. Sometimes it's rough, sometimes it's sentimental, sometimes it's mysterious, but it's all just something that's making a great to-do over nothing.

So all the things in this great stewpot boil up to an absolutely furious level, which is the loudest moment, I expect, in all orchestral music. What one perceives through the sheer blare of it all are dim shapes of one sort of music or another going on, very much like the way one hears music at an enormous parade. You do hear all these large ensembles, but the wind is shifting the sound around. Then in a moment it's all blown away. It's as if the wind comes through and there's nothing left but a few violas desperately trying to play some very rapid sixteenth notes that tail off to nothing ...

The third movement takes up the answer of Congregationalism. Ives himself did attend a church and was an organist for many years. So one can only imagine what they made of all these pieces we've come to know now as *Holidays*. Many of these pieces began as improvisations while the offering was being taken. We can imagine what the congregation of this church must have thought as this wild young man played all of these things. Unfortunately all that he played at Centre Church in New Haven was lost, thrown out. It was one of his stories. Many years after he had gone they just threw it all out. But he did attend church, and his beliefs were of course very individual. Nonetheless he felt that there were important benefits to be obtained by going to an event where other people met together for the purpose of worship and contemplation. Indeed symphony concerts provide a great deal of this sort of experience for many people nowadays.

The third movement is based on the hymn 'From Greenland's Icy Mountains'. It is a fugue, and it is meant to go at a rather vigorous pace. The words themselves are those of the hymn: 'From Greenland's Icy Mountains, from Africa's Sunny Shore, they call us to deliver ...', and so on. A rousing sort of chant, as is the hymn tune 'Ye Christian Heralds Go'. It's very important that this movement goes at the right tempo, the first movement is a slow movement and the second a great stewpot of music and noises and many rhythms which very often counteract each other. For the third movement to be a slow movement also would make the whole piece too slow. The third movement must move along in a committed sort of way. There is a kind of a desperate climax and then a very luminous, tranquil ending in which 'Joy to the World' is quoted: 'And Heaven and Nature Sing, and Heaven and Nature Sing.' A very peaceful, almost sleepy, plagal cadence.

And then the last movement begins. In the first movement we had the Star of Bethlehem group and the orchestra. Now Ives introduces a new group – the percussion ensemble. Actually he asks for a subterranean percussion ensemble, which represents the ticking of the universal clock. I have only recently had the chance to perform this piece with a truly subterranean percussion ensemble in San Francisco. We're now going to do it in Miami and in London. It makes a tremendous difference. It is so remarkable that this man imagined these things and knew exactly what he was talking about. When you read the instructions to the score which say 'a subterranean percussion ensemble', it sounds totally absurd. But if you actually do it, set it up so that they can play in a space that would normally be given over to the pit beneath the stage, it sounds fantastic.

So this ensemble begins playing this odd, rhythmic pattern which suggests the ticking of the universal clock. The theme is the same, the question of human existence. And this time the answer is a sort of procession, a mournful procession, the tune of which is one of Ives's most master-ful combinations of several phrases from different sources, melded together. It is an expressive and sad melody. And what an ensemble it is – the violins of the Star of Bethlehem group play along with one solo violin on stage and gradually more violins join in. The first, second and third violin parts throughout much of the symphony are used to maximum effect. 'Nearer, My God, to Thee' is brought in, with dark and tragic harmonization over a bass line which is at first that of a procession, and then becomes increasing-ly more desperate, lashing and flailing its way through these harmonic turns. The large forces of the orchestra – brass, winds, percussion – come in, bringing various phrases to a glittering, obliterating climax, and then they disappear – one of Ives's favourite effects. This huge sound suddenly clears, and leaves the sound of violins and quarter tone pianos far in the distance playing a beautiful quarter tone harmonization of 'Nearer, My God, to Thee'.

It is these kinds of contrasts which shape the movement, leading to the biggest of big climaxes where 'Nearer, My God, to Thee' in the massed low brass is pitted against a swirling, original combination hymn tune in the upper orchestra. And just at the moment when the happy ending should occur, it turns round this corner into an absolute Calvary-like passage, where sounds occur like souls being borne down through great travail by the immense power of the orchestra.

It's typical of Ives to represent this most exalted moment of spiritual search in ever more dissonant and blaring sound. For example, in the song 'The Camp Meeting', drawn from the Third Symphony, as the text approaches the words 'Flowing round the throne of God', the music grows fiercer and fiercer until on the word 'God' there is a pile-up of major and minor sonorities which are impossible to untangle.

This to me has always suggested the Mount Sinai aspect of the spiritual revelation. Man searches and searches and as he gets too close to the divine it is more than he can bear, the sounds and the harmonies are just too much. This is exactly what happens in Ives's Fourth Symphony. It builds up to a point of such intensity that it's as if we can bear no more, and it sweeps away. We have to turn away and a few little tendrils of singed nerve endings then lead to the beginnings of the long, luminous coda. The choir brings back, wordlessly, the last phrase of 'Nearer, My God, to Thee' – 'Still all my song shall be nearer, my God, to Thee, nearer, my God, to Thee, nearer to Thee'. And as the choir is luminously singing 'to Thee', the rest of the orchestra, divided into many groups, is playing bits of all kinds of other music – 'Westminster Chimes', 'Polly Put the Kettle On' – all manner of things quietly going on in different keys from the top to the bottom of this huge ensemble. And as the chorus reaches its last phrase we come to the *raison d'être* for this Symphony.

In the original hymn tune, 'Nearer, My God, to thee', the chorus sang the raised seventh degree of the scale – C sharp. But the very last time Ives uses the tune in the symphony, he lowers the seventh degree of the scale to c natural. So now 'nearer to Thee' is sung in a modal cadence rather than a diatonic cadence. By doing that, he takes this hymn from a small Congregational church in New England and changes it to bring it into concord with ancient music, with Asian music, with all the musical traditions of the world. And then, with all of this layering of tunes going on, the procession slowly retreats. It's as if all the people on earth are singing, and then the planet itself, with all of its inhabitants singing, passes further away on its orbit, out of our view. The C natural was so important to Ives that he has the tenors of the choir continuing to lean on this note in a rhythm which recalls the end of the *Second Orchestral Set*, which likewise ends with a chorus quietly murmuring, 'Worship Thee, worship Thee, worship Thee', fading into the distance.

This, to me, is what is so extraordinary in Ives's imagination: all the aspects of this piece – the Star of Bethlehem; the percussion ensembles; the quarter tones; the mixed wind ensembles playing in different metres and different rhythms; the different spatial representations of music within the orchestra; the incredible use of dynamics to suggest the shifting of the winds and changes of psychological concentration; the extraordinary complexity of the layering, the textures; the complex reharmonization of familiar tunes in ever new ways; the whole vastness of this expression. And yet the whole Symphony is really about one thing, which is 'Nearer, My God, to Thee'. What is the meaning of existence? Nearer, My God, to Thee, Nearer, My God, to Thee ... To search for this closeness to God, and in searching for it, discover that one's own expression of it changes from being the comfortable little thing you know at home to something that does indeed connect with the great universal search of mankind. And Ives is able to focus all this by simply changing one note of the cadence of this familiar tune. That is a remarkable piece of imagination and musical symbolism.

Now we know that Ives's symbolism with regard to this music – to all music – was intense. When he was writing things like the 'Concord' Sonata, he would actually bring people into the studio and read a passage out of Emerson or Hawthorne or Thoreau. Sometimes there would be this great abstraction, and then he would sit down at the piano and say, 'Now here's how that goes.' And he would play, say, two minutes of music, which was a representation in sound of something that he had just read out of the book. That was a most remarkable sort of imagination.

Now the Universe Symphony, which Ives undertook after the Fourth Symphony, was to take the ideas of the Fourth Symphony even further. The Universe Symphony was conceived to be performed in a valley. The orchestra and the spectators would be in the valley, but as one went up the mountains on either side, there would be different ensembles deployed, so that you would hear all this music coming from this enormous space. And that experience of music in space, or sound in space, was something so important. It somehow evokes an experience from our collective unconsciousness – maybe from the time when we were hunter-gatherers, or whatever.

I find that when I go out to the south-west, or some place in the country, where things are very quiet, suddenly you may hear a sound that is coming from several miles away. It is very faint, but you can nonetheless hear this presence of something at that distance. Not only do your eyes have the perspective of the view, but your ears have this perspective of enormous space. And this is something which I believe human beings need. It is deeply comforting to us, and it is clear how necessary it must be to us, since we live in a mechanized, boxed-in society where this experience is largely denied to us. We have created it synthetically, haven't we? I mean, that is what stereophonic recording is all about. All these technologies of recording get more and more involved, but we're just trying to recreate that sense of spaciousness, grandeur, opulence, surround sound – whatever. That is what that's speaking to, the need that we have to feel this large acoustic space. And this is the sort of space that Ives's music was meant to inhabit.

ES: *Who was it that said that Ives was the Old Testament Prophet crying in the new mythology of the American wilderness.*
MTT: I think that is true.

ES: *It has that Old Testament kind of feeling ...*
MTT: Well, as did Whitman, because Whitman wrote *Leaves of Grass* to be a companion to the Bible. It was supposed to be a book that had everything in it, that spoke to every issue.

ES: *My favourite quote is the one where Ives talks about the frustrations, the limitations of 'the instrument', whatever it may be: 'Is it the composer's fault that man has only ten fingers?'*
MTT: So you can imagine how pleased he would be, and the sort of things he would be doing nowadays, with all these new possibilities. But again,

and I want to make this point strongly, he wasn't just throwing these notes around in order to see if it would be interesting to hear seventeen different parts at once. There was always a very specific expressive purpose to the music he was writing. That was his real mission, to set down these feelings he so powerfully felt. And he had to do it in such a vacuum, since there was really no one, virtually no one, who comprehended him. It is only now that musicians and audiences, even in the United States, are truly coming to appreciate him. Partially this is because the scores were in very bad shape, and only now are we getting materials which are clear enough for the players to read without enormous vexing difficulty. And so the performers are able to present performances which are convincing enough for the public to grab hold of. Therefore audiences are also recognizing that these pieces are events, or rituals in sound – pageants. I don't really know how one would characterize them.

And they come out of very traditional pieces. Ives remembered as a child hearing his father do a piece which was called something like 'Jerusalem'. Not the 'Jerusalem' you know, but a piece in which there was a brass quintet in the centre of the town square, and then in the steeple there was a trumpet soloist, and in the windmill down the road there was another group of brass. And over this vast distance they were all playing, I am sure, some very sentimental thing. It was a kind of event. They would pray, and sing, and do this. And of course the Moravians in American musical tradition also had this tradition of trombone choirs of hundreds of members at different distances from each other, and playing this music in squares. It was very much a part of the homespun American religious musical experience. Wagner would have adored it, I'm sure, if he had ever known it.

ES: *Ives is something completely original. And you're absolutely right. In a sense, everything that came after him in American music he had done already.*
MTT: And not only in American music. The twentieth century has been a century packed with '-isms': impressionism, serialism, primitivism, dadaism, neo-classicism, pan-diatonicism, total serialism. Every one of these '-isms' came on to the stage, and with each one it seemed for a while as if that was the only possible way to write music, the only respectable way to write music. And then of course it went out of fashion and was soon gone. But as we reach the end of the century, there are more composers saying, 'Well, never mind what the "-ism" is, I just have to use whatever notes are necessary to say what I have to say.' Today international composers as diverse as Schnittke, Knussen, Holloway, Matthews and

Carl Ruggles

Lutoslawski are writing music which has a strong similarity to many of the things that Ives did. Schnittke particularly shows a very strong influence of Ives's work.

ES: *Polystylism – that's another one.*
MTT: Yes, that's exactly what Ives was doing, and he was doing it not from an ideal of a particular synthetically created style; he was just saying that this was the way it had to be. It's like when I asked Carl Ruggles one time, 'Are you interested in serial music? Are you interested in twelve-tone writing?' He said, 'Well, I don't know about that twelve-tone stuff. What I would say is I always like to write ten notes or so before I repeat one.' That is such an American homespun approach to things. Just roll up your sleeves and write music.

Roots and Plain Music

ES: *What is it about America, the land and nature of the country, this idea about growing up, of rolling up your sleeves and getting right back to the earth?*

MTT: For us in America I guess it all goes back to our first composer, William Billings. William Billings was a composer of hymns and part-songs, pieces which had a great asperity and a certain kind of rough-hewn quality. Maybe it's good to say something about that. The foundation of American musical language is in religious music, coming primarily through England. The *Bay Psalm Book,* I believe, was published in the United States ten years after the Pilgrims got here. It is remarkable that ten years after they arrived, with everything else they had to deal with, they got round to publishing a psalm book. But because of the rigours of life in the colonies in the early days, and the absence of music teachers, the quality of musical expression declined. Around the beginning of the eighteenth century some people complained that the music sung at religious services sounded like chaos, more like the grunting of beasts than the singing of pious religious people.

And there arose singing schools, taught, in most cases, by amateur musicians. Most of these people were hatters, joiners or blacksmiths, but they also had a mastery of singing and knowledge of notation. They started singing schools, where people would come to learn how to sing by rule. And these composers, like William Billings and Timothy Swan, who had other professions in the guilds, taught singing. They called themselves 'tune-smiths' and they brought some of their hands-on craftsman approach to their musical works. The singing schools were very important, because they were the only opportunity for boys and girls to be together in a social situation. William Billings became a very celebrated composer with his hymns and psalms. Some of his tunes were sung during the War of Independence. He was a religious composer, a patriotic composer, a composer of ensemble music and a popular composer, making the mould for so many American musicians to come after him.

Of course, at this same time there was importation into the colonies of music from England, including all the big religious pieces of Handel. Billings said that he admired this music of Handel, but they didn't think it was the sort of music that Americans should sing, because it was musically unrelated to their culture. Billings said something like, 'When a person sings, he has to sing the sort of music which is appropriate to him, which is right for him. I stand on this ground, which is American, and I feel this earth beneath my feet, and certain tunes and certain songs feel right here in this land. This Handel's music is too prettified, it doesn't suit us, it's not right for us. Americans speak plainly, so they should sing plainly.'

And this idea of plain-speaking music one can hear in Bernstein's 'Simple Song' or in many of Copland's scores, which he wants to be 'plainly sung', 'simply sung.' This ideal of plainly, simply sung music, matching the plainly made quilts of the Amish community, or the plainly but honestly made furniture of the arts-and-crafts makers is a theme that comes back again and again in American music. I think it is the one that we most deeply respect. Somehow, as Americans, we do respect citizens who had written elegantly made music on the model of European masters. But when it comes down to it, fundamentally, we most admire the people who somehow just wrote music that seemed a completely natural expression of that moment, of their time and place in America. If it has a few rough edges around it, never mind, we love those all the more. Just as we love blues singers whose failure to sing 'the perfect' line is the most expressive touch of all.

So we can see in American music, even in the short time it's existed, these continuing themes. This question of plain speaking, plain singing, related to the idea of music expressing a national purpose, a kind of spiritual credo.

Then there's been the curious change in American musical fashion, which, in best American style, has gone at such an accelerated pace. One can see this in several ways. As the American musicologist H. Wiley Hitchcock observed, the history of American music is one of a cultivated and a vernacular tradition. It is fascinating to observe how American composers have dealt with the vernacular musical cultures around them. It has been a constant preoccupation from the first published American music through Gershwin and Copland's obsessions with jazz and beyond.

From Primitivism to Sophistication

One of the first published pieces in the United States is called *The Death Chant of an Indian Chief.* It is a work for baritone and string orchestra, published during the colonial period. I sought it out with great interest, and discovered that it really is quite a straightforward, four-square, English-sounding melody, played by strings with a bit of tom-tom accompaniment, and some words that have a kind of noble savage cast to them. But there is nothing there musically that sounds authentic. It's just a presentation of a kind of cardboard figure of an Indian chief. There is no ethno-musical substance to it at all.

Then, a hundred years later, you have composers like Gottschalk writing a piece around a native melody from the black quarter, or from the folk-song tradition. But he 'corrects' the harmonies to render it compatible with the elegance of salon music. It's a particular kind of turn in the salon music tradition. This continues through the time of the composers influenced by Dvořák's use of American music and black music. The music is corrected, it's manicured to conform to their sense of acceptable practice, which is, of course, a European one. But what a major step forward there is then in Ives's first work, when he begins to say, 'The way the music is originally played is the most interesting; the way people who have no musical education play their own music; the way they instinctively produce the music is the most interesting thing. Never mind that there are too many beats in the bar, never mind that some of the notes are "out of tune", never mind that there are strange meanderings into other keys, and that people get lost and kind of stop and start fitfully – that is all part of it.' This becomes a new perspective for looking at the actual original material, and glorifying and even magnifying the roughness and the rawness of the original. You can see this come in through Ives and then go into the early Copland music – this raw, aggressive music, the kind written by that whole circle of American composers.

Since that time, of course, we have gotten ever closer to the vernacular originals through recordings. It's records that have allowed vernacular musicians like Bessie Smith, Blind Lemon Jefferson or Charley Parker to have such a colossal influence on the whole musical world. In a way, rock and roll and all the other heavily merchandized pop music of today is a kind of tragic triumph of the vernacular over the cultivated. We have come a long way from the time when the only place American teens could properly meet was at the singing school. Now, it's record sales to kids that determine the bottom line of music and the accelerated shifts in musical fashion that change every few months.

But, of course, American music isn't the only art form to try and deal with the vernacular and the cultivated and shifting aesthetic fashion. One can see much the same thing in the development of Chinese song forms. As far as I know, the longest, unbroken aesthetic tradition one can observe is that of Chinese poetical forms. A typical Chinese poem such as the *fu* will have a history like this: A scholar someplace on the frontiers of the empire hears a group of travellers singing a song, or chanting a ritual. He makes some notations of that chant or song, and then brings it back as a specimen to cultivated court circles. He may do a piece himself in that sort of style.

Other writers observe it, analyze its metrical form. They tinker with it over the course of a couple of generations or so, and it evolves into a new kind of song/poem which has both novelty and order. Then people begin to write seriously in that form. It becomes popular. Next come some masters who absolutely cinch that form, giving to it the deepest expression of their own world and society. In the case of Chinese history it's the vitality of the particular dynasty which is coming to its greatest power at that moment.

Then there's a later history, when the great days of that dynasty are waning, but people are still using that same, by now familiar poetic form. Only now they tend to write poems which use quotations and references to earlier famous poems, with oblique endings and strangely wistful elements of yearning. Everything alludes to references from the works of the past, which the reader must know. And finally the sophistication of the allusions becomes so great that only very intellectual, well-read people can understand any of it.

But just around that time, some official from the court, who has been banished to the frontier hears some other group of 'barbarian' people performing some other song or chant. He comes back to the court with a specimen of this new song and the cycle starts all over again.

For thousands of years you can see these new poetic forms come out of their primitive folkloric origins. They become refined, formal shapes, reach fruition, go into artful decadence, then wither away, and something else replaces them. You can see this happening in Western music. You certainly can see it happening in the history of American music. American music has been so much about grasping a new idea, the idea of that particular moment, whether it's an aggressive use of dissonance to recreate the excitement of the clangourous building of skyscrapers and exultant, streamlined, mechanized world, or a concern for folk music, whether it's a work song or a pastoral variety, whatever. There are all these movements, and they all have this very quick rise and fall. Instead of taking several hundred years they take twenty or thirty years maximum in recent times. It's all been much, much quicker.

Nationalism in Music

ES: *American music is very much its own thing: instantly recognizable. What is it about a nation's music that gives it its identity?*
MTT: A nation's music relates to its vigour, politics, wealth, travails, self-confidence. Music reflects society. When you think of English music, you think first of Elizabethan music. In that time England was a very powerful, very sophisticated, forward-looking nation, and therefore there was music

which reflected that. Then you go through a long period where, of course, there was some fine music written, but it did not possess this same kind of brilliant assurance.

Then we come to the Victorian era. Again, England had enormous power, wealth, influence and self-confidence – and this really takes you right through from Elgar to Britten and beyond. The music is expressing '… the Empire was great, the two World Wars were immensely costly and difficult, but England and its allies still sorted things out …' And the music is an expression, even if it is sometimes a despairing one of what it was like to live through those years.

In America too our greatest music was written as we became a powerful and self-confident nation. Ives's music witnesses the pain of losing one's national innocence for the sake of attaining an empire; Gershwin delights in the freedoms of a prosperous land; Copland celebrates the spirit of the people and their desire for fairness, and so on. All these composers were very certain about what they wanted to say. Today, however, life seems much less certain. Perhaps that is why, as we turn the corner into the next century, in America, in nearly every country on earth, people are searching for what they have to say. I don't think there are any nations that feel terribly confident about their future destiny. In a way, some of the Russian composers have recently made their despair and their uncertainty work for them. They really had something to write about, because the nature of their problem was so intense.

ES: *I think that explains the minimalist vogue to some extent – music which is very obviously saying, 'Where do we go now, what do we do now?' But going back to what you were saying about America struggling for recognition by the European community – what sort of influence has Europe had on American music, do you think?*

European Influence on American Music

MTT: Well, America's taste was shaped for a very long time, and probably is still shaped today, by foreign performers, taste arbiters, who are largely conductors. In the mid-nineteenth century there were wonderful characters, like Julian, the showman conductor who came to the United States and made a tremendous amount of money giving concerts which had thematic organization. He'd give a concert on the theme of fire. He wrote grand fantasies about fires. He actually had firebells rung in the hall, and he was rumoured to have set fire to a hall just to make the concert more exciting. He had a velvet pillow on which he used to keep a baton that he reserved exclusively for Beethoven, and it was carried out to him on the podium while his eyes were closed. He had an ebony baton for Beethoven, a silver baton for Mozart, all this kind of thing.

More serious was Theodore Thomas, the founder of the Chicago Symphony Orchestra. He created an audience by having programmes with many short pieces in them. They would seldom play a symphony in its entirety. They would play a movement from Beethoven's Seventh Symphony, an overture by Weber, three arias sung by Madam So-and-So, the Scherzo from Litolff's Concerto Symphonique and so on. So there was never too long a stretch of any sort of music, and this was meant to excite the audience with the idea of variety and novelty. Lots of exotic things were introduced into these programmes, descriptive pieces and so on. But they kept the attention span right down, so as to entertain gently and slowly introduce more serious music to the wider public.

ES: *The Classic FM Radio formula.*
MTT: Right. Gradually, complete symphonies were performed. The programmes had fewer and fewer pieces and fewer composers, until they became the sort of symphony programmes we have today. Of course it's interesting that we're again seeing the decline of the attention span in the latter part of the twentieth century. What with TV programming and the whole *divertissement* world we live in, we seem to be going back to the old approach to classical music. There's no question but that orchestras of today will have to recommit themselves to audience development.

Theodore Thomas paved the way for the group coming after him, which included Stokowski and Koussevitzky. Of course Stokowski and Koussevitzky didn't have to commission small little pieces for novelty's sake, taste had really moved beyond that. Still, they were the ones who found American composers who would write pieces that fitted into the context of standard concert life. So many of Stokowski's commissions and sound experiments had a salon piece, *divertissement* aspect to them. It didn't matter whether the piece was a transcription of Japanese court music, or the evocation of a steel foundry written by a Soviet composer, or the première of Schoenberg's complete *Gurrelieder* in the United States, they were all *attractions* of one sort or another, which were put in to give spice to that week. It was exciting for the audiences to believe that all this novelty placed them right at the centre of the musical world.

With Ira Gershwin, 1981

The Koussevitzky Group

Also from this period came Koussevitzky's amazing work in commissioning American composers. It was because of his association with Stravinsky really. Koussevitzky came to the United States looking around for an American Stravinsky. He found Copland, first and foremost.

Koussevitzky favoured Copland, Harris, Diamond, Piston, William Schuman, Hanson and others because their work had many similarities in form and in sound to some of Koussevitzky's greatest European successes with Stravinsky and Sibelius. These composers used American-sounding materials but with them wrote pieces that were recognizably symphonic. So a trend was occurring with European Maestros commissioning Americans to write symphonic works for the developing American orchestras. Koussevitzky commissioned Copland, Walter Damrosch commissioned Gershwin, and so on. The mythology of the day was: the young American composer aspires to write a piece for the concert hall, however humble his origins, he comes to the big city and writes the piece that sums up the whole voice of the people.

This exact fantasy is represented in a 1931 movie called *Delicious*, from which the Gershwin Second Rhapsody is taken. There are several movies from that time, where the young composer says, 'I'm going to write the piece that'll sum it all up. The songs of the city, the pushcart vendors, the socialites on their penthouse balconies, the organ grinder, the sound of the subway, the people clattering downstairs in the tenements, the cries, the street vendors – all this in one great throbbing cry about the music of the city.'

The Ives Avant-Garde Group

Quite opposite to the Koussevitzky group, was the group around Ives: Henry Cowell, Carl Ruggles, Edgar Varèse, Charles Seeger, his wife Ruth Crawford Seeger, John Joseph Becker and Wallingford Riegger. These people were all much more avant-garde in their thinking. They were 'arty' people, many of them. Of course Ives really wasn't. They were free-spirited people. These were people who were very interested in modern art, in photography. They were all friendly with Westin and Georgia O'Keeffe and people who'd been around the Armory Show in New York. Most of these people lived in downtown New York. They kept irregular hours, many of them. Most of them were politically radical. They were interested in sound for sound's sake. They were not writing music for a concert society. Many of them never expected their pieces to be performed. They felt their only chance for performance was to get a group of people together and put on their own concert, in a loft, in a town hall, wherever they could manage.

And this is the group of people who, in retrospect, contributed so many of the original musical ideas of the twentieth century. They were the people in the United States who were first interested in serial and experimental music; and from them came John Cage, Lou Harrison, Elliot Carter, Morton Feldman, Steve Reich, Philip Glass, and so on.

These two groups formed different societies. One was the group around Varèse, Cowell and Ives, and they had their own publishing company, New Music Edition. Then there was the other group, from the days of Koussevitzky, personified by Aaron Copland and Leonard Bernstein, William Schuman and Samuel Barber and run by Clare Reece. It was a much more upper-crust, New York Upper East Side group.

When I first came to New York in the sixties one still could feel that a bit. Cage, Cunningham, Feldman and Young had their post concert parties at Warhol's factory or John Ashbury's apartment. Barber and Copland had theirs at chic Eastside restaurants or the penthouse of some socialite.

Both of those groups were valid, but there was sense of artistic and social polarity. Of course I had got to know these composers out in Los Angeles. For me they were just folk from New York who came at different times of year to perform their work. So I had no sense of the aesthetic and economic stratification that divided them. I was equally friendly with them all.

ES: *When did the Ives 'avant-garde' group first get going?*
MTT: It was back in the 1920s and 1930s. Ives and his group gave avant-garde concerts conducted by Nicholas Slonimski. Even more radical pieces like Becker's *A Marriage with Space*, where performers were swinging back and forth on pendulums in huge rooms while sustaining notes; and Charles Seeger's vast, happening-like pieces were done. Some really very extraordinary soundscapes. You get some sense of that when you listen to pieces like *Study in Sonority*, for ten violins, by Wallingford Riegger. Or Ruth Crawford Seeger's *Quartet*, with its rising and falling levels of sound. Very abstract, dissonant pieces. This hard-edged dissonant pursuit of sonic architecture, the sort of thing Varèse was doing at that time, was what appealed to the radical crowd. The devil may care adventurousness of that music, was bankrolled by Charles Ives – composer and insurance millionaire. It was he who could put up the money for the concerts and who could pay for the publication of the pieces in New Music Edition.

If you look at New Music Edition volume 1, you have a Ruggles piece, *Men and Mountains*; volume 2, the second movement of Ives's Fourth Symphony; another volume, the music of George Antheil and the Cuban avant-garde composer Amadeo Roldan. The covers were very brightly coloured, and they had great geometric shapes intersecting at odd angles. The whole design aesthetic of it was very radical, self-consciously modern. In comparison, other composers being published by Durand or Boosey and Hawkes, as Copland was, had their wonderful little monograms ... the whole European aesthetic of publishing.

But what is so interesting is that in the 1930s and going into the 1940s all of these composers had the same sort of reaction. Already in the 1930s they felt that their music was becoming too intellectual, too far removed from what the people could actually understand. And quite self-consciously they turned towards creating a simpler musical language. Copland came up with his whole popular style for which he is so adored today. People like Ruth Crawford Seeger and her husband Charles Seeger, and others, completely abandoned musical composition and became editors or collectors of folk songs. Some became folklorists, like Cowell, collecting native musical American material, and that led him on to Oriental musical material. Colin McPhee, who had been a big part of the hard-edge New York radical school, went to live in Bali and wrote the major text on Balinese gamelan music.

This reaction was so pervasive in all these composers at that time, that one has to take this very seriously. There was something happening in America. It was as if the American composers were saying, 'We mustn't get too far away from our audience, we mustn't get too far away from plain speaking, from plain singing. It's all very well, all these theories, these increasingly elaborate displays of defiance and intellectual bravura, but it's not the same thing as walking down the street at night and hearing somebody in an alley whistling a bit of something that you've written. That is a very, central experience.' And they wanted that. Now maybe that was part of them, because, being Americans, they were closer to pop music, pop culture. They wanted to be that kid in the film who said, 'I'm going to write this piece, it'll sum up all the songs in the city, it'll be played by Stokowski – but it'll also be on all the juke boxes.' That really was their secret dream.

ES: *So what happened in American music after the 'Let's back-track and keep it simple' movement in the 1930s?*
MTT: Well, the Second World War happened. There was a transference from pre-war political radicalism to a sense of conscious patriotism during the war; and a desire afterwards to sum up everything that had hopefully been learned in the war in a message of re-dedication, of thankfulness, of forgiveness.

The next major new direction came through a continuation of the radical group – the Ives, Varèse, Cowell, Ruggles group. And this was the direction taken by Cage, Feldman, Earle Brown, Harrison, these people. Actually there was another influence also on Cage – the influence of dance. Cage very early on became very much involved in writing music for the burgeoning of American modern dance. American modern dance, you must remember, had its own continuum from Isadora Duncan to Ruth St Dennis, Denis Shawn, Martha Graham, and many others.

ES: *Did these dance people have anything in common? Were they a specific group?*
MTT: They were people who started doing exotic, folkloric sorts of dances, often with incense and feathered costumes, and then they gradually pared all this away to a very stark aesthetic of motion. There is so often a relationship between the world of the exotic or the salon piece and the later avant-garde. Likewise, Cage's early pieces, like *Bacchanal*, were written for a prepared piano which was meant to reproduce the effect of an exotic percussion orchestra.

From this musical exoticism, a much more pared down, stark, ultimately Zen-like aesthetic was developed. You got the introduction of the idea of Zen for a performer, the idea of not performing all the time, but simply sitting and listening a great deal and waiting for just the right moment to do something, to play a note, or perhaps more important, not play a note. This seems now to have been the central message of such figures as John Cage, and Miles Davis also. 'Don't play too many notes, don't play too many high notes, don't play too many long notes, don't feel you must play something all the time.' And then, through geographic proximity, if you were living out on the end of Long Island or down in Greenwich Village, came the bonding with the visuals of the aesthetic, with the painters of that time.

Morton Feldman, Lukas Foss, Lamont Young, Steve Reich

If there's any area in American music that I feel is still greatly underestimated it is this music, particularly Morton Feldman's music. I think it so beautiful and important. I was very lucky to know him. He was first trained by Edgar Varèse, and influenced by Cage. He was totally a product of New

Morton Feldman

York's Greenwich Village and its avant-garde painters. His music went through a period of very indeterminate sound happenings, but he came back to writing very specific sonorities and notes. Do you know much of his music?

ES: *Very little. Very little's been performed.*
MTT: Morty's music is extremely quiet. And it presents a very luminous, floating world. I think on first hearing it might impress you as a kind of very *de luxe* Webern. But there are a lot of other elements in it. There is a haunting melodic sense in it all – he had a very oblique melodic sense. And there is a fabulous choice of sonority and profound use of silence.

I knew Morty very well because he was in Buffalo the whole time that I was Music Director of the Buffalo Philharmonic. He was composer in residence there, and we made music and spent quite a lot of time together. There was a tremendous contrast in Morty between his music and him. He was a very large man. He loved to eat, loved to cook, loved paintings, loved carpets, loved music of all sorts, Eastern and Western. He was a man of great refinement, who spoke with the thickest Brooklyn accent you've ever heard. He would describe these ecstatic, aesthetic worlds he was creating in this thick accent ... He would say things like, 'Michael, I tell you, dat woik dat I wrote heah is dee most beeyoutiful ting what I ever did.' I remember him telling me one night, 'Michael, you're too anxious about your composin'. I'm woiking on dis piece, I got dis choid, I really like dis choid. So I wrote de choid, den I wrote dis next bar ... den I jus' wrote rests, an' I'm jus' waitin' for what I know should be the next choid. Maybe I'll repeat dis choid. Maybe I'll subtract one note – I'm waitin' for somtin' to come to me ...'

ES: *When he said to you, 'Michael, you're getting too anxious about your composition,' did that affect you in any way? Did that, or his music, have a noticeable effect on you at this point in your career, on your conducting maybe, as well as your ideas about composition?*
MTT: I knew at that moment he was re-confirming to me, as other people have done, that this was something I could do if I wanted to; but I would first have to put aside preconceived agendas of what it is to write, how much work one is meant to get done in how much time – and what constitutes a piece of music, for that matter. Just thinking of what note you want to write next. I wasn't ready to do it at that particular time, even though in those years I sketched so much music. If I ever get past this hurdle and start doing some more of my own music, doing something that really matters to

people, most of it will come from the sketchbooks and the tune books I wrote during that period of time.

But so many people went through that. Lukas Foss is another composer for whom I have a very great admiration. Lukas is so talented and so misunderstood a person in many ways; he is a great pianist and performer, and could collaborated with the most distinguished virtuosi, like Heifetz, Piatigorsky, Schnabel and Lord knows who else. At the same time he had a drive to write American music, and to take American music beyond the neo-classical prairie school – which he wrote so well. During the 1960s he wrote two pieces, *Time Cycle* and *Echoi,* both of which really stand up as masterpieces, taking many of the cries and echoes of the American urban lonely nightmare and combining them with some of the musical ideas of post-Webernistic musical language which were in vogue at that time. His experiments with indeterminacy and layering in pieces like *Phorion* (taking a Bach Partita and deconstructing it) also remain fascinating. But Lukas became trapped by the idea of always having a new piece ready in whatever musical line was coming into vogue at that moment, a very American problem. One feels there were many wonderful pieces he could have written, but which were not written because he was more concerned about 'keeping up' than about what he really wanted to say. It is hard to maintain your own identity on the shifting sands of international art fashion. It is equally limiting to take hard lines and swear allegiance to an aesthetic, a class, a neighbourhood. Real battles had to be won to bring the most original American music of that time out of its obscure downtown haunts into the mainstream of concert life.

You'll get an idea of just how obscure some of these concert events were if I describe Lamont Young's music. Lamont was a important early minimalist, obsessed by the sounds of electric devices, like large high tension power lines and electric transformers. One of Lamont's works in the 1960s was an installation which he called 'Theatre of Eternal Music'. There was a loft downtown somewhere, and in the loft there were banks of oscillators continuously playing. Very slowly they would be placed in or out of phase with one another. And a few of the upper harmonics would be tuned in and out, using filters. All this was meant to approximate that strange buzzing, shifting sort of sound which one hears round high tension lines. Drones were chanted by live performers. A big part of the experience was you yourself singing against the sound of the electronics. Of course, it was much too loud for you to hear yourself, but as you went slightly out of tune with the buzz, enormous standing waves would begin to vibrate in your chest. You could actually feel these great violent pulsations in your own abdomen as you went in and out of tune with this great mass of sound in the room.

This work was played continuously, day and night. There was always someone there playing it or attending it. It was called *The Tortoise, His Dreams, His Journeys.* The original plan was that the work should be one year in length. So even with primitive light projections that were done with cut-up doilies and several different coloured projectors on the walls and some bubbles – all part of the 1960s aesthetic – it was quite arduous for the uninitiated to sit through a long session of this music.

You must remember that this was the time when John Cage was still giving concerts of his more extreme music. In the 1950s he'd given concerts where you'd pay perhaps ten dollars to enter the concert, and if you stayed till the intermission you got back five dollars. If you stayed until the end of the concert, you could get back another two dollars. If you really did make it through the whole evening, it was quite good value!

I had played, or heard most of these composers in Los Angeles. A new East Coast discovery for me was Steve Reich. The first piece of his I heard was *It's Gonna Rain*, an early piece using taped loops. I was immediately taken by the great richness of texture, nuance, and scale that emerged from the recorded sounds of the gospel preacher. The process of moving from the intelligible common place to the abstract remoteness was a profound journey that interested me greatly. Shortly after this I heard a few early instrumental pieces like *Violin Phase* and realized that Steve Reich was not only a composer of ideas, but of wonderfully chosen notes. The pieces seemed to hover in a world between East and West, Gamelon and Motown, folk and classical, continua which suited me just fine. Around that same time I was starting a series with the Boston Symphony Orchestra called Spectrum Concerts. These concerts were unified by a central idea of juxtaposed music of the greatest stylistic contrasts. Composers like Perotin, Elliot Carter, Monteverdi and Stockhausen found themselves competing for the audience's attention. The first programme was called 'Multiples' and explored music written for multiple ensembles. The programme consisted of *Divertimento for Four Orchestras* by Mozart (with Arthur Fiedler conducting one of the orchestras) Bartók's *Music for Strings, Percussion and Celesta*, some Gabrielli brass choir pieces and Liszt's outrageous *Hexameron* for six pianos and orchestra. I was very keen to add one of Steve's pieces to this programme in the featured spot after intermission. At first he was reluctant. He felt his music was suited only for his musicians and for loft spaces in New York's Soho. I convinced him that his music could stand before any audience and how important I felt it was for him to do his work with members of the Boston Symphony. Steve finally agreed to let us programme

With Steve Reich, 1984

Four Organs, which was for four rock organs and maracas. The piece would be played by Steve, myself, and two other keyboard players from the BSO and maraca players drawn from the orchestra's percussion section. The concert took place in Boston and was very successful.

A bit later we repeated it in New York, at Carnegie Hall. It's nearly twenty years ago now, but I can still remember everything about that extraordinary evening quite vividly. We presented the concert on a regular subscription programme for the Boston Symphony devotees in New York. We knew that the audience was somewhat conservative, priding itself on attending the New York concerts of the self-styled 'aristocrat of orchestras'. But nothing prepared us for what took place. During Steve's piece there was a riot in the auditorium. People in the audience began making disparaging noises which grew louder and more threatening. There were three definite attempts to halt the performance. People were standing up and screaming very loudly. At one point a woman left her seat and came down the aisle to the edge of the stage and banged her head repeatedly against it, screaming, 'Stop, stop, I confess!' This prompted the audience to make still greater amounts of noise until, even over the electronic amplification of the instruments we were playing, it was impossible to hear where we were. So I was obliged to look at Steve and the other performers and mouth and yell out the beats of the bar so that we could stay together. This was quite difficult as the piece is written in long rhythmic cycles, some of which are 256 beats long.

Finally, at the end of the piece, there was a moment of silence – and then an avalanche of boos and bravos, a pandemonium of noise such as I've never heard in a concert hall. It was quite unbelievable. People had to be restrained, taken back to their seats. It was a total circus.

Poor Steve was absolutely white – green even. He just didn't know what to think. I kept telling him, 'Steve, this is the greatest thing that could happen. This is fantastic. People don't react this way to music. You really have done something, you've really challenged the whole public here in New York. They never imagined that you or your music existed and now, suddenly, it does. They, and you, will not be able to ignore this.'

Then the Liszt *Hexameron* came on. It is a set of variations for six pianos and orchestra, which Liszt and Chopin and various virtuosi of the day had done. It's all based on a march from *I puritani*. During this piece the members of the audience who were pro avant-garde music and had been outraged at the behaviour of the conservatives who didn't like Steve's piece, had their revenge. After the introduction, when the big Bellini tune was first stated people began screaming, 'Bourgeois trash!', and other insults. The commotion continued on and off until the end of the evening. It was really a fascinating exhibition of two ideas of music and two audiences – a downtown, avant-garde audience and an uptown society audience coming smack into collision right there in Carnegie Hall. We all felt that we were at a turning point in history.

So you see we haven't really been all over the shop in our discussion today – there is a thread we can see that goes through this. There are those two audiences put together. And I would say in the time since then, in the last twenty years, those barriers have broken down considerably. Symphonic audiences now are much more used to the idea of being challenged, even though they perhaps feel that they must be challenged at a certain level of intellectual involvement. There is a small hard core group of serious music lovers everywhere which thinks that unless a piece is complex and tough enough, it can't really be that good. Like aged bolsheviks they zealously extol the theory and lambaste the proletariat – the audience – for failing to fulfil its mission.

Minimalism

ES: *So the emergence of the so-called minimalist movement, and the other minimalist composers, was very reactionary, a complete inversion of that, Philip Glass, particularly. Suddenly this cult emerged which was based on a kind of reaction to this toughness and complexity ...*

MTT: Yes. Minimalism was a reaction against the impenetrability, the aesthetic of the 1950s and the 1960s. Music, largely influenced by total serialism and other intellectual conceits, was very modish at that time. The theories were great but audiences could not accept the music, or they couldn't accept a great deal of it. A hostility grew between many composers and their audiences. Some of these composers felt that if the audience didn't understand them then, 'to hell with them.' The audience, of course, would not be treated this way and so an estrangement resulted. Into this communications gap moved minimalism.

Many people have written music which falls under the large descriptive label called minimalist music. There is some really great minimalist music, and there is some really unnecessary minimalist music. Minimalism is very easy to imitate, so a lot of people have done just that, and a lots of it is not very good. But a composer like Steve Reich is to me a very interesting and profound musician.

Steve's writing developed from his work with tapes. He listened to recordings of voices speaking, observing qualities in the voice's cadences that could be developed or organized into a composition. He discovered that in the sounds of even one or two spoken words there was terrific expressive potential. So, instead of being obsessed as the total serialists were with throwing every note of the scale at us in every bar, he began to see to many beautiful and profound possibilities contained within very few notes. If, of course, they're the right notes. Steve chooses the right notes.

In some ways minimalism was an expression of Cage's exhortation that people should want to discover the music in everything, should use their ears to make music out of whatever was sounding at that particular moment. There's a thin line there, though. To what degree can a composer release himself to observing, to being open to whatever may happen without abandoning his crucial role as someone who must choose what is actually going to happen?

ES: *I know they have just recorded Cage's 4'33". Four minutes, thirty-three seconds of silence. Wayne Marshall doesn't play it. Brilliantly.*
MTT: Did they get it in one take?

ES: *No, they did several takes.*

MTT: Are there any surprises? Can you hear the edits?

ES: *One or two extraneous noises. I heard a dog bark. The timbers of the church creak.*

MTT: Well, minimalism has had its day now. But the rise of minimalism was news. It gave many music journalists a chance to write articles about it, to propagandize for it, and to advance their own causes through it. We all know that one aspect of the arts is, 'What's happening? What direction are things going? What's in fashion now?'

ES: *Yes, exactly. But the fashion actually went too far the other way.*

MTT: It did. Well, there you are. Minimalism came into fashion and went out of fashion in, what, fifteen years? The '-ism' that preceded it, tough avant-gardism, I suppose lasted about twenty years. And the '-ism' before that, the neo-classical diatonic world, lasted about twenty-five years. So we go in and out of these fashions quickly. After the fashions are gone what remains are the great works. Once again, the classics will transcend their time.

Elliott Carter

Of course, particular parts of the audience remain loyal and interested in their favourite composers no matter what. The patriots, performers, and friendly critics of a particular composer continue to propagandize for them, as is necessary and proper. For example, Elliott Carter, whose music is currently unfashionable is regarded by many people as the most serious, most important living American composer. I can't dismiss his music, I know too many people who greatly admire his work and are very devoted to performing it. I love the first seven minutes of most of his pieces, but after that point I feel that it's time for him to make a move towards us, as audience members. This is something that Berg and Ives did so well. They stretch us out to the limits of our perception and then, for one moment, they let us understand what it is they are saying with unmistakable clarity and communicative power.

In Ives, and Berg, there are self-defining, beauteous moments that even on first hearing draw you in to the sound world of an otherwise very tough piece.

Back to Melody

I probably should be more patient with Carter's music considering how very patient I am with Ives's often murky meanderings. But with Ives it comes back to the power of those melodic moments – and maybe for me, as an American, everything finally comes back to those moments. Yes, I adore the Berg Chamber Concerto, and I adore his Three Pieces for Orchestra, and the Violin Concerto, I adore all those pieces, and all their form and all their structure and their essence and everything about them ... But when I walk down the street all by myself on a rainy night I hear a phrase from the Violin Concerto, or from an interlude in *Wozzeck,* or a particular turn of harmony in the Three Orchestral Pieces – a phrase just comes into my heart, comes into my mind, it's with me, it's a part of me. And it's not the intellectual, structural part of the piece that's with me at that moment. It's the message of what those notes say that's with me. Just as the message of what Ives says is with me at that moment. Just as the cadences of Bernstein's 'Some Other Time', or Gershwin's 'How Long Has This Been Going On?' or Schubert's A major Rondo for piano four hands, back through the whole history of music – it's these turns of phrase which ultimately have the real communicative power. Is it just Americans that feel that, or is it everyone that feels that?

If we *all* feel that, why have we all been made to feel so guilty? Why has this dichotomy been allowed to come into existence? Why is there the brainy, serious, abstract side of music on the one side, and the melodic, experiential on the other? Why haven't we been able to tell people who want to make these barriers, 'Just do what you're going to do, but please, now and then, give us a tune, a motive or something to hang on to.' The power of melody is so great, it can draw us to works in musical styles very far from the familiar.

ES: *That's interesting. I had a conversation quite recently with Lutoslawski; and he's saying that people are not writing melodically any more, that people should start writing melodically again. He's got a point.*
MTT: He has. Melody reaches out to us equally in works that point to the far future or come from the remote past. For example, one of my favourite pieces is the *Missa Pange lingua* by Josquin des Prez. I listen to it just about more than any other recording. Of course, I appreciate the polyphonic mastery of the piece, but, ultimately, it's the tune itself that sticks with me. Josquin has an amazing ability to allow the tune to be clearly heard, even in the midst of his most dazzling intellectual inventions. It is as if the tune is a

key unlocking his powers of imagination for us, his listeners. So again, with my science-fiction turn of mind, I imagine some time in the future when people are on starships, with vast banks of computers, and the thing that they have to give them a sense of identity is tunes coming from one era of mankind, or from one planet or another. Then, given what they have at hand, they can have these computers turn those tunes into any sort of piece they happen to need at that moment. It can have text, rhythm, grandeur. It can be as dramatic or romantic as you require. But it is the tune itself which will be the essential element that will give it soul.

In a way that's like going back to this idea of a song form or a tune that comes in from the barbarian frontier, comes in from where people are perhaps experiencing things more directly, less self-consciously, more innocently, more intuitively. And out of intuition come these tunes, these melodies, which trace some very important spiritual journey in ourselves. And then comes the question of technique and what's done with that. Well, fine, human beings have occupied themselves with that up to this point, but in the future it may well be that technology will begin to take over many of the tasks that compositional technique formerly did. Can't say.

So what's happening now? I can tell you that when I meet young composers, they are concerned again about their music sounding beautiful, about having communicative power. I think a lot of American composers feel that a lot of very tough music has been forced down their throats for a long period of time. They know they can't write minimalist music anymore, they've got to get past that. Learn from it, but get past it.

I think many of them feel a bit betrayed, actually. I think they feel that the academic institutions in the United States, the direction of concert societies and orchestras, denied so many of the most important musical traditions of the country. It was the same attitude I encountered as a young musician when certain 'very important managers' said, 'Don't play too much Gershwin, too much Copland. Don't get typed as someone who plays American music.' That same influence has had an effect on the curriculum of so many schools. In every country of the world today, really, young musicians are made to feel that the ultimate prize is an international career. In this quest for internationalism (which really means salability in the world music market) important traditions and qualities can suddenly disappear.

It's extraordinary, isn't it, that even a place in the United States like Tanglewood, which was the centre of American musical thinking, has been affected by this attitude. While it is still an important international music festival it's no longer an American cultural centre. It's lost whatever connection it had with the sort of musicians who thought along the direction of what Koussevitzky liked to call 'the central line' – humanist path blazed by Ives, Ruggles, Copland, and so on – the composers whose concern was to sound in the largest and freest sense, American. Some of the soul has been lost, some of the courage to say, 'What are my true feelings, what do I have to plainly sing, or to plainly speak, or to set forth?'

I think young composers are now trying to look back at the tradition of the country and ask, 'We once seemed to have so much to say in this country. What has happened? What has happened to our personal voice? Did we lose it simply because we lost our political, economic domination of the world, and therefore we are a bit more halting in our speech and in our tune-smithing? Is it as simple as that? Are we the first people to whom this has happened?' I think not.

ES: *Do you think it's inevitable that American music will in future be drawn more and more into the world of European music?*
MTT: The United States is still trying to get over the catastrophic cultural blink of the 1960s and 1970s. These were times when our susceptibility to international music fashions and international music merchandizing caused us to back down and turn away from our central line. We forgot that the value of our music was always its directness of expression, its plain speaking. We thought that internationalism was hip and slick. But it just turned out to be empty. It's time to go back to the old neighbourhoods and remember the songs we sing on the street corners.

ES: *Well, as the world has become smaller and as communications have increased, as the barriers between countries have come down, so the individual identities, I think, have disappeared.*
MTT: There's one terrible danger that I'm aware of when I listen to the more international music that's being produced now. Just think of pop music for a moment. When you hear some, wherever it may originate, it's likely to be a sort of synthetic village music or global funk. It may have a bit of melody, some African percussion and Asiatic drones and some Western street noise and lot of Western techno-noise. Because of the riffs and the hooks and whatnot that are in it it may be momentarily arresting, very good for pro-pelling you around a dance floor or a circuit of exercise machines for an extra ten minutes or so. But finally you notice that it is empty. The refer-ences to one musical culture or another are being eaten up and all that remains is this great, inexhaustingly hungry maw of backbeat. All the tunes, all the cadences and nuances are ultimately stripped away, and all that remains is, 'Bunk, chung, bunga chunk, bunk chung, bunga chunk.'

After all, backbeat just represents sex. Blasting backbeat into the ears of kids is just a ploy for merchandizing what is nearly always of low quality and without spiritual value.

ES: *Those appalling Hooked-on-Classics discs, where all these wonderfully disparate tunes are simply strung together, all robbed of their identity.*
MTT: Another issue in American music to be thought, with respect to modishness, is the way, for example, a composer like Gershwin was treated. Since he came from the pop side, those around him felt that his pieces should be updated, re-arranged, every five or ten years or so as a new sound came in. It's only in the last fifteen years or so that a few people have begun to say, 'Hold on a minute, these original versions are very important, and the way they were first written is the way they should be preserved and played, more often that not.' And that is part of the American classic tradition. But again, that shows you how far we have had to come in America, because no one in Vienna would have ever thought, 'Oh, stay away from Johann Strauss, don't play too much Johann Strauss. And oh, Lehár, be careful; and maybe we should update the Johann Strauss pieces after all ...' No one would ever have thought that. From the very beginning it was recognized how important and how central they were.

ES: *But isn't that just the insecurity of a new nation as opposed to a very old one?*
MTT: It may be so, but I think it comes back to the merchandizing of music. And I suppose, sadly, America has led the world in its merchandizing, of pop culture artifacts particularly.

ES: *One does think of America as being the father of popular music, really – rock, pop music, jazz or whatever.*
MTT: Yes, but it's also the place where the barriers broke down between classical and popular. I personally feel such a debt to specifically American musical culture. There are many moments when I think this is the only thing I should do. Yes, I love to conduct Mahler and Bruckner and play Mozart, but perhaps more important for me are all those pieces of Morty Feldman's, Marc Blitzstein's and Leon Kirchner's, and so many other American composers who are not actively championed.

American music is as vast and wide as our continent. To be an American musician you have to know American music. That means, just for openers, knowing Indian song, folk songs, hymn tunes, cowboy songs, ragtime, blues, jazz standards, show music, Latin music, bebop, swing, bluegrass, country, rock, and Billings, Gottschalk, Foster, Ives, Ruggles, Cowell,

Copland, Bernstein, Ellington, Gershwin, Schuman, Barber, Rogers, Cage, Feldman, Piston, Foss, Schuller, Carter, Sessions, Wuorinen, Del Tredici, Adams, Reich, Glass, Riegger, Ruth Crawford Seeger and Harriet Beecher Stowe. Not bad for two hundred years.

French Music

ES: *It's not really surprising that the French repertoire should be one of your specialties. Indeed, part of your central nervous system, given that your first full-time conducting appointment was with the Boston Symphony, with its amazing French tradition.*

MTT: Actually, my first awareness of French music came through my father, who loved Debussy's music very, very much. My father had written a play for Paul Muni on the subject of the madness of Nijinsky, and one of the major scenes in the play had to do with the choreography of *The Afternoon of a Faun*, the choreography that was being done when Nijinsky met Romola. So from the time I was two or three, I was aware of these names – Nijinsky, Diaghilev, Bronislava, Romola and Debussy. All these Ballets Russe names and stories were part of our dinner time conversation. I heard the *Faun*, both on an orchestral recording (I have no idea by whom), and by my father playing it by ear on the piano, which he could do very well. The hauntedness of that piece was apparent to me from the first time I heard it; it was one of my favourites.

Shortly after that, there was an early television programme that used *Syrinx* as its theme music. I didn't much care for this television programme, which was some kind adult metaphysical chat show. I remember that sometimes I would tune it in just to watch the final credits so I could hear that mysterious flute piece. I had no idea what the music was and didn't know until years later. I was attending a summer music camp in the mountains of California. One of the traditions of the camp was a sunset ceremony held at a dramatic outlook called 'Inspiration Point'. We campers aged eleven or so were assembled, sitting on blankets, looking at the spectacular Western sky. Just as the sun touched the horizon, an old Indian woman, who lived on the camp grounds, began to sing the traditional 'end-of-day chant' of her people. Her name was Attahloah, and she accompanied herself with a low tom-tom singing in a cracked, but melodious voice, 'Ah-zoo-ee ma watah zoo-ee.' (I swear those are the exact words she sang!) The chant continued until the sun completely disappeared. Then, from a rocky grotto, came the sound of a flute playing the mysterious piece whose name I had so longed to discover – *Syrinx.* That experience cinched my obsession with Debussy.

I sought out piano music by Debussy and began playing the few pieces simple enough for me to get my fingers around. Other more difficult pieces I sort of played at. Even just a couple of bars of the music felt so wonderful under my hands, and the gestures of the sound in the air were magical. And after that came Ravel. The first piece I adored was the Quartet. I was initially very attracted by the Pizzicato movement. Then came *Introduction and Allegro.* Gradually, through recorded music and through playing more of the music myself, I set out to explore Debussy and Ravel more completely. Around the same time, *Carmen* came into my life. I remember we had the Rise Stevens/Reiner record of *Carmen.* I learned to sing the whole opera by heart. But what most impressed me was the incredible precision and intensity of the orchestral playing, from which the expression of the voices seemed to naturally arise.

Debussy and Ravel with the Boston Symphony

Many years later, conducting in Boston, Debussy became a major part of my repertoire. I had done some Debussy and Ravel in Los Angeles, with the Young Musicians Foundation Orchestra, but the big musical breakthrough happened for me one summer in Tanglewood. I learned *La Mer,* and I learned a lot from looking at the parts used then by the Boston Symphony Orchestra. These parts were full of interpretive markings from Koussevitzky and Munch and Monteux even. I talked with some of the veteran French musicians in the orchestra about their approach to this music, and learned a great deal. A great source of wisdom and encouragement was Louis Speyer, who had been solo English Horn in the première of the *Rite of Spring* and Roger Voisin, the remarkable trumpet player. Both of these artists gave me insights into approaching the music in an articulate and daringly flexible manner. That summer, I gave a performance of *La Mer* with the student orchestra in Tanglewood. It worked well. A year or so later, I had to make a programme for my first concert ever with the Boston Symphony, and I wanted to end the concert with *La Mer.* The programme was characteristic. It was Haydn's Symphony No. 98, Ives's *Three Places in New England*, Stravinsky's *Huxley Variations* and *La Mer.* That was my initiation, my baby programme.

I felt very confident about all this music, but everybody said to me, 'Whatever you do, don't do *La Mer* with the Boston Symphony Orchestra. Are you crazy? They did this piece for breakfast with Munch and Monteux and everybody else – just don't do it.' But I said, 'I have to do it. I know the piece. I love it.' I mostly rehearsed just textures and dynamics. I didn't take the whole piece apart. I couldn't, because I had much more to do, rehearsing the Ives and the Stravinsky and the Haydn, which they didn't know. My basic instincts about the music were similar to theirs, so that in the performance I was able to conduct them in a way that encouraged them to play with the sort of freedom and opportunity for panache that they had had in the performances they did with Munch and Monteux. In the first performance, I really let go. I conducted with daring and abandon. They really liked it. I still remember the gleam in their eyes and the tremendous approval from them for this performance of *La Mer*. It so astounded me, because I had heard them playing wonderfully with other conductors, but I hadn't had that experience of standing in front of them and hearing them play really full out with complete enthusiasm a piece that I so much loved. It was extraordinary, transporting. I was right there in the middle of it. It was what I dreamed conducting would be like.

Over the next years I did quite a lot of Debussy and Ravel with them. I didn't have to rehearse every little stylistic matter because they knew it. They knew it thoroughly. It was just a question of a little nuance here, a little time there, and how energetic or how serene it needed to be. The sound of the orchestra in those performances became my model for French music. Each reading was different, growing more mercurial and dangerous. A year or two later we went on tour to Germany taking many of these French pieces with us. The reviewers didn't know what to make of this torrent of free music making led by a young man whom they described as 'conducting in a state of ecstasy and jubilation'. It certainly felt like that. It was magical.

The next stage of Debussy consciousness came in an unusual way. Leonard Bernstein came to Boston to do the Elliot Norton lectures. One of the pieces he did was *Afternoon of a Faun*. He rehearsed it, so I was told, forever. I was somewhere else, guest-conducting. When I returned, there was a repeat concert which took repertoire from various programmes. One of the pieces was *Faun*. I had done the piece with the orchestra on the European Tour the previous year, so I was just going to do it in concert with no rehearsal. As I conducted the piece I became aware that it was absolutely transformed. The orchestra was following me and responding to all the give-and-take nuances we mutually understood, but all of the *pianissimi*, and the quality of the sound – every burnished, wonderful, half-gleaming, golden sparkle in the midst of the haze – had been refined by Lenny's hard work. I realized that those 'for-ever-long' rehearsals had really produced a conception of sound which would inspire me to think of the music in a deeper way.

A Paradox

That began the process of working on the French pieces with more of a sense of what I myself imagined. Boulez was of course an influence at this time too. His immense sense of clarity and precision in these pieces set a new standard. I still believe that there is a paradox in French music. On the one hand, you have the French saying, 'Oh yes, everything must be *tout règle*, absolutely in tempo, except where it's marked otherwise.' But there is more than that in the music. Yes, everything must be clear and in order, but at the same time, when you play a Debussy piano piece, like *L'isle Joyeuse*, you really are not concerned whether the melody in the right hand lines up exactly with the quintuplet accompaniment in the left hand. One hand must murmur quietly along, and the other must have a more ardent, expansive quality. There is a certain amount of *rubato* between the hands, aided and abetted by the clever use of the pedal. This produces the illusion of the whole piece. I feel very much that the same is true for the orchestral music. To be slavishly concerned about whether you get the notes exactly in the right place can rob the piece of some of its mysteries. More importantly the piece must have a certain swing. It's more important that each part have its own character, even if that means that at a particular instant it is slightly out of time. As long as it works out evenly at the end of the phrases, at the cadence points, it's fine. In fact, the streams of music moving slightly in and out of synchronicity with each other is a part of the magic and excitement of these pieces. It is the responsibility of the conductor to decide which parts of the music must be exactly together and which parts have the possibility of greater freedom.

This approach has led me to performances which were more and more risk-taking. Certain pieces seem to inspire the most daredevil perspectives, Ravel's *La Valse*, in particular. *La Valse* is one of the most challenging pieces for an orchestra to perform. Although it is only twelve or thirteen minutes long, it stretches the abilities and endurance of the performers to the very limits. It requires such constant attention to balance, to nuance, to articulation and, of course, to continual changes of tempo. Orchestras have described the experience of doing *La Valse* with me as accelerating around a racecourse without flinching in the turns. I do like to take the piece as close to the edge of chaos as is possible before pulling it back on track at the last possible moment. I do enjoy that.

ES: *That's the piece.*
MTT: That's what I believe the piece to be. *La Valse* brings to fruition the

terrifying aspects of the waltz as revealed in all the E.T.A. Hoffman stories, Max Klinger drawings and so on. The ecstatic and fatalistic whirling of this dance has captured so many composers' imaginations. It is extraordinary that the same dance form can be so utterly charming and at the same time be so frighteningly powerful. Ravel developed the piece far beyond his original idea of transmogrifying Vienna's musical predilections.

ES: *I don't think the audience quite understands this. After all, things turn very ugly at the end.*
MTT: Yes, the music can't remain in a mist the whole time. It must come forth, first suavely, then brutally. It finally has to reveal its true intention, which is total domination of *ein, swei, drei.*

The Nature of French Music

ES: *What is it about French music that elicits such strong reactions from people?*
MTT: Well, I suppose it's music that focuses very much on the sacred and profane, like Debussy's famous *Danses sacrées et profanes.* Throughout his life he wrote pieces referring to subjects from classical mythology, and from oriental mythologies and cosmologies, and then things from the Christian side, or the Bardic middle ages, the troubadour side of things. All those images are there, and that's very much the tradition of the French song, the clearly modulated text, the attention to surface, which has been so much a part of French art and of French music.

But in the case of Debussy, it's of course modulated through the fact that one of the major geniuses in music spent a very formative part of his life in Russia. You can certainly hear lots of Mussorgsky and Tchaikovsky and Rimsky-Korsakov, among others, in Debussy. Debussy was Nadezhda von Meck's pianist. There was also his enormous awe of Wagner. But he was saying, 'Well, this is the way Wagner should really have done it. If he'd got it right it would have sounded like this.' That amazing mixture in Debussy is what gives all the mystery in his music; all the aching, lonely spaces in his music, the sense of exotic vision, and at the same time the Tristan-like warmth of the phrasing and the harmonies. You get two composers like that around the same time, and they're two of my all-time favourites. Debussy and Puccini.

Debussy and Puccini

I know that people don't usually think of them in the same breath, but I

With Leslie Caron at the recording of Debussy's *Le martyre de St Sébastien*, 1991

really do. Never mind that Puccini only wrote operas. If you listen to his musical language, it's an Italian's conception of all kinds of musical ideas coming from Mussorgsky and the others, and Wagner, as re-interpreted through the idea of Italian songs. You can also hear a great deal of Monteverdi in Puccini and also touches of Bellini and Verdi. But still more I think Monteverdi shows through, especially in Puccini's extraordinary gift of making the most commonplace chords sound wondrously new, and in making major chords sound so utterly sad. Puccini really succeeded in doing what Wagner dreamed of, writing an opera with continuous melody and combining it with Mussorgsky's great dramatic insights as well. Debussy did the same thing within the tradition of French song and French musical tradition. Here then are two artists, in two different countries, who shared the same influences but realized them in their own personal ways.

Returning to the music, Debussy and Ravel is always one of the parts of my musical year to which I most look forward. As we've been having these conversations, I have been recording Debussy's *Le martyre de St Sébastien*. This project has been one of the most enjoyable on which I have ever worked. Why is that? Because, as Debussy left this piece in an incomplete and fragmentary state, it has required all of my performing instincts and critical abilities to imagine a satisfying realization of the score. When I mention the piece to my musical colleagues, there is always a special gleam in their eyes, remembering some particularly deluxe moment of the piece, such as when the six horns first make their entrance, one by one. It has been so wonderful using the medium of a CD recording and the perfect silence it affords to connect the fragments of this piece into a completed whole. As we were recording it, the profundity of the piece swept us all away. Everything worked. The solo singers, the chorus, the orchestra, Leslie Caron's wonderful narration, the superb engineering – all coalesced to reveal Debussy's extraordinarily imagined score. I can't speak enthusiastically enough about this piece, which is at once so opulent and expressive, so spare and abstract. Of all the Debussy projects I have done over the years, this has been my favourite.

This experience has increased my desire to do more French vocal music and opera. I must find the time to do *Pelleas*. And I also must do *Carmen*. I'll probably wind up doing it in concert version since it is so terribly difficult to stage. You have to have a director who knows how to move crowds. So often when I go to see a new production of *Carmen* it looks like the year end sale at Harrods. I've never seen so much buying and selling going on on stage.

Messiaen

As for music since Debussy, I at one time performed a great deal of Messiaen's and Boulez's music. Boulez's music I now seldom perform because the pieces I know the best are chamber pieces like *Marteau Sans Maître*. It is simply no longer a part of the schedule of my life to spend so long a time with a small group of people to rehearse these pieces the way they need to be done. Some of the pieces that involve very large forces perhaps eliminate themselves only because Pierre is apt to be here in London himself doing his pieces with the LSO.

The case of Messiaen is rather different. There are a few pieces of Messiaen I still do, like *Couleurs de la cité céleste*, but the years during which I would have done *Turangalîla* at the drop of a hat are long gone. I do appreciate Messiaen, and there are still movements in his music I like, but honestly I feel the continuing obsession with Messiaen on the part of many people is old-fashioned. I don't find that there's much mystery left in his music. I know how to perform it. I know what is necessary to make it work, but there's not that intangible element which remains to be discovered. Their lasting importance, I think, will be seen in their syncretism – the daring use of tonal and atonal, and serial and Western–Eastern and world-music-type elements to create a large and diverse work. The big architecture of his pieces, the musical symbols he throws in your face, the shocking juxtapositions and perverse discontinuities strike me as cinematic, a lot like Alfred Hitchcock. Who knows? He might wind up being thought of as a quirky late romantic figure rather than as a radical, pioneer figure. If he were lucky, some of his work might attain the affection the public now holds for Janáček. I personally think that Janáček has survived his reputation as a sort of acerbic avant-gardist, and is now recognized for the profound Romantic composer that he is.

ES: *You won't find the emotional complexity of Janáček's music in Messiaen. Messiaen is more of a naïve idealist ...*
MTT: Well, I guess if you want to be quite wicked about it you could say there's a similarity between the works of Messiaen and what's happened to Paris in these last years. In Paris you can have an incredible seventeenth-century arcade, and it's decided to put stumpy, unfinished plasticene columns, or whatever they are, in the middle of it. Or there's one of the great views through the Jardins les Tuileries all the way to the Arc de Triomphe, and it's lined up with the Arc de Carousel and the Tuileries, and it's all on a certain axis, then you build a modern glass pyramid which is deliberately put off the axis of all these other things. You could, perhaps, compare this to the idea of a Messiaen piece in which you've got a bit of plain chant and then suddenly great monolithic chords of serial construction interlaced with birdsong played on cacophonous percussion instruments.

ES: *I find it brings out the sceptic in me. It's the Lurex view of heaven I can't handle.*
MTT: I think *Colours* is a wonderful piece. *Sept Haikai*, *Chronochromie* and a couple of movements of *Turangalîla* really hold up. But I must say that the last time I heard a very committed artist play *Vingt Regards*, I thought, 'I really would much rather listen to Rachmaninov ...' His music holds up better for me because it is based on a kind of life-long dialogue that Rachmaninov was having between his melancholy spirit and the rapid-fire virtuoso impulses of his lower nervous system. That's my kind of dichotomy.

Of course there are other wonderful French composers today such as Dutilleux, who has a real lyric gift. There are haunting, really memorable turns of phrases in his music. But he too is preoccupied with creating a new luxurious sound world for each new piece. While it is always wonderful to admire the sheen and sophistication of his new works, I always wish there were more of them and that they were more centred on what is for me the most important issue in music ... the actual expression of the notes.

With French music today, as in so many musical traditions, what we are awaiting is a composer young enough and free enough to be able to take on board the whole varied musical language now available and decide just how it can most effectively be used. We don't need another pioneer sound explorer. We need a composer who can take what have become the 'clichés' of late twentieth-century music and turn them to real purpose even as Mozart did with the 'clichés' of eighteenth-century music before him.

Mahler

MTT: (singing to the tune of the second subject of the Rondo Burlesque of Mahler's Ninth Symphony)

> Gustav Mahler's the bloke drives me round the bend,
> With his nine symphonies what don't never end ...

ES: *Who was that created for?*
MTT: Cyril Reuben in the LSO. He's a violinist – a spirited and veteran player. But, strangely, he's not too keen on Mahler so we always kid him about it.

ES: *One of the things that always astounds me about Mahler's music is that it should have lain dormant for so long. Was it simply the lack of exposure? Did the time have to be right for it to emerge? A time when it was fashionable to bare one's soul again?*

How Mahler Became Mahler

MTT: I think the root of the answer to that question is to be found in considering how the music itself came into existence. The most extraordinary thing about Mahler's work is that it just seems to come from nowhere. All we have surviving from the earliest period of Mahler's composition are some songs and the fragment of his Piano Quartet. What is so interesting about those songs, and particularly the piano quartet, is that you can already hear that they are by Gustav Mahler. He was only seventeen years old when he wrote the piano quartet, and you can hear the kind of depression, melancholy, turbulence, yearning, and a kind of odd, ungainly awkwardness that would be lifelong characteristics of his style. The Piano Quartet climaxes with a little violin cadenza at the very end of the first movement. It is a most extraordinary passage in a very distorted gypsy mode. It bears the most striking resemblance to some of the wildest music Mahler was to write in his last symphonies, particularly the amazing *leidenschaftlich* A flat minor section that is the most daring utterance of the Ninth Symphony's first movement.

This early piece is an extraordinary example of someone who as a teenager was so in touch already with the basics of his musical language ... a musical language that was such a clear expression of tremendous loneliness and frustration. It is the true outcry of an outcast, there's no denying it. And very highly tinged with Jewish music. Music like this could have developed into entertainments for a bar mitzvah or a wedding, but instead it somehow stumbles into a very a primitive sonata form. It is all very deeply felt, but technically inexpert.

The emotional states that he yearned to express were already so vivid for him, and all were associated with one genre of music or another. This is the essence of the Mahler style – the big symphonic shapes, sonata, rondo and so on, built from miniature worlds of musical remembrances, such as folk music, Jewish music, military music, funeral music, pastoral music and sounds, like ironic cadences of the spoken voice (remembered from some specific conversation). All these bits and pieces are made into themes and counter-subjects for his life-sized epic symphonies. Of course this idea wasn't new. Much of this work had been done already, if not as daringly, by Brahms and Dvořák. It was Brahms who consistently used themes alluding to pastoral music, folk music and cabaret music as a feature of his style. It was Brahms, whose piano ballades and choral pieces (*Songs for Women's Voices, Horns and Harp* and *Gesang der Parzan*) opened up the folk and forest world with its ghost marches and all. But Brahms covered his tracks. His orchestrations and his method of working tended to disguise his sources or at least blur them. Mahler's inclination was to throw all the disparate elements of a piece into as sharp a relief as possible. It's what gives even his early music its 3D movie score quality.

Song and the First Three Symphonies

By the time Mahler came to write his first symphony he already had a nice little nest egg of songs in various forms and states of completion that would be his sources. His big cantata *Das Klagende Lied* had almost held together. It's a big hulking torso of a piece containing many beautiful things and other moments that are so clumsy.

There are even clumsy things in the first symphony itself, which is, in many ways, the most difficult Mahler symphony to perform, because it is not that well written. It is terribly awkward for the instrumentalists. They are always so exposed. The very opening, for example, where all of the strings of the orchestra must play *pianissimo* harmonics on the note 'A' from the basses right up through the violins. It's not easy to get the notes to sound properly and to have them in tune. It's meant to sound peaceful and serene. But if not perfectly played it can be as annoying as chalk scraping on a blackboard. But, never mind. It's worth doing perfectly because here Mahler finds the canvas that he's been looking for. He calls this opening sound *naturlaut* – nature sound. What it really represents is the span from horizon to horizon – the listener's acoustic space. The experience of this acoustic space is, I think, one of mankind's essential needs, as is fire. To be in the country and hear from far off someone calling, or a church bell, or a bird singing, or whatever, gives us a sense of perspective on ourselves and our relationship to the earth. It's because most people don't experience this perspective in nature any more that we are so obsessed with high-tech sound production. We substitute stereo systems for the experience of natural space, just as we substitute the light of television for the light of the fireplace. But in the First Symphony, Mahler creates his own horizon with his *naturlaut*. Now within this sound he can place all the little sounds of nature and man that he has been hearing. Then, over them all, he slowly spins out his main motifs, simply contrasting minor and major, leading us deftly into his world.

Meanwhile, whilst the audience is enjoying all of this, the musicians are in torment. The first few minutes of the piece are like walking on egg-shells. It's one of the most frightening things for an orchestra to have to play. Each one of the little bits and pieces of songs and ditties from which Mahler is weaving his symphonic design must be played with an absolute perfection of intonation, articulation, character and, above all, quietness. It's torture. But, of course, it can't sound like torture. It must sound like little sing-song motifs such as one sings to oneself while walking along. It's from the casual relaxation, the improvised mood of the music, that Mahler will build up his big symphonic form and create the emotional narrative panorama that comes from his forest, his village, and the heartbreak and sadness of his family life.

ES: *And always the deaths. All those children.*
MTT: Yes. Mahler uses music to express sorrow, but also to drive away sorrow by revealing what in nature and in life remains wondrous. So much of the First Symphony is spent exploring these two worlds of music. Most of the symphony is either tentative introduction or exultant postlude. You can really see the First Symphony itself as a kind of introduction to all those that would follow. Its somewhat rambling quality makes it, I think, the

hardest of his symphonies to conduct. To some degree, the First Symphony, and absolutely the Second and Third, follow the Romantic era's favourite symphonic format, the trail first blazed by Beethoven's Fifth Symphony, namely sorrowful minor finds its way to joyous major. This very simple but satisfying idea is carried out on a mega-scale. His basic plan becomes sonata/march, minuet, scherzo, march/rondo, with various songs introduced here and there for emotional variety. In a way, the first three symphonies are three different versions of the same piece, growing ever more assured. The joyous endings become ever more majestic, but the discursions on route to it become more extreme, more tranquil, more grotesque on their way to the Handelian cum Beethoven burn out. By the time he's finished the Third, he's just about exhausted his ideas and materials, but he's still got a few bits left over to try to use in the Fourth.

ES: *Including the original last movement – the song 'Das himmlische Leben'.*

The Second Period: Symphonies Four to Seven

MTT: Right. But that process of having to write a piece without having some enormous gripping dramatic narrative idea changed his whole work greatly. Because you get the Fourth, which is a little introduction to the second period of his writing. You could think of the Fourth as a delightful vacation sketchbook. Mahler seems at ease, trying out new combinations of counterpoint and form. Even the main themes of the piece seem more like descants or counter melodies to the symphonies that came before or will come after. The Fourth is such a gentle, Schubert-like symphony. It is many people's favourite, particularly those whose *Weltschmerz* tolerance is low. The Fourth also tries out telling new uses of a small, 'simple', but artfully placed movement in a very large piece. In fact, this symphony takes the daring step of ending with a superb little understated song, which is the first sign of the great spans of music of resignation with which Mahler will end his musical life. It is a unique challenge as a performer to approach these little movements. You finish one of the great hulking pieces that precede them with your breathing and pulse rate pounding away, and you have to calm yourself down. You have to completely reset your whole physical and emotional state so that you can approach this slow and simple music which requires total emotional commitment. It's not easy.

This is especially true in the Fifth Symphony. What a curious work. You wrestle through the first two hulking parts of it, bringing yourself to full finale fervor already at the end of the Olympian Scherzo. Then you have the

Adagietto with its apparently simple expression and of course inescapable associations with wide-screen pathos. Really, it's a salon piece like Grieg's 'Last Spring' or Debussy's *'Plus Que Lent'*. Or even Rubenstein's 'Melody in F'. But it is a perfect, transcendent salon piece, whose subtext could be, 'Ach ja, I remember, I still remember that beautiful summer such a long time ago. So many difficult things have happened in my wanderings since then, and now seeing you here I recall that time again. I suppose you must have forgotten all about it, but I just wanted you to know that I still remember that one moment that we shared, which was the most important of my life.'

I can see that I am provoking you to smile, Edward, but I assure you this ad hoc subtext that I have proposed is most effective in creating a performance. Two summers ago in Japan, I did the Adagietto with the Pacific Music Festival Orchestra and coaches from the Vienna Philharmonic. We had the hardest time getting the young musicians to play the piece with true feeling. Almost as a joke, I took them through the piece with this improvised subtext, and the instant understanding that came into their playing was amazing. We veterans also smiled, but the feeling was there. Mahler himself has a laugh on his own Adagietto in the next movement of the symphony. This funny Rondo, with its displays of virtuoso counter-point, and country bumpkin music has, as its main purpose, to bring back the Adagietto in a flirtatious and slyly playful form. There is an enormous amount of knitting of the themes and then an almost Broadway or 'That's All Folks' cartoon finale.

Then, Lord help us, comes the Sixth, the symphony I am most afraid of. It's such an unflinching statement of despair. I find it wonderful and nearly unbearable. When I perform the Sixth it wrecks my health. It is an obsessional thing. I cannot sleep. I'm awakened from sleep with my heart thumping wildly and motifs from the piece going through my mind. It totally affects my day-to-day existence. I can't eat, I can't function. It is a piece that completely takes over. It's such a powerful statement of agony and despair that it can't help but affect you in this way. And it obviously affected Mahler in that way. He too was frightened of the piece. The message of this piece, that all man's deeds, hopes and aspirations come to naught, that everything is fated to end in ruin, could really drive you around the bend. The most remarkable thing for me is that Mahler felt all of this but instead of taking up a gun to end his life, as many of his colleagues did, he took up a pen to write down as much as he could of exactly what he felt. So, although the mood of the piece is tragic, its very existence is a reaffirmation of the healing power of music, and its fundamental nature, which is to communicate. When we listen to a piece like this and hear this naked despair, we realize that we are not the only ones who have felt this way.

Of course, examination of psychological states has been a preoccupation in music, really, I suppose, since the rise of opera in the seventeenth century. Mahler, in his symphonies, was just continuing the line of investigation so daringly advanced by Wagner. He is exploring more and more all of the aching and ambivalent thoughts that are so much a part of our times. The Sixth Symphony seems to take us down the road that leads from 'wrong' to 'wronger' to 'wrongest.' By contrast, the Seventh Symphony seems to reflect the more analytical side, one might say psychoanalytical side, of musical expression. The meaning of the phrases, the emotional direction of the music, seems constantly to turn back on itself, as if it were asking, 'Did I really mean this?' It's really a schizophrenic piece, intellectually more advanced than anything else Mahler ever did, but absolutely nuts. There is a real 'mad-scientist' aspect to lots of it. And as for the Finale, it poses maybe the greatest challenge to maintain coherency that the performer faces in any of the standard repertoire. Performing it makes you feel as if you are trapped inside a video-game. There are so many starts and stops, changes of direction, profound and utterly trivial ideas, alternating in what is at first a completely bewildering way. It seems as if Mahler is toying with us, enjoying telling us with a slightly malicious sneer, 'And now for something completely different!'

ES: *So how do you really feel about the black sheep of the family, this Seventh Symphony?*

The Black Sheep

MTT: It's so odd with the Seventh, which I really like so much. I'm just now entering on this point of Seventh Symphony-itis. I remember seeing this expression come over Klemperer's face, Steinberg's face, Bernstein's face – all them thinking, 'Oh yes, the Seventh Symphony, it's so great, now at last I see how I can make it work. It's really the greatest piece, and I see how it can be done.' I've seen this come over many conductors' faces, and now, God help me, I look in the mirror and see that same expression on my face!

ES: *It's a very original sounding piece though. I always look at it in terms of pure music rather than in the light of associations I usually get from Mahler; there are fewer of them in the Seventh.*

MTT: But it does have references to cabaret music, Bulgarian music, almost

With William Steinberg, 1974

Mikado sounding music. It reflects all the places he was travelling to. But, as I said, it's a symphony I would call the 'psychoanalysis symphony', because it continuously second-guesses itself. So much goes off into these speculative passages that make one ask, 'Which direction are we really going in? and is this really a happy ending or is it a sad ending?, or maybe I just thought it was sad. Maybe it was neither happy nor sad. What does it all mean anyway?' All we know for sure is that Mahler is struggling in this symphony with the same issues that were tormenting him in his own life. He called it *Song of the Night*, but maybe it should really be the 'Insomnia Symphony'. 'Oh God, I'm up all night again wrestling with these same problems. I don't know what the answer may be.'

The Third Period: Symphonies Eight and Nine, and *Das Lied von der Erde*

The Eighth, although written for much larger forces, is actually musically a good deal simpler than the Seventh.

ES: *Yes, I actually see it as a wholesale return to the* Wunderhorn *world.*
MTT: That's right. The Eighth, *Das Lied* and the Ninth return to the *Wunderhorn* world, to the world of simple themes coming out of the old *naturlaut*. But, of course, Mahler now has a vastly greater developmental

technique. This can be seen in the way the whole amazing Ninth Symphony is unified by the simplest little motives, such as occur in the most familiar and naive music. For example, a simple descending *appoggiatura*, just two notes, one lower than the other, is made into the first movement's opening lullaby, the second movement's waltz, the third movement's jeering parody, and the forth movement's heartfelt hymn.

Even more astonishing is Mahler's use of the other unifying theme of this symphony, a simple little musical ornament called a 'turn'. This had been used by Viennese musical pastry chefs for over a hundred years to dress up their confectionery compositions, but Mahler's use of it is far more than decorative. In the first movement he uses this motif just once, at the very climax of the movement. In the second movement it becomes the end of one of the waltzes. In the Burlesque movement it is presented as a theme in its own right, first transmogrified and then transfigured. And then, in the last movement, little by little, it becomes the most emotionally telling theme in the entire symphony. In fact, it is the very last notes of the entire work. Mahler conceived a piece that would last ninety minutes in which a musical motif heard only once in the first movement could gradually, almost geologically, emerge as the central, urgent idea. This is a level of musical technique which very few composers have possessed, and which Mahler learned during the part of his life when he was composing those difficult middle symphonies, the Fourth, Fifth, Sixth and Seventh.

Letting It All Out

ES: *As far as the performing of Mahler is concerned, style is so crucial – getting players to lose their inhibitions and take those extremes. How do you prepare an orchestra for that?*

MTT: Well, if I'm working with an orchestra I've never done any Mahler with before I say, 'Look, you must remember this piece is a portrait of a whole person's psyche, of everything, and that in this piece, at some time or another, we are going to have to play in the loudest, the quietest, the shortest, the longest, the most acerbic and aggressive, the most tender and caressing way – the entire spectrum will have to be there in its most heightened sense. There will also have to be times when things will change abruptly and terrifyingly, and at times things will need to move at an almost geological, scarcely perceptible, inexorable pace. And all of this happens in the course of this one piece. We have to be very clear about what exactly we need to do at any particular moment in the piece.'

It's easy for the conductor to understand this, but much more difficult for a member of the orchestra. Perhaps you are a wind player, a second oboist, and you are struggling to play a low B *legato pianissimo*. Right behind you there's a gang of clarinets and bassoons playing as *fortissimo*, *staccato* and generally over-the-top as they can. Next to them are horns giving out distorted hunting calls of all sorts. Quite naturally you want to play with the colleagues surrounding you, but very specifically the composer is saying, 'Don't you do this, don't you get louder, whatever happens all around you, you must stick to your own part.' Or perhaps just the reverse, everyone around you is playing very quietly and you have to perform some outrageous, loud, grotesque shriek. It is quite scary having to do that. You have to be totally certain it is what the composer really wants you to do.

ES: *Can the extremes ever be too extreme in Mahler?*
MTT: Well yes, because there is a large scheme of priorities involved. For example, taking the performance of the Mahler Ninth we just did, one or two of your colleagues wrote very nice things about the performance, but one said, 'Well, the first movement was fantastic, the third movement was astoundingly vicious, and the last movement was fine. However, the second movement wasn't quite as characterful, aggressive, biting.' Actually that was quite a conscious decision on my part, because I felt that if the second movement of the Mahler Ninth (one of those big *ländler* waltz movements) is done too aggressively, too grotesquely, and if the *fortissimos* and the accents are too much exaggerated, then there is no place to go in the third movement. Now it is true that the second movement functions in the symphony as would a *scherzo*, but the third movement is called the Rondo-Burlesque. You have to leave room so that the Burlesque can really be completely crazed, completely grotesque, completely aggressive, completely mad.

ES: *Yes, there's also this idea of geniality going sour, isn't there? There's a lot of charm in that music but it's always bordering on collapse.*

Mahler the Jew

MTT: I remember when someone gave Leonard Bernstein a book called *Tunes of the Viennese Ghetto*. It turns out that the opening theme of the third movement of Mahler's Ninth was based on an actual tune sung by Jews in the ghetto. Mahler, as was his wont, took this little tune and made it into a colossal construction. But what's so searing about the third movement is that it is a representation by Mahler of the way he believes his enemies think of him. It is a monstrous self-portrait, in which he is saying, 'This is what they think of me, this is how they imagine me to be, this crazed, obsessive, grotesque, hard person.'

Cartoon satirizing the instrumentation of Mahler's Sixth Symphony

ES: *There was that wonderful caricature cartoon of the Sixth Symphony, a crazed Mahler blasting his unsuspecting public with motor horns and the like ...*
MTT: Oh yes. But you also have to remember that during the time he was writing the Ninth Symphony, everybody knew he was very ill. There were debates in the papers concerning whether or not the 'Jew Mahler' should be allowed to be buried in the honorary cemetery next to Brahms and Beethoven. Anti-Semitic writers railed against it. And there were horrible caricatures of him lying on his deathbed writing crazy music. This is what the man was enduring. So, in response, he wrote the Burlesque movement, which is a biting satire first of the little Jewish tune, but also of other Viennese music. 'Radetzky March' and *Fledermaus* are all over it, but in the most warped way. And then this little tune that I mentioned before, based around an ornament, is introduced in this wheedling, transmogrified, horrible way. There is this great crash of cymbals, and suddenly it all clears away, and in that wonderful middle section we hear the same notes, the same shape of the same tune, but now it's as if he's saying, 'But this is how I really am inside. What I really am feeling inside is a warm yearning need to make

music and communicate with you. Why can't you hear this? Can't you understand? Can't you meet me halfway, somehow?' It is all so heart-on-the-sleeve, but so perfect. Then the orchestra has a few moments of embarrassed twitching before the grotesque parody resumes in all-out savagery.

ES: *Yes. You get that terrible mocking from the clarinets – derisive, just turning the thing around. But the idea that he should compose his own mockery ...*
MTT: That is extraordinary. Perhaps unique. In painting I can think of painters such as Goya and Picasso who have done self-portraits that present themselves in not the most flattering light. But musically I'm not sure that any other composer has.

Why the Big Sleep?

But coming back to what you were asking right at the beginning, about why people didn't take up this music earlier – it's because it was too honest. It was so frank, nothing was disguised, nothing. It was a spiritual testimony, it was an outcrying for understanding, for justice, for love. It was absolutely undisguised, even in the way the orchestra was meant to play. Mahler wanted his orchestra to sing, but he also wanted it to speak, whisper and bellow. Consider the number of *vorschlags*, the grace notes that precede the beats in the string parts. These are meant to represent the breaking of the voice or the spitting out of a rough group of consonants. The compulsive use of this device coupled with the use of the instruments and the wild extremes of their registers and the most bizarre dynamics, causing the orchestra to howl and rage and whimper and carry on histrionically like the most crazed melodramatic performer, was not what the world of serious symphonic classical music lovers was expecting at all. Perhaps his music was too tied to his highly imaginative specifications of the nuance of performance. Certainly his obssessiveness as a conductor is well documented. His rehearsals were long, demanding and emotionally exhausting. It is clear that he must have demanded the same range of colour and expression for his interpretations of Beethoven, Wagner, all the other masters, as he did for his own music. He certainly was a taskmaster. I was shocked as a teenager in Los Angeles to hear the hostility retired members of the New York Philharmonic still felt towards him more than fifty years later. He had no patience with complacency on the part of performer or listener. You had to accept his whole musical world in one big piece. Parts of it were, of course, even on first hearing, so beautiful. But other parts, for the audience of his day, seemed like the incarnation of ugliness.

ES: *Well, the critics of the time refer to 'these ugly sounds' ...*

MTT: I think the melodrama aspect is very apt. You can imagine an actor on stage, ranting and bellowing and weeping and collapsing, and going through a whole enormous exhibition . . . birth, life, death, resurrection in a single performance. And then, imagine all that transferred into an orchestral composition. It was so honest. It was like psychotherapy. It was his therapy. He was writing all of these terribly painful things that he felt, and putting them right out there on the stage. Not just the notes, not just references to them, not the way in which Brahms says, 'I have an old story to tell you, it's a very old and sad story, and I want to tell it to you so you understand that I do not want to lose my control. I do not want to be weeping or blubbering in my beard, so I'm going to tell it to you with a certain coolness, a certain reserve.' On the contrary, Mahler is saying, 'I hold nothing in reserve. This is exactly how horrible, how exalted it feels.' It was desperate, and it was just too much at first for most people to take.

ES: *You hit upon something else there, when you were talking about melodramatics and the stage. I sometimes wonder whether these great symphonies were really surrogate operas.*

Influences on Mahler

MTT: If not opera, then surely music-drama, musical-panorama, or music-epic. On another level it was musical, social criticism. Of course, this side of the music, as I mentioned earlier, came from the radical side of Brahms's work, because Brahms was in many ways a very radical composer. It is in Brahms's symphonies that we find all of these references to other kinds of music, in which various themes, the subjects of the work or the developmental processes of the work, refer to all kinds of other music.

ES: *On your score of Brahms's Second Symphony you have all these notes ...*
MTT: Which say, 'This work points towards a Brahms concept.' The warm and the cool, the extrovert and the introvert; starting from a position of introversion and then, suddenly, outbursts of extroverted utterance. Making a plan for a symphony. This is the form of the symphony; and then making a drama out of either carrying through the plan, or breaking the plan, or losing one's way, or dawdling or becoming impatient, or whatever. The formal process is made to have drama. All this Mahler picked up on.

But, even more, the fact that in the course of a Brahms symphony you will have references to dance music, cabaret music, organ music, pastoral music, Hungarian music, Bach, Beethoven, Schubert, folk music of all sorts, ballads, reflections of moments in time such as *intermezzos*. And what Brahms does with all of his references to these musics is sort of smooth them over, so it all fits nicely into the well-formed and dignified utterance that he wants to make. And of course Mahler does just the opposite. He puts in every raw edge, every sharp contrast. He disjoints changes – it's all there. And nonetheless this mood, this kind of bardic, story-telling, hanging-in-space mood – a lot of that came from Bruckner, but a lot of it also came from Brahms. Pieces like the first Brahms Ballad, which Brahms refers to again and again. His music has this great, vast, almost movie music kind of sound that Mahler used.

And, for that matter, he used Brahms's harmonic language. I think the piece that I hear right through all of Mahler's symphonies is Brahms's Lullaby, which is another great similarity of course, because Brahms was primarily a song composer. What we hear in the symphonies, what we hear in the concerti, is the sort of music which is distilled from moments that come from songs. So this was again Mahler's plan, he had the same way of working. But the melody of Brahms's Lullaby is again one in which there is an oscillating, hovering minor third in the basses, and then it goes up to the sixth and plays with those, 'Oh! Is it happy, is it sad, is it sad, is it happy?' changes of perception that occur in that situation. And of course Mahler even quoted the Brahms's Lullaby extensively in the bass line of the second movement of the Ninth.

ES: *That's something I'd never heard before you pointed it out. I can well believe that you only hear these things when you have to play every note on the piano.*
MTT: But Brahms had not very much use for the one piece of Mahler's that he heard. He heard *Klagende Lied* or something, didn't he?

ES: *At the big competition. The Beethoven Prize, wasn't it? They gave it to someone else.*
MTT: Sure. 'Get a hold of yourself, young man!'

ES: *Absolutely! Hans von Bulow said, when he played through 'Todtenfeier' – the first movement of the Second Symphony-to-be – 'This makes* Tristan und Isolde *sound like a Haydn symphony.'*

The Eighth

MTT: I hope to do it staged. I think it cries out for staging. It should be an enormous pageant.

ES: *Are you going to fly in the* Mater Gloriosa?
MTT: Absolutely! But let's talk about Eight. I love Eight. A lot of people don't like it. I love it because it has such humour. True, it has immense pathos, but it also has tremendous humour, especially in the second movement. It's a difficult piece to shape because, of course, the first movement is like an enormous rush of jubilation. A great gasp is what it actually is. A kind of twenty-minute long 'aaaaaaaahhhhhh', and then suddenly it's over. In the course of this amazing first movement, *Veni Creator Spiritus*, it's interesting to note that at the recapitulation of this movement, where there is a rolling river of accumulating quavers and semi-quavers, you have a big almost-Handelian choral build-up, but blown up to enormous size, and it rushes forward, and then we come to the *Veni, Veni Creator Spiritus*, repeated. Now, every conductor I've ever heard do this piece makes a big *rallentando*.

ES: *Tennstedt and Bernstein with a vengeance ... But – I know what you're going to say – no* rallentando *is marked ...*
MTT: *Yes.* But perhaps even more curiously, it doesn't say '*Nicht ritenuto*' either. Such was Mahler's nature that he often wrote cautionary statements for the conductor, saying, 'Whatever happens, make sure you do this,' or 'Whatever happens, make sure you don't do this.' And so this would have been a very logical place for him to say, 'Don't go slower.' But he doesn't say that. He doesn't say anything. Very puzzling.

ES: *It's interesting that you should bring this up because I've written many reviews about this piece, and I've always been struck by this huge moment. I think it needs a big* rallentando.
MTT: I don't.

ES: *I could see you were working up to this!*
MTT: You know what I do? I go right in tempo to the *Veni*, and then on the second Veni I make a big hold, a big *fermata*. I like this better, because then you get the full effect of this great sweep going straight into the climax. Everyone takes an enormous breath, and then at the high note, which is a sensible place to make a *tenuto*, you have a *fermata* climax. The last

movement is so huge it is difficult to take in all of its details. Or, perhaps because of its details it is difficult to perceive its real shape. I remember how my fingers used to ache playing it on the piano, turning page after page that seemed to never end. But the main point of this movement is something so simple and yet so powerfully symbolic. At one evanescent moment the spirit, formerly known as Gretchen (Faust's betrayed love) sees Faust's spirit ascending into heaven. With casual grace, she sings this wonderful text:

Die früh Geliebte,
Nicht mehr Getrübte,
Er kommt zurück.

My first beloved,
Now no longer troubled,
Comes back.

Then we are off into something else. Everybody is singing, 'My first beloved, now no longer troubled, comes back, he comes back, he comes back.' And then we're off into something else. And everybody's singing, philosophers and saints and sages and angel choirs − everybody's got something to say. But the little tune she sings has only one set of words associated with it, 'My first beloved, now no longer troubled, comes back, he comes back, he comes back.' And then at the climax of the whole piece, everybody's singing full out about the Mater Gloriosa and the whole design of the universe, this adoration of the Virgin, the Eternal Feminine, whoever she is. The cosmos is united in song. And at exactly this moment, horns and trombones blare out that formerly tremulous tune, 'My first beloved, now no longer troubled, comes back.' Mahler set this up so you would have no other associations for this tune, but just those words. And what this moment in the music is saying is that somehow, the joy and the love of one simple person are equal to, as important as, the whole design of the universe. That is the point of the piece.

Of course, on the way to this incredible mystical fusion, there are so many digressions in all manner of moods, some angry, some wistful, representing the meandering way up the mountain of salvation. And some of these episodes are really quite amusing, like the Three Penitent Ladies, who are in Heaven, nostalgically recalling their forty years of penitence in the desert. The music evokes a nostalgic chatty mood ... Well yes, Heaven's nice but there's nothing like those days of bread and water out in the Sinai

Desert.' He's caught that aspect of it he's caught so wonderfully. It would be so easy to turn that into another very dark and tragic utterance, but he's set it as a kind of café clutch of ladies, saying, 'Oh, yes, wasn't it fun? Loved the jackals. They used to come round at night, sniffing around my cell. They were so charming. I made friends with several of them.' His dramatic imagination is just marvellous. He could probably have written a wonderful comic opera. You'd first think of him writing a tragedy piece, but if he'd had a libretto like *Rosenkavalier* it could have been delicious. He certainly had it in him to do it.

So, you see, in this last movement, because it is so vast and the forces are so huge it's terribly easy to get bogged down. I think most people have problems with Mahler's Eighth because it gets bogged down. In spite of the grandiosity, the discursiveness, you just have to say, 'I must keep going, I must keep it on track.'

I was responsible for one of the most bogged-down performances ever given of the Mahler Eighth, although it was not my fault. The performance took place in the Hollywood Bowl. It was with the Los Angeles Philharmonic and the Summer Institute student orchestra, which meant the orchestra was around 250. With the added choral forces, it made a colossal gathering.

We did the first movement and all was well. I started the second movement – this hushed, depressed, morning-after, can-I-pick-myself-off-the-floor mood – and suddenly I heard a humming, a kind of buzzing and humming. At first I ignored it, and then I began to recognize that it was the sound of a helicopter. Then it became clear that the helicopter was circling, because of course from the air at night the Hollywood Bowl with this whole force laid out there must be quite a sight to see. It started to circle, and it made smaller and smaller circles. The helicopter noise got louder and louder just as the orchestra was playing this most quiet music. Then came the first big agonized climax. We're supposed to have the men of the choirs whisper, very quietly. But the helicopter was closer than ever – this horrible, deafening drone. I'm thinking, 'I cannot believe this, what am I supposed to do?' Suddenly, something snapped. I suppose it was all my frustration of years of doing outdoor concerts, which really is a curse laid upon mankind by I don't know whom. Something just snapped in my brain, and I yelled out, '*Basta cosi!*' I broke my baton, threw it down and walked off the stage.

Imagine. The Hollywood Bowl. The stage packed with many hundreds of musicians and singers and an audience of eighteen thousand. As I walked off I looked up and the expression on everyone's face in the orchestra and choir was really extraordinary. It was just like, 'What in God's name is going to happen?' Staff members were running from all directions saying, 'What are we going to do? Call the civil air patrol. Tell the audience not to leave. Who the hell is up there anyway?' Through all this the helicopter continued to circle.

It took about a quarter of an hour for them to locate, through air control, whose helicopter it was. It turned out that the helicopter belonged to the police department of a Los Angeles suburb who had taken possession of it only the day before. In spite of all the rulings forbidding any aircraft from going any where near the Bowl during a performance, there they were, up in their helicopter, joy riding and taking in the view. When asked why they were violating the Bowl's air space they said that they were pursuing a suspect who was known to be at large in Los Angeles and who was a great fan of classical music! Only when we threatened them with paying the overtime charges for the entire ensemble did they beat a hasty retreat and buzz off.

Half an hour later I came back on to the stage to huge applause from the audience who had had suffered years of frustration from having beautiful music obliterated in the Hollywood Bowl by noises. We started from the beginning of the second movement and went through to the end. It turned out to be quite a wonderful performance, but I suppose I was the cause of perhaps the most protracted Mahler's Eighth ever done!

Mahler's Eighth, Hollywood Bowl, 1985

Part Four

Recording session of *Ein Heldenleben*, 1988

On Recording

Is Recording Different from Live Concerts?

ES: *Do you view recording as a completely different experience from actually perform-*
ing that music in a concert? Is the process so very different?

MTT: Yes, it is a different experience. Of course, some of the elements are
the same – the music, the performers – but nothing else is. It is like making
a movie of what was originally a stage play. The microphones, the studio,
the absence of a live audience, the quest for perfection (which is, of course, a
reflection of the high-tech side of it all), these things create an entirely different atmosphere, perspective and priorities for the musician. When you
play for an audience, your goal is communication. You can feel the electrici-
ty in the air, the depth of the audience's concentration, the sense of whether
the music is going over or not. But in the studio, you can find yourself in a
very empty clinical space, where little problems that in concert would never
bother you can become so magnified that the joy of music making can disappear. The tension can mount, and all at once you feel you are no longer in
a music hall, but rather in a torture chamber or a padded cell. It can be
quite a Sisyphean task. The most difficult thing in performing music is to
be actually able to hear what you are playing, to really sense the quality of
what is coming across. The music may feel one way under your fingers and
sound quite another. Performing, after all, is the art of creating illusion.
You want the audience to perceive the music in a particular way, and you
must do whatever is necessary to create that perception. It's what I call the
Parthenon question.

When you look at the Parthenon the columns appear absolutely straight
up and down, and all equidistant. But in fact they are not, the columns are
angled. We know, in fact, that every single dimension of the Parthenon has
been altered in order to create the illusion of perfection. It is exactly the
same in music. Yes, you want to create the illusion that everything is
absolutely even – absolutely rhythmically perfect – although that probably
means that you distort the rhythm slightly by holding the tempo back a
little, so creating moments of silence measured in thousandths of seconds

that go in between the ictus, the attack of the notes. Or you may slightly accent the notes on the beat, or perhaps emphasize patterns of notes lying between the main beats in a heightened way. All this to create the illusion that it's exactly in tempo, which, of course, it is not. The whole sense of sound, how quickly or slowly it begins – the length of the breaths of the phrases – these are just some of the artifices that you use to create a certain mood. That's what happens in a live performance. You create illusion using your ears as a guide.

Now when you are recording, you have the orchestra in an artificially arranged configuration, usually in a studio, town hall, or generic large live space. Immediately everything that you hear is quite different. It is not at all the sound that you have gotten used to in the rehearsals and performances. You have to find it anew. Of course, you are not starting from scratch, but still, it is quite tricky since the space and layout of the orchestra are meant to make the music sound good, not to you necessarily, but to the microphones. The musicians are much further apart, to help, in theory, get greater separation and individual brilliance. Of course, this makes it harder for them to hear one another and harder for me to know how it is really sounding.

There will be many microphones. Two or three main microphones are grouped somewhere around the conductor, and a quite variable number of spot or solo microphones are scattered throughout the orchestra. The number of these microphones depends on the style and philosophy of the record company and of the producer and engineering team on those sessions. I always think of the microphones as cameras. They give you wide shots, close ups, long shots, diffused shots. Each kind of microphone, like different lenses of a camera, gives another quality to the sound. The final sound of the record comes from the mix of the signals from all these mikes, either at the session, or later in an editing room. It is always essential for the conductor to come to an understanding with the producer as to what the sound will be. You run through a section, and then you must go listen to it to find out how the mikes are taking it. It is always a total surprise. It usually takes several tries to get it right. After you have worked out the quality of the sound you can then go back in the studio and start to make music, using your now informed ears to guess how the mikes are perceiving what you are hearing.

All of these questions of how the music should sound on disc reflect the drive of fashion and the merchandizing of recordings. People like to sense a breadth of sound in recording. That's what sells records, you know. There is a feeling of lush, slightly over-upholstered luxuriance to most of the records we listen to. One can delight in that, sure, but it can be exaggerated. I think that film music has had an influence on the way we hear recordings. Film music was a sort of caricature of the music of composers such as Strauss, Mahler, Debussy, Mussorgsky. It was recorded in a way which was absolutely as grandiose, wide and luxuriant as it could possibly be. It is our old primitive need for vast acoustic space reasserting itself.

But when you come back to recording the original music on which the film music was based, in the audiophiles' imagination the sort of sound it should have is that of film music. When they hear *Heldenleben*, they want to hear that super wide-screen sound, giant banks of speakers, big studio sound. And the recording I quite enjoyed making that way was a recording with the LSO of *Heldenleben*, which was fun, in that we decided from the beginning that we were going to make that kind of recording. We were going to use the technology to make a very, very lush sound, and use spot mikes to highlight the perspective of the overall microphones. We said, 'This is that sort of piece, and this is what we're going to do.'

ES: *Do you approach each kind of repertoire with your producer and engineers in a different way, according to the nature of the piece?*
MTT: I have done so, and I'd like to be able to do that more. I like to have contact and to plan with the recording team from the very beginning. 'This is a particular piece, and we are now going to treat it in this way.' There are all kinds of techniques in recording. I really do believe it is a completely separate thing from performing.

ES: *You wouldn't just want to re-create an all-purpose concert hall balance?*
MTT: If we had the luxury of recording *in situ* in the hall in which we perform, yes. I actually like to record live because so often the live performances are better than the recorded ones. Live performances can be taken, and then patched, that is, corrected. Many of the recordings that I love the most are recordings made in the early days when they were done live, or virtually live. They have something about them. Who cares if you hear a page turn, or a cough, or somebody plays one wrong note, it doesn't really matter. There's something in the body of the performance. The only performance of *Das Lied von der Erde* to listen to is still Ferrier, Patzak and Walter, which has innumerable things 'wrong' with it – but who cares? That's a real performance.

ES: *Yes, a classic. There's no substitute for the presence of an audience.*
MTT: That's right. When you make a recording, you win some, you lose

some, and you really can't know when you start out which way it's going to be. You could have just given the greatest performances ever in the concert hall, and you go into the studio and suddenly nothing works at all. That is when you really rely on your colleagues' patience and professionalism to pull it out of the fire. It can be very hard. I've had the experience of doing a wonderful performance of a major piece of repertoire – and then going into a recording hall where certain people in the orchestra were too far from other sections, or certain sections of the orchestra were too far apart, or part of the sections were too close to a particular surface, which produced an artificial echo. In the end it was all but impossible to record the piece. It had to be done in such tiny little fragments that I left the studio not having any idea at all of what it was we had accomplished. I would never agree to have a recording released that was made under those circumstances.

ES: *You've recently set down three of the most difficult pieces imaginable. I mean the two Debussy pieces,* Jeux *and* Le martyre de St Sébastien, *and Stravinsky's* Symphony in C.
MTT: Yes, and these three experiences were some of the most pleasurable I have ever had. The LSO was in top form, the concerts went wonderfully and the studios we used were perfectly chosen for the different works: Abbey Road for the brittle Stravinsky and highly detailed *Jeux*, and Tooting for the expansive *Martyre*. Tooting is actually a church and choral

With Sylvia McNair, recording *Le martyre de St Sébastien*, 1991

music sounds great there. The Sony recording team was able to get great solo sounds of bass harmonics and low harp noises, as well as the huge grandiose sections. The only frustrating thing was that the church is not very sound-proof. There is always a motor bike going by or kids in the neighbourhood playing football. *Martyre* is a piece all about extreme quietness and lots of profound silences. We constantly had to be on the alert for noises from outside getting into the recording. It can be quite maddening to have an absolutely wonderful take spoiled by a plane making an approach to Heathrow or an ambulance wailing blocks away. But the end result was really worth it. In fact, the silence of the CD format gives a whole dimension and importance to this work. The silences themselves have a depth and expression that seems to draw the fragments of the piece together. It is awesome, and I never say that about my own records. What, never? Well, hardly ever.

Serendipity and the *Fountains of Rome*

But let me give you a classic example of the way a recording can work. I was recording some Respighi pieces in Los Angeles, the Rome pieces, for which I have great affection. I know they're totally over the top and out of fashion now, but, you know, they'll come back. At the end of the first movement of the *Fountains of Rome*, there's a little epilogue. The idea is that the flute plays the tune twice in a very quiet misty way, and at the end of each flute phrase there is a punctuation, a little two-note fanfare (ta-ta!). The first time it's played by the first harp and first horn, and the second time it's second harp and third horn.

So this is what happens at the session: the flute finishes his phrase, and the first horn and first harp play quite crisply a two-note fanfare punctuation – 'ta-ta'. Lovely. The flutist then plays his second phrase, and then the second harp and the third horn, because of reasons we won't go into here, absolutely cannot play their two notes together. Instead of a nice quiet 'ta-ta', we hear a disorganized clattering mess. Fine, so we do a re-take. It's a recording, you go back, so that you can patch it. We do a re-take. We do another re-take. We do yet another re-take. We make nine or ten attempts to get this second harp, third horn bit together. It doesn't work. At a certain point the producer has to step in and tell us we must move on to something else. The clock is ticking. The money is running out.

It's a great comfort, by the way, as a performer in the studio, to develop a relationship with a producer you really trust, so that you can totally release yourself to performing and not have to be thinking about cosmetic issues, or laundry lists or glitches. The producer must stay very alert because it can be that an otherwise great take is flawed by some small noise or glitch that may be very obvious on a particular mike, but in the boomy obscurity of the studio is inaudible. Steve Epstein, one of my oldest friends, and a great producer, was making this particular record, and he said, 'Right, we have to go on. We've tried nine times, we have all the rest, we'll work around it. If we have time we'll come back to it.' Famous last words. The record is finally edited. They use the take where the flute plays his first phrase crisply and quietly, punctuated by the fanfare of the first harp and first horn. No problem. For the second phrase, since it was impossible to get the second harp and the third horn together, the producer relies on the device of cutting out the main microphones entirely and shifting to the ambient microphones. These microphones are so far away from the orchestra they produce a vague wash of atmospheric sound. So, after the first phrase we have a perfect close up little fanfare. Then, after the second phrase, we have a vague, wispy echo which disguises the inaccuracy of the take.

So, fine, that's the way it is, we leave it. The record comes out and the reviews appear. One of the most prestigious record magazine says, 'This performance of Respighi's *Rome* pieces is a most insightful and interestingly coloured and inflected performance ... Even with Toscanini you don't hear anything like this. To cite only one of the masterful touches, there is a moment at the end of the first movement where Tilson Thomas has made the first harp and horn so crisp and clear, and then comes this wonderful distant *sfumato* effect ...'

You just don't know. You just don't know when something like that is going to happen, or if it's going to be an absolute catastrophe – there's no way of knowing.

ES: *You get people writing in to* Gramophone *all the time, saying, 'You'd think they could have got this right, you'd think this could have been better,' so on. What they don't realize is that there are the same restrictions, the same pressures on one's time in a studio situation as there would be anywhere else. There are only so many things you can do in one recording session.*

MTT: It's true. It's very frustrating to do things in little bits. It's far better to do it in longer takes, and then to do small patches. The first producer that I worked with extensively was a very interesting man named Rainer Brock, who was a classmate of Claudio Abbado's in Swarowsky's conducting course. He had an absolutely brilliant mind, deeply loved music and was immensely knowledgeable. He was a fantastic colleague for a young artist. He was the producer who made all my very first records with Deutsche

Gramophone. Because he let me just perform, I could conduct absolutely freely, as I would in a performance. Then he would quietly say, 'We have this, but we don't have the third bar after G, we need just these two bars.' I could completely rely on him. Since that time I have had the good fortune to work with outstanding producers, but always I find that I must keep my own critical faculties quite active, even while performing. I imagine the score in my mind, and, as I am listening to the performance, whenever I hear a bar really well played, I mentally cross it out. When all the bars have been crossed out, I know that the recording has been accomplished. It is quite a balancing act to maintain these two faculties at once – the performing spontaneity and the critical observation.

The Role of Technology

While we were recording Debussy's *Jeux*, you heard me say to the producer, 'I'm going to fool around with multi-track on this one.' Because there we had one wonderful take; but for two bars someplace the *mezzo forte* in the trombones was just too much into the main mikes compared to the second piccolo, second harp and lower divisi violas, which are supposed to have the lead line. It would be so silly to go back and do an entirely new take for that, when it's possible with multi-track to make a minor re-adjustment with balance. It can be done only to a minor degree, because otherwise it really does sound ridiculous. There are record companies who have actually made a lot of money making rather ridiculous recordings. There are recordings of Mahler symphonies, for example, where you have an entire string orchestra playing a *furioso forte tremolo*, and somehow in the middle of it you can hear a bass clarinet, absolutely as if it were surgically implanted in your sternum.

ES: *Well, this is back to the question of how far one is prepared to allow technology to create the illusion. If it serves the piece, or if you can achieve a balance on a record that you could never possibly achieve in the concert hall, then it is valid, I suppose?*
MTT: It could be valid. The good thing about recording is that it has allowed us to hear so much music and have access to so much music. But the danger is that it has reinforced people's natural tendency to have a conservative viewpoint towards an original conception of a piece, an original interpretative idea.

Why Recordings Are Dangerous

The classical music audience, to a great degree, is like a wonderful child ... a child who is deeply devoted to a particular nursery rhyme or fairy-tale, and always wants to hear the same story told in exactly the same way. You know the experience of reading a story to a child. You're trying to read *Goldilocks and the Three Bears*, and it's getting late and you think, 'Well, I'll just leave out the bit about the bowls of porridge this time.' But they won't have it. They want every single detail of the story, the same presentation, the way they've always heard it before. There's a very strong part of the classical music audience which is just like that. They want to hear the same pieces, done the same way every time – and very often the way they want to hear them is the way they've heard them on their gramophone recordings, probably because they've heard that performance more than any other. They've got used to it ... not only the tempi, not only the dynamics, but the general perspective of it. Then they go to a live performance, and they think, 'Well, this isn't like what I hear at home, this is rather disappointing, it's not right, I'm not happy.' So in a way I think the best thing for music would be if there were records which would self-destruct after five playings. And maybe there would be some licensing system whereby if you had previously bought the Haitink performance of Mahler's Sixth, you'd be obliged next time to buy the Bernstein, and then you'd have to have the Solti one, or whatever. At least it would give you the correct idea, which is that there are many views of these pieces.

Actually, what will probably happen in the future is that we'll come to a point where, through telephone lines or fibre optic cable systems, we'll be able to access a performance by anyone in the world, instantaneously. That might very well change lots of things about the music business.

ES: *It's frightening that there are actually some people who only ever listen to recorded music; and when you ask them, 'Why do you not go and listen to live music?' they say, 'Because it's always such a disappointment.'*
MTT: Yes, it is frightening, but it's common. We feel this so powerfully here in London because we don't have proper venues to listen to music. If you listen to a concert in the Musikverein in Vienna, or if you listen to a concert in the Teatro Colon in Buenos Aires, I assure you that you do not experience the sense of alienation which it is possible to have in some other halls. At a live performance you're supposed to have a sense of immediacy and excitement, but in some venues this is completely impossible. It's just that, for whatever reasons, the models of great concert halls were arrogantly

abandoned by acousticians. I think they take a course of study, and at the end of it decide whether they want a degree in economics or in acoustics – both subjects seem to me to be so utterly unpredictable, imprecise and unreliable.

Tilson Thomas's Recordings

ES: *How do you view your own recorded legacy? Does it worry you that in five years time you might feel quite differently about a piece, and your old view will still be circulating?*
MTT: I'm happy about some of them, and I have a few pirate ones too, which I find amusing.

ES: *Of your concerts?*
MTT: Yes. I didn't make them, but they're out there, and I do find those amusing. Almost all of them are of live performances. You see, in the United States nearly all of the major orchestras record their performances, edit them a little bit, and then release them as radio broadcasts. So there's a whole network of people across the United States who record those broadcasts and then issue them as privately circulated tapes or LPs. Now there may be pirate CDs about. There is a performance I did years back of the *Symphonie Fantastique* with the Cleveland Orchestra, which is still around. That's quite thrilling. It's fun.

ES: *Do you have favourite recordings among those you've made?*
MTT: Well, the *Sacre* I did with the Boston Symphony I like very much. Also the Tchaikovsky First. And some of the Debussy I did at that time. I like the Gershwin record I made in Los Angeles, which includes both rhapsodies for piano. I love the record of Gershwin Sarah Vaughan and I made together. What an astonishingly new experience to work with such an intuitive genius. I do like the *La Mer* recording I did with the Philharmonia, and the *Heldenleben* with the LSO. The Mahler Third – I like lots of that too. Also the Brahms First Serenade with the LSO, the Glagolitic Mass, and, of course *Le martyre de St Sébastien*. I'm also fond of the first recording I made with the New World Symphony, *Tangazo*.

ES: *The Debussy* Images *with the Boston Symphony is very fine, though it's also very 'microphoned'.*
MTT: Mmm ... That was the style at that period. But it really was a remarkable experience because, of course, I love those pieces, and I had my

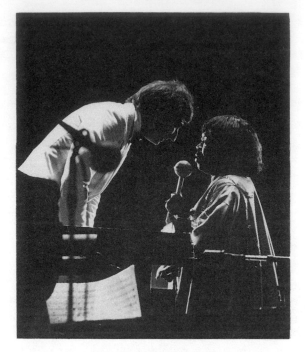

With Sarah Vaughan, 1982

own perspective on them. I was working with the Boston Symphony, and at that particular point it was filled with people who had a lifetime of working with Koussevitzky and Munch and Monteux, and who were, a lot of them, in their late sixties, and still in great shape. So the whole sense of tradition in that music, coupled with my youthful enthusiasm, was a very good match. In the same way that, for example, Horenstein and the LSO was a very good match. Horenstein, you know, was old, expansive and mystical, and the LSO at that point was very young, hard-edged and tough – it was a very good combination.

Composing the Recording

There are certain moments when for a particular piece a particularly favourable situation happens. I keep coming back to cinema. We know that lots of the great classic movies, like *Casablanca*, were really made almost by accident. No one was quite sure what character they were meant to be playing, or who was shooting what, or what order scenes were being done, or who was in what, the dialogue hadn't been written for the next day's shoot – it was really quite chaotic. I think that's part of the whole experience. You're really happy when it all works, and when it doesn't work you shrug your shoulders. It's interesting for me that some of the older musicians whom I really revere, very experienced artists who have made recordings for many years, won't come into the booth and listen to things. Because they have played for so many recordings, and they've had the experience of playing something and feeling that they have played particularly well, and then in the end, for whatever reason, it wasn't used. That is just too frustrating for them, too emotional and perplexing, and they just won't do it.

ES: *You suggested in the studio that making a recording was a little like composing the piece.*
MTT: If only you could make a recording which would give people that feeling. Who was it who said that there should only be three recordings of every piece – beginning, intermediate and advanced? In the beginning all the main themes are played very loudly, in the intermediate one all the secondary themes, and then in the advanced one it's all absolutely equal, and it's up to the listeners to decide what they want to hear. I think I said that.

You see, it's odd. As I said, as I'm conducting in a recording session, I'm trying to perform, and at the same time I'm crossing off bars in my mind, which is a kind of split personality thing. I'm performing but I'm also saying, 'Well, I just heard that bar and it's beautiful, so I will now cross that out, I won't think about it any more. Even though I'm going to go back and do other takes, I'm not going to think about it.' But it's difficult with a piece like *Jeux.* You have the opening of the Allegro, interlocking semiquavers between violas, cellos, percussion, horn, and the players are spread all over the studio, and yet you want this to be very crisp. So I go in and listen to a take and I think, 'This is too slow, and too ponderous, and it's all too long and too boomy and too mushy and everything ...' So I'll want to go and do a take to correct that.

However, it may be that just those bars in an earlier take are fine, and everything else in the Allegro is no problem, because it's covered in later takes; but it's hard to remember that, and so it can easily happen that the first thing to change, if you're not careful, is the tempo. You think, 'This is not crisp enough,' so you start going a little bit faster. You don't want to be faster, you just want to be crisper, but you're trying to look at these players who are so far away from you that you can barely see them ... And the horrendous communication problem becomes clear when a musician asks you a question. Usually what I hear is my name, and perhaps, 'Could you tell me, three bars after ...', and then suddenly it's a complete blur because the whole end of their sentence has been washed away by the acoustic of the room, or by the little noises going on, or whatever. It's can be very perplexing.

ES: *Yes. in a live performance, things are prepared, and then you perform them, and that's that. But recording is different, because of the scrutiny of those microphones.*
MTT: Also because you could do a take which you think is great, and at the other end of the room the percussionist has knocked over his music stand. Maybe you don't hear a noise like that at all because it's at the other end of the room, but some microphone there does hear it, and if his track is cut off at that point it produces a noticeable little gap.

Analogue versus Digital

ES: *Where do you stand in the debate about analogue versus digital recordings?*
MTT: I suppose it was inevitable that people would come up with digital recording. Digital recording is a process in which a computer samples things, which is really just a way of saying that the computer points at something an incredible number of times. It says, 'Listen to this, listen to this, listen to this,' very, very rapidly, and records all these tiny discrete moments which it has sampled, and calls your attention to them. Then it relies on your brain to fill in the blank spots, which really are there. There are actual gaps between the samples. They are very tiny, they are microseconds, but they are there. I hear those things. Digital recordings sound different. Yes, digital is more accurate. It has many more possibilities because it's done numerically. It can be processed in many more ways and it's convenient – but there is not the same smooth sort of continuity that analogue recording used to have. You hear that particularly with the bass response. I'm sure I'm speaking like a real dinosaur, saying all this. But just the idea – analogue, analogy – sounds like a very humanist, noble, civilized sort of thing – this is to this as this is to that. Digital recording somehow has a rather simian aspect to it. It's like monkeys pointing at everything they can see saying, 'Look at this, look at this, look at this, this, this …' It's frantic and crazy making. Of course, I am not really a fanatic on this subject. I appreciate the magic digital can accomplish, but I know there are folks out there who feel quite pasionate about the issue of analogue versus digital. I once received an invitation from a group of audiophiles in Boston inviting me to a new Boston Tea Party, only instead of dumping tea into the harbour, they were dumping CDs.

Controlling the Recording

ES: *Do you feel you're as much in control in the recording studio as you are in the concert hall?*

MTT: Control of the recording process ... the question of just how much time is going to be spent doing the recording, just how painstaking it's going to get, is what it's all about. The conductor is not like the director of a film in those situations. He does not have that kind of power. He doesn't have the final cut in many cases, let alone the kind of final cut a director in a film gets, where he says, 'Okay, that's it, cut and print.' You don't get to say that. In the first place you're not actually looking through the lens, so to speak, you're out there performing. How people who are director-performers do it, I'd be very interested to know.

ES: *I bet Karajan had the final cut ...*

MTT: Well, von Karajan had the system entirely mastered. He had such musical and economic power in the sphere of German music-making that he worked on recording as he would work on a film or video, or whatever. He just worked on it until it was done. He would perform something, record it, and then it would be edited together, and he would listen to it, and reflect, and ask himself if he really liked it or not. And if he didn't like some bit of it, he could go back and re-do it. In some cases he would throw out the whole thing and start all over again.

I was at a couple of recording sessions that he did with the Berlin Philharmonic where the orchestra was assembled, but no one was quite sure what he planned to record that day. There were teams of librarians standing outside, all with music tightly clutched in their hands. In the course of those two sessions he worked on bits and pieces of Mahler's Ninth, two or three movements of the Dvořák *Serenade for Strings,* a couple of orchestral bits from *Falstaff,* the Pizzicato Polka, the Barcarolle from the *Tales of Hoffman* and, I think, a movement of the 'Prague' Symphony. He would work on these things, then stop and go up and listen to it. The whole orchestra was sitting below. He would listen to the music, listen to it again, tell stories, say, 'Do this, do that,' go back, carry on. There was absolutely no sense of pressure, no sense of 'it must be done'.

I don't expect anyone else will ever work in that way again.

Fashion in Music

ES: *Why are some composers suddenly more in vogue than others? Is it just to do with exposure, or the mood of the times, or a combination of those things?*

MTT: If we're to talk about musical fashion, we have to make a clear demarcation between musical fashion before and after electronic media came into the picture. The course of musical fashion was enormously altered by the introduction of electronic media. It's true that, to some extent, the fashion of the concert hall and the fashion of the electronic media existed in parallel for a long time. But increasingly, I think, they are separating, and we are beginning to see a situation in which fashion and marketing in the electronic-media world are having more effect on the concert hall than the other way round.

The History of Performance and the Role of the Patron

ES: *So where shall we begin?*

MTT: I guess we have to begin with the fact that of the music we most perform – say the music from Bach's time up to the present – the earliest of this music is from a time when it was written for court orchestras or court ensembles. It was music designed to be played initially for very few people, and it was also designed, for the most part, to be played once. A very outstanding or expensive piece, like an opera, might, of course, be repeated if the patron or the public desired it. For the most part, audience and patron alike wanted to hear something new.

If you liked a composer, you had to like that composer enough to hire him to work in a certain style which you as a patron liked. If the composer pleased his patron they would settle down together, and there would be a stream of new works which would be in the same sort of style. This was also the case with those composers who were lucky enough to become opera composers. Everyone, of course, wanted to become one, because it meant such international recognition. The first mega-international careers made by composers who were not virtuosi were made by people writing operas.

Always there was the issue of the public's taste, which was a balance between what they found familiar and the excitement of diverting or surprising novelties. Each country's taste was different. The taste of one nation versus another, the taste of France versus the taste of Austria versus the taste of Italy, and so on. The sudden introduction of the Italian style into England had an enormous effect during Handel's time; the sudden introduction of Gluck's style into France had an equally dramatic effect. Later on, there were increasingly revolutionary steps, by Wagner and others. As time went on the public seemed to demand more and more sensational turnabouts of style. Fashion movements, fashion statements, were very often ushered in by scandals of one sort or another. An initially scandalous première might create such furore as to create a new fashion overnight. After all, when we go to the theatre, we love to see something wonderful that we truly like but seeing something shocking that we really hate can be equally entertaining. One can dine out for weeks recounting one's impressions of either the good or the terrible evening. It is the so-so middle of the road performance that are truly the most unendurable.

Let's think about that for a minute. Can we think of a major composer who didn't start with a scandal? I guess Handel. By the time Handel arrived in London we were ready for him. On the other hand John Gay's *Beggar's Opera* caused a scandal when it was first done, didn't it? And it reversed fashion against Handel. So very often I guess it was a single piece which created a furore of some sort – but the piece itself was designed to appeal to the tastes of some group within the public which was dissatisfied. Perhaps people, up to that point, hadn't really had enough money or enough control over the concerts there to make their say worth listening to. It always came round to that issue of economics.

Haydn was very lucky to find, in Esterházy, a patron who had great taste, who would listen to him and basically accommodate Haydn's view of things. That's very clear when you go to the room in the Esterházy Palace where Haydn performed. It's a whole room of marble, very ornate surfaces, but the floor is plain wood. The floor is plain wood because when Haydn first came into the chamber he said, 'I'm sorry, your Highness, it is not good when music is played in a room that has a stone floor. You really must change the floor.' And the Prince did change it to a wooden floor. He listened.

As a contrast to that we see the situation with Mozart and his patron Archbishop Colloredo. Colloredo knew what he wanted – background music, whereas Mozart was trying to write music that was searching for a more profound level of musical expression. It just wasn't to Colloredo's taste. Therefore, it wasn't fashionable. It wasn't his idea of what music should be, that is, decorous and entertaining. Poor Mozart's whole life was spent trying to find a patron who would support him so he could take the sort of daring spiritual voyages of which he dreamed.

A few years ago I attended a formal dinner in London. We were privileged to be serenaded by a group of players from the LSO. Through two or three courses they tootled away quite pleasantly as we ate and chatted with pleasure, then, all at once, they began playing music, while not any louder, was so much more assertive in its harmony, melody and expression it was impossible to ignore. I had to get up from the table and ask them what it was they were playing. Of course, it was Mozart. One couldn't go on eating or gossiping. The music, even in its quiet elegance, was far too vivid and intense. For the first time in my life, I felt myself agreeing with the Philistine Colloredo, who said to Mozart, 'The trouble with your music is that it calls too much attention to itself.' He was right. The music is far too powerful to accompany gossip or gourmandry. The archbishop didn't really want a profound composer, but rather an acoustic interior decorator.

It's interesting to follow how in different nations the edge of fashion finds itself at a different point at different times. While Mozart was battling with a conservative public in Vienna, Salomon was putting on concerts in England, where the innovations of Haydn were being acclaimed. Each new, revolutionary device which Haydn devised, each new surprise, each artful misdirection of the ear, the public loved more and more. Salomon had of course planned to invite Mozart to come to England and follow in Haydn's footsteps. Mozart had accepted. Haydn had only gone first because he was a much older man. Mozart, they thought, could come to London in later years. No one expected that Mozart would die before Haydn. If Mozart had ever come to England, and had played for the audience whose ears were opened by Haydn's late symphonies, then suddenly Mozart could have become the height of fashion, as he had been earlier in his life, when he was a curiosity as a child performer.

Music as Show Business

So those themes are still with us. The theme of how advanced is the music, how attractive is the performer? Is it a young performer, is it a performer from an exotic country? Is it a very young prodigy performer? Is the repertoire based on folkloric or national airs of some sort, which may possibly bring in another audience? I think impresarios have probably always manipulated these same elements, as far as the concert-hall audience is concerned. And indeed, Mozart, Beethoven, all the other composers who were themselves virtuosi, used the art of manipulating an occasion for the sense of its dramatic impact, that is, creating a spectacle.

Mozart as a child astounded his audiences by playing the piano blindfolded and demonstrating his perfect pitch. Later he tried to overwhelm the public with his programmes, playing many symphonies and concerti and concert arias and all manner of pieces in the one concert. Beethoven tried to do the same thing in some of his early public concerts, such as the one where he premièred the Fifth Symphony, the Sixth symphony, the Fourth Piano Concerto and the Choral Fantasy on one evening. Then he got on to the line of putting on concerts with novelties like Mälzel's mechanical clock instruments, or automatons that played trumpet pieces, or ladies of Vienna who did *tableaux vivants* based on Greek statues while Beethoven improvised. After that of course there was Beethoven's mammoth Ninth Symphony concert, which was designed to be a huge spectacle. By this time he himself was a wild man of music, and it was a last chance to see him in action.

You can see the idea of musical taste changing in the course of Beethoven's career. At first he was a drawing-room performer, then he became a musical curiosity and a revolutionary figure – but his big successes in the concert hall, in the actual concert hall, sold tickets. And then the biggest ticket of his entire life, his funeral. Beethoven's funeral. The ultimate event.

The performers instinct to find whatever is necessary to put the piece over is a reflection of music as a part of show business. This is something that many of our most serious tenders of the eternal flame would prefer not to recognize. In fact, music is a very elevated, transcendent form of show business, or at least it has been since the seventeenth century. Before that time much music aspired to be a model of God's universe, and had a more meditative function. But certainly since the creation of opera it's man's thoughts and feelings that have held centre stage. Symphonic music takes the same dramatic questions to a more abstract level. Nevertheless, there is still a platform, performers, an audience, lights, ushers and tickets. That's a show. Sometimes the show may have a prayerful intention which can unite people in a spiritual way. There is nothing more wonderful than the moments of silence that the audience and orchestra share together at the end of Tchaikovky's *Pathétique*, or Mahler's Ninth Symphony. These moments have arisen from the huge spectacles that preceded them. In this spectacle the conductor can be a kind of master of ceremonies, celebrant, cheerleader, drill sergeant, band leader, and so on. Whatever role he may take on relates to the occasion, to the chemistry of those particular performers and audience members gathered in that concert hall.

Educating the Public's Palate

A part of the conductor's job is to surprise people and shake them up a bit. He has to give them some inkling of what composers are writing in their own time. Since Beethoven's time, the history of music has been filled with angry young men, who seemed at first to want to shock or to annoy the audience. But in the course of a generation their music was often accepted and loved. I think it was Varèse who said that the composer is never ahead of his time, but the audience is quite far behind its time ... that there was about a fifty-year gap between the audience and the composer. The gap seems to be getting shorter.

ES: *You said the other day it's more like twenty-five years now.*
MTT: Except for those pieces which really go out on a limb – pieces that seem more interested in demonstrating intellectual theories than in musical expression. It's interesting to see that many pieces by Stravinsky, and a few by Schoenberg, have been accepted into the standard repertoire. So what are we to do about pieces by Schoenberg, for example, which are older than fifty years and still haven't been accepted into the standard repertoire? What kind of fashion does that represent? Is there some threshold still up ahead where the audience will accept this music? And, if they do accept it, how often will they want to hear it? Every few seasons as they do with some of the classic masterpieces? Every decade? Fashion in music reflects why we need music. What purpose in our lives does it fulfil? And, of course, the influence of recording and television has changed the way we use music in all kinds of ways.

The Influence of Records and Record Companies

ES: *Yes, in a sense the record companies are now the impresarios of the present day. They are the fashion dictators. The image makers, if you like. But for how long?*
MTT: The big record companies want to market artists, and, in the classic relationship between an artist and a record company, if you become an exclusive artist with a company, they will try to market you as ubiquitously as they can. It's expected that under your name will come out recordings of all the Beethoven symphonies, all the Brahms symphonies, all the Bruckner symphonies, all the Mahler symphonies, all the Wagner overtures, all the French pieces – *La Mer, Daphnis et Chloë*, and so on. There are, what, seventy or ninety pieces you're expected to do.

ES: *Core repertoire.*

MTT: Yes. You do the core repertoire because it is necessary for the company, in order to promote you and to represent you as an international musical brand name. However, it may not be necessary for you, the artist, to do all those pieces, or certainly not at that particular time. Or indeed I can not think of any artist who wanted to record or perform the entire repertoire, or who was suited to record the entire core repertoire.

ES: *You were saying you think that the arrival of recordings changed things in the music world.*

MTT: The fact is that listening to music on a recording is a different experience from listening to music in the concert hall. The sort of music that you want to hear at home, that you want to fall back in a big chair and have wash over you, or have going on round the house whilst you take care of minor domestic activities, the sort of music that you want to fill up the space of your house, may be quite different from the kind of music that you actually like to listen to in a concert hall. The music that was written for the concert hall was designed to make a very strong effect, often a very startling effect on people in the concert hall. That's part of the excitement, why you sit there. Seeing a large ensemble get itself together to play this very virtuoso and daring piece live, with no safety nets, is part of the thrill of a concert. But when you're listening to music at home, I think you may want to hear music that is a bit longer-lined, more spacious, and perhaps not music of such dynamic extreme. After all, the credo of pop radio became that the dynamic range of a piece must be very limited and discrete. Either it is loud, or medium-loud, or quiet. It doesn't have the wide dynamic range of classical music. It is 'middle-of-the-road' – dynamically, harmonically, emotionally. But middle-of-the-road music did have an influence on classical musicians who realized that the comfortable acoustic space could be vastly extended beyond a three minute single to a twenty minute or longer work that would combine ancient elements of meditative music with the 'feel-good' aesthetics of our pop culture.

ES: *And of course radio and records, in turn, influence people's taste in music.*

MTT: Right. Look what's happened with a piece like John Taverner's *The Protecting Veil*. It had its first performance at the London Proms and was a notable success, and of course the programme was broadcast, so it got to a much larger audience. Shortly after that the disc came out, sold thousands, and the disc and that broadcast together stimulated many more performances of the piece, and really quite a turnaround in the composer's career.

With John Taverner and Steven Isserlis, Carnegie Hall, 1993

I love this piece and have loved performing it with Steven Isserlis. However, I suspect that the piece may be better experienced on CD rather than in the concert hall. In a live performance of a piece like this it really matters what seat you have.

It is wonderful that there are contemporary pieces which reach a large audience through recordings and create for a time a new musical fashion. However these fashions come and go very quickly nowadays, some of them arising, peaking and receding in only five years. During that time the influence of a hit record or a hot performer can be powerful. The goal of recording companies is to sell records. Their involvement in backing artists and repertoire which they think will sell is an influence on the way the music business goes. Many projects are done in partnership with recording companies and video companies, and this can have an effect on what sort of projects are undertaken in the concert hall.

Lots of what passes for innovation or new fashions in concert giving is just a form of repackaging. For example, the theme concerts or festival concerts so popular in London now are an attempt to make familiar music seem new by putting it in a different context or package. One can't foresee how long this will be in vogue.

Current Trends in Public Taste

The main difference is that early in the twentieth century people still wanted to hear mostly new pieces – up till, what, 1910, 1920 or so. The concert societies still had to come up with new symphonies, new concerti, new possibilities that the audience was going to listen to, going to take in. Nowadays most programmes are centred around repetition of music that people have already heard. Classical music has become music of reassurance and historical reference, rather than music expressing where the feelings and concerns of members of the audience actually lie. That's a very big difference. Which is not to say there isn't music being written which does deal with the themes of right now, but it tends to be characterized either as the realm of avant-garde music, or some kind of serious music or intellectual music or academic music.

ES: *Do you think, though, that people at the moment are more prepared to go and hear a new piece, and feel less threatened by it than they were ten or fifteen years ago?*
MTT: I think so. And I think people are also more aware that musical values are askew, because so much hype has been given to one form of music, namely rock and roll music, and the sorts of music that are associated with it – pop, disco, rap and so on. There is so much money behind the presentation of this, let's face it, rather limited material. That's not to say there aren't some very interesting and inspired people who've worked within these genres, but there are also many who are not. And all that material is presented with so many adverts, so many freebies, so much exposure, that it is the one music that everyone is aware of, to the exclusion of all the other musical traditions that are operating.

This puts all these other musics into the position of being a sort of dodo music, in which dodo stands for 'dementia of deficit operations'. There is this craziness in classical music, because you feel no matter how much of a success you may have, it just means you're losing a little bit less money than you might have done otherwise. That's a problem in society, because the overall tastes of musical fashion have been pushed towards one particular style of music. It's a very sober thought for me to reflect on this, because certainly as a kid I was someone who was saying, 'I'm a classical musician, but I really love rock and roll, leave it alone, it's fine.' And now, in many ways, I look back and say, 'It really hasn't been all that fine. A lot of very terrible things have happened to music because of rock music. Not because of the music itself, but because of the way it's just been crammed down everybody's throats worldwide. We've been exploited.

ES: *What about something like opera? Selling popular Italian arias in the way the Italians might sing those arias in the street – suddenly that's the way it's being marketed over here. They become the pop songs of the day – the world's favourite signature tunes, like 'Nessun Dorma!' and the World Cup.*
MTT: Right. That's all very self-consciously done. The Three Tenors Concert, all this kind of musical ballyhoo. It reminds me of what Sol Hurok used to say. He called himself an impresario, and he described those he represented as his 'attractions'. I was the last attraction to be signed by Sol Hurok. Some of his other attractions had been Anna Pavlova, Vladimir Horowitz, the Barnum Bailey Circus, the Concertgebouworchest, the Bolshoi Ballet, the Ice Capades, the Grenadier Guards, Sviatoslav Richter – and now Michael Tilson Thomas. He was interested in box office and how it could be manipulated. He was very sympathetic to the artists, seeing after their needs, coddling them, almost like precocious children. He had a great instinct for seeing the spark in a performer. But no one more than he would have agreed with that old saying, 'They don't call it show-art. They call it show-business.'

Out of the Fashion Trap

Now, what is the way out of this craziness of fashion? The way out is by encouraging artists who are really interested in exploring music, and who have a sense of responsibility to their audience, and who will present interesting pieces to their audience. The audience must have faith in the artists' vision to such an extent that they can see an item they don't know on a programme and accept it, knowing that it will be important for them to hear. That's a way out of it. True audience development is the way out of it, both by educating people from an early age, and by creating musical events which are perhaps less daunting to experience, so that a wider public can participate and hopefully be inspired to explore other repertoire. In my view, a good programme should have three elements: something diverting, something challenging (perhaps provoking) and something reaffirming. When the audience can trust that the performers will provide them with programmes that fulfil these three important needs then you have the basis of a sophisticated, forward looking and fun musical community.

Audience development is an area that must be continually explored. But, again, fashion enters into this. Any artist discovers that he or she becomes an object of fashion, in that a particular record company or a particular concert society may decide that you are a good singer for lyric parts but not for dramatic parts, or that you are a good pianist for Schubert but not for Prokofiev, or that you are an ideal conductor for Mozart but not for Mahler, or for Stravinsky and Debussy but not for Schumann, for example. The way it works is that it's mostly the people who are rather limited who benefit most by this, because they stake out their territories and then they're happy within them. If they can develop enough clout based on the specialty they first stake out, then they can force the company or the music society into letting them branch out into wider areas and taking risks.

ES: *So are we constantly going to be exploiting the fashion of the day in arts like music?*
MTT: If it only were the fashion of the day, that would be fine. If we were walking up the street, and we heard somebody interesting playing out of a window, and we thought, 'Oh, that's interesting music, let's hear that next week,' that would be exciting. All too often the music and many of the artists we hear on recordings of concert programmes are the result of managerial feeding frenzies and resultant media blitzes originating in music's 'high fashion' centres, such as Salzburg. There can be a certain distortion in people's perspectives of these events. People often find it very difficult to dislike something for which they paid a very high price. The snob values of the event, the gossip surrounding the cast or the post-performance intrigues can outweigh the actual musical or dramatic values of the project. A perfectly 'OK' performance dropped into the musical puddle can generate concentric ripples which can be made to seem like an artistic tidal wave by the time it has arrived at your local record store.

But don't get me wrong. I have nothing against Salzburg, where I have quite enjoyed working. It is a kind of theme park of classical music. The nicest part about it is that so many artists are working there at one time it gives one the rare chance to hear many of one's colleagues work and appreciate anew how wonderful they are. Nevertheless, I find it amusing to watch record labels plugging a few of the same artists into every piece in the repertoire with sometimes absurd results.

ES: *I think you're right when you talk about audiences needing a feeling of reassurance. When people say, 'I know what I like,' it's the desire to hear something they are familiar with rather than to hear something fresh. I think that's what gets exploited. More and more, at the concerts I now go to , I can feel audiences are more receptive to things they've never heard before.*

MTT: I must say that's true. I never would have thought there'd be an audience in London that would respond in the way it did to the Ives Fourth this year. That's all on the good side. On the slightly scary side at this moment is that the future of classical music, particularly on record, is by no means certain. There seems to be less recording being done, and it is more difficult for people not living in major music centres to hear interesting new work and artists. On the other hand, there is a kind of provincial limitation that comes from living in a major music centre where one imagines that whatever is important must be happening there. London, as astonishing as its musical life is, is still just one little point on the globe. The greatest excitement for the future of music is that worldwide there are artists exploring who knows how many new ideas.

As always with music we come back to the central line – communication. Ideally musicians are people who have the talent and the need to sing songs for other people. Whatever allows them to do this the most directly is good. Record companies have had a very good effect on the level of musical culture worldwide. For years record companies were producers of projects. They backed an artist, a composer, a style, in the building of a catalogue. They were willing to risk large sums of capital to do this. But now, more often, the companies are packagers, manufacturers and distributors of what is increasingly a musical artifact – the disc. The cost of doing this are so great that flexibility, imagination and daring on the production front are faltering.

However, in the future, with new technology, it may be feasible for the artists themselves to produce and distribute their own performances world wide. How I would love to be able to license my performances of Morton Feldman, Robin Holloway, or Mozart's A minor Rondo through a 'sophisticated music lovers' network to interested listeners all over the world. If civilization will only survive long enough we could have some very productive times ahead.

ES: *Well, it's an extension of recorded music, isn't it?*

MTT: There should also be a TV channel. I mean, consider the amount of video of classical music that's been done. There should be a worldwide classical music channel showing these videos, so if you have a satellite dish you can tune in anytime twenty-four hours a day and always find a serious classical music programme on. Why not? The product is there, the distribution possibility is there. It could be very interesting. 'What is on now? Oh, it's *Die Soldaten* by Zimmerman!'

Then there could be a computer or a video line which would be a sampler line. You could have all different kinds of people as a sampler, much in the way pay-for-view television works in America now. You get to see two or three minutes of it and you're not charged anything. If you want to continue watching it you press a confirm button and then you see it. Some variation on that.

A system like this would give the artists a much more direct possibility of achieving a project that they want to do, and having it reach the public, and let it be there in the market place to find its own level. I still believe that a lot in the classical music world happens through people telling one another that a certain performance or certain artist is good.

Word of Mouth and Reviews

ES: *There's no substitute. Word of mouth is the best advertising. People rely upon it. I think that's why they still read reviews. If they're well-written, if they whet their appetite, then people will investigate. Reviews still have a purpose.*

MTT: But, as you say, it's very difficult when you have only so much money to buy a recording. You think, 'I'll take a chance and buy this or that.' It would be much better to be able to sit at home and sample it in some way, and decide if you like it or not.

ES: *Yes, in the way that one used to be able to do in the record shop. You still can, in some places, do that with CDs. You can sample, because they have players in the shop. I think that's important. On the other hand, people are prepared to spend, in the UK, £10 or £12 on a symphony they've not heard a note of, simply on the strength of a review. That was certainly the case with Górecki. That, plus the air time on Classic FM Radio.*

MTT: And it's interesting too that people are saying, 'Here's a piece, and I want to hear it, and I want to take it home and play it over and over again, and have it around,' in just the same way that people would say, 'I want to buy the new Sinatra record, or I'm going to buy the Beatles' new record and have it around and play it again.' That is different from the time when people would say, 'Fine, I just heard Beethoven's Fifth Symphony, that was very interesting, now what's his Sixth Symphony like?'

Back to Basics

ES: *Where do you think music is going right now?*

MTT: People are coming back to the basics, there's no question. Melody, harmony, these fundamental things. The importance of minimalism was that it brought people back to those things. Of course there's a terrible danger in simplicity. It's one thing for a composer like Górecki, who has gone on a musical journey and then come back to writing a simpler form of music, somewhat along the lines of what Aaron Copland was saying, that you write a lot of notes and then finally dispense with the unnecessary ones, but it's a different thing perhaps for someone at the beginning of their career to write this way. There's somehow a very big difference between what Górecki does and what a 'New Ager' may do. New Age music is a vastly different thing from the best of simple soulful writing. I think I would have to leave it in capable hands like yours to try to analyze where the borderline is, where it becomes wallpaper music.

ES: *I worry about people making that distinction. That's what worries me about trends we've seen, because there is, as you've just said, a world of difference between something that is simple but comes from somewhere and has a history, and something which is a meander that appeals to people's laziness.*

MTT: You can see ways in which that's manifested in America. On American cable television there are all sorts of things advertised. One of them is a piano course in which you can learn to play the piano in two lessons. It says, 'The reason people can't play the piano is just that they're so inhibited by all of these restrictive ideas that previously written music has presented to them. You just have to be there at the piano, and you go with the flow, and then in two minutes I'll have you entertaining and astounding your friends.' And then out comes a former *Playboy* magazine bunny, and she says, 'Yes, I just had two lessons and now I've released my first CD and here it is.' And she starts playing this music, which is all the white notes of the piano, all strung together, with the pedal down all of the time. It's just musical wallpaper, and not all that good a wallpaper.

ES: *But in a sense it has purged music of the kind of complexities that were simply alienating.*

MTT: There still are people writing in that manner. People get very defensive about defending their little musical territories. Not only the people who are making music, but the people who are administering music, and the people promoting music, and the people writing about music. But I think things have hopefully brought us to the point where we don't feel there has to be a certain level of complexity in a piece of music for it to be taken seriously. A piece can be more or less complex, entirely according to what the composer needs to say, what he needs to do, and trusting the performer to recognize a good situation in the music and make the most of it. I have a suspicion that, in the long run, a better course for the composer to follow might be to let people perceive what the notes are, what the shape of it is, and what the intent of it is, and then to rely on the performer's instinct to take it and do interesting things with it.

Crossing Over

ES: *You said a minute ago that people were protective about their territories. One thing I see as being a hopeful sign for the future is that people are accepting that it is possible to switch from one style to another, to enter different worlds of music. Understanding that one style is not necessarily better, or less worthy, than another. I think we're seeing more acceptance of the whole spectrum of music. Except that nowadays they're calling it 'cross-over'.*

MTT: Yes, there are some great moments. Kathleen Battle singing 'Caravan' by Duke Ellington is a wonderful moment of cross-over. There are other moments, even sung by that same artist, that are not so wonderful. It's a very, very delicate balance point to find and maintain. It's wonderful to know that so many young musicians now have accepted that these bound-aries are really artificial and arbitrary, and can be comfortable and at home in many musical styles. I am very proud that American artists have brought this message to classical music. Of course, there were great European singers, like Richard Tauber, who sang light repertoire as well, with great artistry. I would hope that we Americans, like Bernstein, Previn, von Stade, Hampson and myself, have brought an ease to all of this which will have a lasting musical effect. It is no laughing matter for a classical artist to abandon vibrato, pearl-shaped tones and self-conscious beauty of expression for the sake of the more conversational and spontaneous musical language of 'pop music'. The toughest issue of all seems to be vibrato. I remember being part of a classical gala concert once which turned out to be one of those 'famous people perform repertoire they have no business going near' evenings. As I listened to the third or fourth intensely undulated perfor-mance of Bach and Jerome Kern, I remarked to one of my colleagues, 'Wasn't it da Ponte who said, "As a young man two thing troubled me greatly: infidelity and excessive or inappropriate use of vibrato. Over time I have come to accept the former. But the latter I shall never be able to endure." '

Sometimes one is lucky enough to find a piece which is balanced perfect-ly between the classical and pop worlds. There's a piece by Astor Piazzolla I've recently been performing, and he calls it 'Fantasy on Buenos Aires', and it's absolutely wonderful and original and terrific. I recently played it in New York, and a number of composers, like David del Tredici and Steve Reich and Charles Wuorinen, came back and said, 'This is so wonderful, where did you find this piece?' They were so happy it was on the programme; and yet there were a few people writing to the papers who were deeply concerned about whether a piece of this sort really belonged in a concert of serious music, and where does the borderline go? I should mention this was a Sunday matinee concert in Avery Fisher Hall in New York, with quite a programme. It was being done with Ives, Gershwin and Ginestera. It was not as if we were following the Bruckner Ninth with *An American in Paris*.

Walt Whitman wrote, 'Showing the best and dividing it from the worst, age vexes age.' Ain't it the truth! These taste wars battled out in the press and arts management circles are pointless and fatiguing.

I thought of this when visiting Bali. I was staying in a dance pavilion in a small village outside Ubud. My hosts had told the villagers that I was a 'famous musician', but they had no idea of what I did or what kind of music I played. Over the next week I tried to explain it to the many Balinese musicians I met.

They would usually say, right at the start, 'I'm sorry, but I don't know much about Western music.'

I'd ask, 'Do you know Bach?'

They'd answer, 'No.'

'Mozart?'

'No.'

'Beethoven?'

'No.'

I'd sing the opening of Beethoven's Fifth Symphony. They answered, 'No, but it's an interesting melody.'

I asked, 'Do you know Barbra Streisand?'

'No.'

'Michael Jackson?'

Incredibly, 'No. As I told you, I don't know much about Western music.'

God, it was refreshing.

Later in the week, I met a few of them who said that they had once attended a concert of the Concertgebouworkest when it was once on tour in Java. They said that they hadn't understood the music at all but thought that the dancer was wonderful.

That night I gave a 'performance' for them of Mahler's Fifth Symphony. Attired in white tie, tail coat and sarong, I conducted the first movement singing all the orchestra parts as best as I could. They were quite startled and amused by it all. They couldn't imagine that the enormous sound of the many instruments I was directing could be drawn and controlled just by using a little stick – the baton. In a gamelan orchestra, of course, that role is fulfilled by the drummer.

Over the next days I played music for many musicians using my little Yamaha synthesizer, which I take everywhere. After the astonishing hours of gamelan that they treated me, I wanted to play something for them. While they listened attentively I could tell that none of the Bach, Mozart, Gershwin or Beatles tunes made any impression on them. Then, one day I hit on playing one of my favorite Hassidic tunes, *Die Evige Kashe*, the one that goes:

Freygte mann die alte kashe – tra la la la liri la?

Or in English:

Man asks the eternal question – tra la la la liri la?
Man asks the eternal question – tra la la la liri la?
Then man answers, if he can, tra la la la tra la la la
And still it remains the eternal question, tra la la la liri la?

This little Jewish tune, with all its resigned singsong cadences, they took to immediately. They asked me to play it again and again. I could still hear them singing it as they disappeared along the trail into the bamboo jungle ... 'tra la la la liri la.'

So, perhaps my most important contribution to music and greatest effect on international 'art fashion' will have been that I introduced Yiddishkeit into Bali.

On Composing

Early Improvisations

ES: *You're a composer as well as a conductor. How important is this to you?*
MTT: Well, I'm a fledgling composer, but I think I have always inhabited, and still do inhabit, much of the imaginative space, the dream world, that composers know and experience. The earliest musical memories I have are of playing my own music, or playing music made up with my father. The very first song I knew was called 'The Toodles Song'. My father had gone to a nightclub that had been opened in Los Angeles by a former heavyweight prize fighter, trying to make his way into cabaret society, and this guy's name was Slapsie Maxie Rosenblum. He had a big opening night at his nightclub, and my father had been invited there by some friends of his from New York, and he had stayed out too late and knew my mother would not be very pleased about this escapade. So, hoping to make the best of it, he had bought a little toy from a cigarette girl at the nightclub to take home to me. It was a little toy dog. It had shortish, wire-haired fur and black ears; it was meant to be some kind of terrier. He came home with this, quite early in the morning, at five or six o'clock, and presented it to me at break-fast. It was really a peace offering to assuage my mother's doubtful feelings.

The dog was given the name Toodles, which was my father's nickname when he was a little boy. And then Teddy, my father, took me over to the piano and put me on his lap and began making up a little song, which went, 'I love a Toodles song, I love a Toodles song, I sing it all day long.' As he sang he played the piano holding the dog in one hand and moving it down the keyboard, its forepaws striking the appropriate keys. But of course the paws, as they struck the keys, actually produced dissonant splodges of notes, that are called tone clusters in the parlance of avant-garde music. So the first piece that I remember adoring so much was the 'Toodles Song', in F major – but all of the melody notes were outlined in tone clusters. To this I attribute my love of contemporary music and dissonance, and my conviction that dissonance can be an expression of excitement and joy. This unusual mix of consonance and dissonance is still a part of my

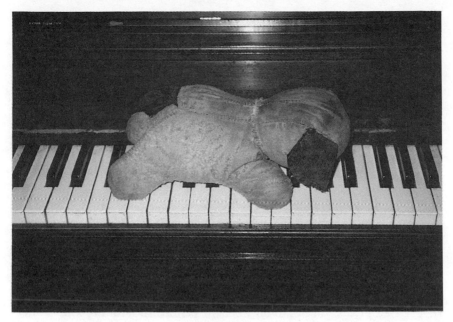

Toodles

music today.

I've already told you about improvising at the piano, watching the light coming into the room. The point is I really began making music by improvising and making up my own music. And that continued during my childhood. I always had little tunes and pieces and things that I was playing. As I began playing more repertoire by other composers, I would write more complicated pieces; so I could play pieces of my own improvised in the style of Shostakovich or Prokofiev or Kabalevsky or Chopin or Bach or whatever I was working on.

I was quite fearless about playing these in public. I had got a scholarship given by the Parent-Teacher Association at school, and every six months or so I'd get a $100 scholarship towards my lessons. One of the results of getting this scholarship seemed to be that I was always asked to play at meetings of the PTA, so of course I had the problem of running out of repertoire. Very early on I started making things up. I presented these improvisations as 'Sonatina by Prokofiev', or 'Concert Etude by Tchaikovsky', or something like that. As my pieces got more individual and difficult to classify, I would begin to pick composers' names who were less well known: 'This is an *Etude Chromatique* by Roussel,' or, '*Bagatelle* by Szymanowski.' I was around twelve or so.

I would usually start these mini-recitals by playing a movement of Beethoven or Chopin, and then end with one of my wilder improvisations with one of their *outré* attributions. I was particularly delighted when a member of the audience would approach me and say, 'Well, the piece I really liked the most was that Roussel piece, or that Szymanowski piece.' I remember I so enjoyed doing this, and the fact that no one ever suspected or caught me at it, I kept pushing it further and further. By the time I was in high school I was announcing pieces like, 'Contrapuntal Fantasy by Hindemith, written during the brief period of his life when he was under the influence of Eric Satie.' It was completely absurd and I quite enjoyed it.

Ballet Concrète

I was notating a bit of music around that time, mostly piano music, plus a few sketches of pieces for orchestra. Then, in my early college years, I had the opportunity to write a ballet score for David Lechine, the famous choreographer from the Ballets Russe. Lechine, who must have been in his seventies, arrived in Los Angeles to do a benefit performance for his wife's ballet school. They asked my Young Musician's Foundation Debut Orchestra to play the performance, the centrepiece of which was Lechine's famous 'Graduation Ball', to music by Johann Strauss. At some rehearsal, during a break, I was improvising on the piano. David, hearing my music, cried out, 'Zat's it! Zat's the music I vant for my new ballet vhich vill show how inspiration is transformed through invention into dance. I vill call it *La Création.*' I was struck dumb. Suddenly I was in the middle of some Diana Durbin movie, or in *The Red Shoes*!

Lechine's idea for the ballet was the representation of an unformed world – a kind of chaos of possible ideas. Then, somehow or another, the artist found a little thread in this unformed world, which he gradually spun into a composition. The music which I composed for the ballet was a mixture of symphonic music and *musique concrète*. For the beginning of the piece I made a multi-channel collage of sounds mostly produced by using a piano in unorthodox ways. The most interesting noise was made by sliding metal bars of different dimensions and densities across the strings of the piano and picking up the eerie wailing with contact microphones. It was all very primitive live-electronic stuff – very West Coast. This tape music represented the world of the unformed. Then I wrote some instrumental music, using the orchestra, where little solo strands came out of the wash of *musique concrète* and gradually turned into motifs and themes. The themes were then developed into duets and trios and ensembles that grad-

ually worked their way towards a climax. The music was gestural, dissonant, a bit on the late Stravinsky side. It was very primitive, but I had a
very good time doing it.

In this ballet the prima ballerina was Chris Harman, the daughter of the
famous American football player and sportscaster, Tom Harman. She had
recently married the famous TV personality, rock singer and teen heart-
throb, Ricky Nelson. So there we all were trying to get the ballet together,
with me improvising music and David Lechine saying whether he liked it
or not. Work on the project went very slowly. One major problem was that
there weren't enough strong male dancers to carry out Lechine's vision.
There were a lot of big lifts and very athletic stomping sections in the work,
and Lechine finally announced that he couldn't possibly complete the ballet
unless really 'strong' men were found. The solution came from Chris
Nelson's father, the ex-football player. Through his contacts he got a few
line backers from the LA Rams football team to come in and be the male
corps. It was a real LA project of its time: ageing Russian émigrés, young
avant-garde university musicians, teen ballerinas, television superstars,
Hollywood celebrity sponsors, and, of course, football players.

Nevertheless, things were getting a bit desperate because David was old
and felt that he lacked the energy to push the project through. He became
depressed and despondent. At this point, someone in that circle of demi-
monde Hollywood people he was surrounded with suggested to him that he
could get a lot of inspiration and energy if he took LSD. So suddenly we had
David Lechine, Ballets Russe émigré legend coming to rehearsals absolutely
bouncing off the ceiling.

In spite of all odds, we actually performed this monster. It didn't quite
work because there was an old stage-hand who was very, very drunk and
neglected to give the cue backstage to turn on the tape of the *musique
concrète*. He passed out and never gave the cue. By this time everybody was
on stage, so the whole piece took place without the thread of *musique concrète*
that I had planned to hold it together. As a result it was a series of fragments played against silences that seemed absolutely eternal. I got savagely
reviewed for the piece, which the critics quite rightly said amounted mostly
to nothing. By that time I was inured to getting sometimes savage com-
mentary about my work in the press, but nothing hurt so much as reading
such hostile words about something that I had written. Somehow circumstances had decreed that the piece was not heard as I had imagined in my
mind it would be.

Around that same time I was getting many opportunities as a performer,
particularly of contemporary music. I played many first performances of

Stockhausen, Berio, Boulez, Cage and other avant-garde composers. It was very easy for me to find a niche being an improviser/performer in that world. There was a kind of excitement in playing this very intellectual, and yet free, music. Suddenly, I found myself at the head of the A-list of per-former/personalities, taking music into what was then supposed to be 'fearless new frontiers'.

As I began to play that sort of music as a pianist, I also began to conduct it, and deal with its musical challenges in ensemble situations. I was a young man who could cope with the complexity of it all. I was frequently asked to play and conduct these kinds of pieces. As a result I could say, 'Well, could I also do *Siegfried Idyll, La Mer,* a Mozart Serenade, whatever.' The politics of my career worked in this way. So my fortunes as a performer in the earliest days were associated with the challenge that the avant-garde music of the 1960s and 1970s posed. I truly believed then that this musical language was the only valid direction for the future. As my own musical impulses were melodic and expressive, I left my own writing behind, and became fully active as a performer, moving more and more into the standard repertoire as the years went on.

Songs on the Side

ES: *Did you abandon composition altogether at this time?*
MTT: Not quite. I thought, 'Well, the sort of music that I really want to write isn't like anything I am playing. Actually the music I want to write is more like my father's music. It's melodies, it's songs, it's theatre music.' So at that point in my early twenties I just stopped pursuing the idea of com-posing.

But along the way I was of course writing things. When I was in Buffalo I would stay up writing very late into the night. I had a wonderful studio upstairs, and I would play music by the hour. I began writing songs, and then imagined larger pieces that developed from them. I tended to write these numbers which developed into many sections, and had developmental characteristics, and really were large scenes, almost in a pop-operatic sense. In later years I played these pieces for Bernstein and Sondheim, and they said, 'This is what you should really be doing.'

I used to play this music for friends. It was my late night music. It became a feature of the many happy gatherings of musicians we had at my house. I discovered that people did not really want to go home until I had played some of these pieces. The music became a part of the expression of that group of friends who were together in those years.

With Aaron Copland, 1975

There were a few serious moments when I thought about all this. I was always saying, 'Well, what am I going to do about my writing?' Copland came up to do a concert in Buffalo, and I got all my courage up, and I said, 'Aaron, I really want to play you some of this music I'm writing. I want to get your opinion.' So I played a couple of hours of music to him. What he basically said was, 'You haven't written down enough music to be able to distinguish the notes that really matter from the ones that don't. Yes, I can hear a soul, I can hear a voice running through all of your music, but I can also hear a lot of other things that are just convenient for you to play. What you have to do is get rid of all of those things that are just convenient, and leave only what is really you.'

In the following years I became more courageous about playing music for other people, even for Lenny. He was always very encouraging. He turned to me one day and said, 'Look, I don't know what to tell you about this. You just don't have the compulsion that I have of hearing something wonderful in your head and then sharing it with other people. You have to have the compulsion to wrestle the notes down on to the paper. If someone is lucky enough to be sitting next to you at the piano while you are playing then they can share in your dream. But what about all those other people. That's the only thing. You have to develop the compulsion to share your music and then you'll do something about it. When you're ready, you'll be ready. Not all the lecturing I can do will change that.'

Three Public Pieces

My first public performance of one of my pieces was at Leonard Bernstein's birthday at Tanglewood. I really wanted to write something for his birthday. I was asked to write something for a programme in which many composers were contributing short pieces. I wrote a song called 'Grace', a little song in C major. It's a humorous yet rather sad little song. Roberta Alexander sang it.

This concert of musical offerings turned in to a very long and exhausting event. So many distinguished composers had written such clever and tough pieces that the audience's attention was sorely tested. My song was scheduled next to last. (Stephen Sondheim's song, a paraphrase of a Brecht and Weill piece, actually ended the programme.) I think I was never so nervous in my life as standing there backstage wondering how my little piece would go over.

Roberta and I came on and did my song. The first line of this song is, 'Thanks to whoever is there for this tasty plate of herring.' She sang that first phrase so beautifully, and immediately we got a very warm laugh. From then on the audience followed the piece straight to the end and they loved it. That was an amazing feeling, very different from all the other applause experiences I have had in my life.

A year or so later I wrote a brass piece. That developed from a few songs that were stitched together very quickly because of the ruthless enthusiasm of my friend Rolf Smedvig, who's the leader of the Empire Brass Quintet. He had heard me play my music at late night parties, and kept after me. He was always saying, 'I must have a piece from you.' He was absolutely relentless. He called me up, and then actually showed up even when I was on vacation. He said, 'Well, you're sitting around here on vacation, why don't you write?' I said, 'Well, I don't know what I would write.' I played something on the piano. He said, 'That. Write that.' Then, later, while I was stuck in the middle of the piece, and I said, 'I'm not sure what to do next. What shall I do next? Perhaps I could do something like this ...' he'd say, 'Stop worrying about it, just write it down.' He was very persistent and I am very grateful to him for being so. Suddenly the brass quintet *Street Song* came into existence. The Empire Brass Quintet played it and recorded it, even though I could hear the ways in which it was primitively joined together. I played it for Lenny and he said, 'Never mind, never mind. Now

you're really on the right track – keep going.' A few days he sent me a red
baseball hat with a note saying, 'This is your composing hat. wear it often.'

Then came the Anne Frank project. I met Audrey Hepburn. She had
heard some of my music, which she liked. She talked to me about the possibility of doing a series of benefits for UNICEF which would involve a piece
about Anne Frank. At first I imagined she would do a reading from the
Diary of Anne Frank with a bit of music in the background, and confidently
I accepted her proposal to work on it together. Little did I then know that
she really had in mind a major piece which would inevitably have passages
involving the holocaust. However, I think even from that first moment,
perhaps unconsciously, I knew that this piece would have a big dramatic
shape. There was a lot of uncertainty about whether or not the project
would take place. I worked a little, sketching some ideas, but not really
thinking about it.

And then, suddenly, one day, it was happening. All the organizational
details of the project fell into place and the concerts were suddenly just
around the corner. I basically had a month to write thirty-five minutes of
orchestral music, which I knew was practically an impossible task. I did my
last concert with the New World Symphony in Miami on 6 December
1989, and then I just stayed at my house and wrote every minute of every
day until 6 January. I lost thirteen pounds during that time. I pushed
myself to the limit, but shortly after New Year I had nearly done the short
score of the piece. Since that time, through a couple of revisions, it has
become still more substantial. I've gone back to it and respectfully put in
order some things which were just not possible at the frantic speed at which
it was first written.

What was so good about this project was that it was a piece about the
world of a teenager. It was an opportunity for me to return to writing the
sort of music that I might have done just at the point where I left off composition – as a teenager. I could musically return to that sixteen-, eighteen-
year-old world. It was a perfect re-entry point for me The text moves around
a lot from one sort of subject to another, so it was a chance to write music in
all sorts of styles – sometimes terribly sad and sometimes giddy and exuber-
ant. I had great fun imagining the orchestra and combining musical styles –
some tonal, some serial, some dissonant, some nostalgic – playing with
them and seeing how they could be intermixed. I took full advantage of the
fact that Anne Frank herself was an adolescent and was speaking about
feeling sometimes as an adult, sometime as a child. Sometimes she's so
scared. Sometimes she's so hopeful. Sometimes she's so philosophical. I tried
to use the diversity of the text as a way of trying out lots of musical situa-

tions. I learned so much in the course of writing it.

The most difficult thing was to commence writing the section on the holocaust, which I really resisted. I finally had to start writing it, and then it was so frightening, because once I began, I couldn't stop writing about it. That section got bigger and bigger, and began to dominate the whole work. I didn't want this to happen, because ultimately I wanted the piece to be optimistic. Audrey and I both wanted it to be a very positive piece about who Anne Frank was and what she had to say. We recognized, of course what she went through, but also we wanted a sense of her joy of life and hope for the future.

Anne was given its initial performance with Audrey me and the New World Symphony in Miami, and on tour in the United States. It was then revised and done in London by the LSO. The final revision was accomplished for performances in Japan, culminating in Hiroshima on the Day of Remembrance. I now see that this piece is as much a portrait of Audrey Hepburn as it is of Anne Frank. In so many ways the piece reflects Audrey's remarkable spirit. It was Audrey's devotion to the *Diary* that drew me back to it. We read the *Diary* together and she made me a tape of her reading the

With Audrey Hepburn, 1990

sections that we both liked the most. I listened to the tape and the inflections of her voice for countless hours. So much was there – whimsy, wistfulness, hope, compassion, courage. The way she read the text gave shape to many of the musical gestures, and her friendship and confidence gave me the strength to finish it. The piece exists because of her. It is dedicated to her. Other wonderful actresses have done it in many languages, but for me it will always be her piece.

Pulling to the Centre

Anne had begun with what I thought was a lot of very disparate music, some coming from Hebraic musical tradition, some coming from American pop music, some from serial writing, some from Balinese, Oriental-influenced writing. There was a bunch of tunes which I had invented, some of them coming from rather tuneless incantations that I heard my father and my uncle do at various points, and a couple of very lush tunes. As I worked on it I began to see that the material, disparate as it was, had common elements. Actually the whole piece was a series of variations on four themes, though the variations were quite far-flung at one point or another. In the process of composing the piece I took these things that seemed to be so far apart and pulled them towards the centre. And as they were pulled towards the centre, there was a kind of fusion point, and at that fusion point was the music which sounded to me the most personal. I recognized that it was me. And that is what I think the process of composition is going to be for me. It's this pulling towards the centre of lots of different languages and influences and things that I like about all kinds of other musical styles. At a certain point they link up, and the point where they do is where my writing really starts.

What these three experiences ('Grace', *Street Song* and *Anne*) did, was to cause me to take my writing seriously, to care about it, and to care about wanting to have people hear what was going on inside my head. When I did *Anne* in Japan, it was an incredible experience for me to rehearse this piece and see all these young musicians of the Pacific Music Festival, from Singapore and Australia and Indonesia and Japan and mainland China, laugh, cry and get involved with the piece and actually understand what I was trying to say. I thought, 'God, this is so touching. Here are people I can barely mumble two words to suddenly understanding what my music is expressing.'

I think that experience has really spurred me on. I also think that my father's wonderful music, the music that he improvised on the piano every day, which I can play, has inspired me. I recognize that he was someone who was at home in the dream world. If you happened to be lucky enough to sit next to him, you could catch parts of the dream. I now understand what Aaron and Lenny said about committing oneself to writing it down and to selecting more carefully what really is essential.

So it was after writing *From the Diary of Anne Frank* that I looked back at my own songs and other music, and I thought, 'Well, you know, really, there are so many things I love in music. I love Schubert songs, I love gamelan music, I love rhythm and blues, I love Bulgarian music, I love cowboy songs, I love all these things. There are all these twists of phrases and moves in these pieces that I love; all these different things – but there are certain things that all these musics have in common, and those are the moments that draw me to them. And the reason I like those things is I'm saying, "Yes, I recognize myself in that passage." '

And that has a lot to do with why people like music in the first place. It is extraordinary that sometimes you can hear a piece that you've never heard before, and it suddenly does something, and you think, 'Oh, I recognize that, that's happened to me, I've felt that, I've gone through that.' And that's the sort of direction I want to take with composition now.

Future Plans

ES: *Do you ever see yourself putting down the baton and not conducting any more?*
MTT: Anything is possible. No matter what, I always want to be a musician. I've been so lucky to work with some really great musicians and with really great orchestras. At this point in my life I'm working with this great virtuoso instrument, the LSO, and now the San Francisco Symphony is on the horizon. After performances like this last group of Mahler Fifths with the LSO, or the Bartók Second Violin Concerto with Midori, I think, 'But this is the way it's meant to sound. This is wonderful. How much better than this do I expect it to be?'

The simple fact is that I've enjoyed doing the big pieces with the LSO, and with other wonderful orchestras, since my mid-twenties. I did forty performances with the Boston Symphony Orchestra when I was twenty-four years old, and my schedule's been like that continuously ever since, so that, approaching twenty-five years of working at that intensity, I am asking myself what is next for me. Is it more of the same, or is it perhaps more composition? Is it more piano playing, a different sort of commitment in teaching? What is it?

Certainly, a major part of it will be the work that I will do with the New World Symphony. Just recently, rehearsing Brahms's First with them, I was struck by this anew. It is a wonderful and humbling experience to explore an old warhorse like this through the enthusiasm and sense of spiritual adventure of these young musicians. With them, there are frontiers not only of greater technical mastery, still more gossamer *pianissimos,* more scintillating staccatos, but of musical understanding and vulnerability. They challenge me, even as I challenged orchestras when I was their age, to have the courage to enter the space where the music must truly be made.

Working with them reminds me that the most important quality in music-making is communication. As each musician discovers Mahler, Janáček, Mozart, he can share his joy with his friends, his colleagues, his whole generation. That is a very big part of the mission of music. I very much want to share that with the musicians I work with, and with the members of the audience.

The passing away of my parents has been a final piece of a puzzle. I'm no longer wondering what I should do, but only concerned of how much I can

Roberta Meritzer Thomas and Theodor Herzl Thomashefsky, 1991

do in the time I have. I know, as a performer, I have much to contribute, but there are, of course, others who can perform those pieces I so love to do. It is nice to think that I bring something special and individual to them. But I know for sure that I am the only one who can write down the songs I hear in my head, or write down the history of my family. I know I have to get these things down. I know that my own music is a lot like my father's. It has melodic twists which are like his. His music was a combination of Broadway and Yiddish music and jazz form that he used to improvise and so is mine. He never had any music lessons, he was completely self-taught. He had a very good ear, even though he was quite deaf. I played some of his music to Bernstein once, and he said, 'It's so interesting about your dad's music, because of course you can hear Broadway and Yiddish theatre and you can hear the twenties and thirties, but you also can hear cowboy music.' I said, 'Yes, my father's music has always reminded me of cowboy songs written by Brahms.'

That's also true of me. A certain genre of my music is sort of midway between Brahms, Schubert and Red River Valley. I love that overlap. My music will always be tuneful and will always be written for performers who can handle melody. The pieces that I've managed to get down on paper so far have only been because of my devotion to various performers; to Roberta Alexander, and to Leonard Bernstein, to Rolf Smedvig and the Empire Brass Quintet, and to Audrey Hepburn. The pieces were expressions of my friendship for them. The sense of family that I have towards fellow performers, ensembles and orchestras, I know, comes from my mother. It was she who sustained my father's sometimes lonely vision, encouraged him and tried to bring him closer to other people. She taught me to appreciate the good and see the original in all kinds of people. My devotion to teaching and bringing people together through music is inspired by her. It will be interesting to see if in the next piece, *Orchestral Piece in Two Movements*, which will not be for any particular performer, I can expand my feelings of friendship and desire to communicate to all people. We will see how compelling it will be. And I mustn't forget that one day I really must write a trombone concerto. I'm a great fan of the trombone. It's such an amazing instrument. It can do such remarkable things that you'd never guess.

Life has so many possibilities. Years ago, while on a trip to the Far East, I had my fortune told. There was a party for a group of aged Chinese diplomats. Everybody was at least seventy-five. Some were as old as ninety. They were all veterans of the foreign service – diplomats. Some were from the mainland, some were from Taiwan. They had all grown up together back in Beijing, and had formed different loyalties during the revolutionary years, some moving to the left and some to the right. But this evening was a wonderful moment of reunion. They had all gotten together again to honour the ninety-fifth birthday of a woman named Mei-tzu, who was at one time a celebrated courtesan of Beijing. Years before, all these very elderly diplomats had been instructed in the arts of love by Mei-tzu, who was now in very honourable retirement. Their political differences forgotten, they joined together for the purposes of honouring this wonderful old lady.

By chance I was at this banquet. There was a fortune-teller, a very eminent fortune-teller he seemed to be. He asked my birth date, he made various calculations, and he looked at my palm. He said, 'First I'm going to tell you things that have already happened to you in your life so that you can judge what I'm telling you is true.' Then he said, 'When you were four years old you fell from a very high place and you hurt yourself very badly.' This was true. I was on a slide and I fell over backwards and had concussion. He said many more things like this, all of which were true and none of which he could possibly have known. Then he said, 'You are well known for doing something, but it is not what you will ultimately do. What you are really going to do you will not start doing until you are in your fifties.' I always remembered that, and wondered what it could be. Wherever it is it's about to happen.

At the Golden Gate Bridge, 1994

Index